SO-AEN-941

50 Hikes in Central Florida

50 *Hikes*
in Central Florida

**Walks, Hikes, and Backpacking Trips in the
Heart of the Florida Peninsula**

Second Edition

SANDRA FRIEND

The Countryman Press
Woodstock, Vermont

AN INVITATION TO THE READER

Over time trails can be rerouted and signs and landmarks altered. If you find that changes have occurred on the routes described in this book, please let us know so that corrections may be made in future editions. The author and publisher also welcome other comments and suggestions. Address all correspondence to:

Editor, 50 Hikes Series
The Countryman Press
P.O. Box 748
Woodstock, VT 05091

Copyright © 2011 by Sandra Friend
Second Edition
All rights reserved. No part of this book may be reproduced in any form or by any electronic or mechanical means including information storage and retrieval systems without permission in writing from the publisher, except by a reviewer, who may quote brief passages.

50 Hikes in Central Florida
ISBN 978-0-88150-902-1

Maps by Erin Greb Cartography,
    © The Countryman Press
Book design by Glenn Suokko
Text composition by Eugenie S. Delaney
Interior photographs by the author

Published by The Countryman Press,
P.O. Box 748, Woodstock, VT 05091
Distributed by W. W. Norton & Company, Inc.,
500 Fifth Avenue, New York, NY 10110
Printed in the United States of America

10 9 8 7 6 5 4 3 2 1

For Jim and Ginny Owen, who taught me that the only boundaries to what you can do are in your own mind.

"I go to Nature to be soothed and healed, and to have my senses put in tune once more."

—John Burroughs

50 Hikes in Central Florida at a Glance

	HIKE	LOCATION	MILES	KEY
	1 Rainbow Springs State Park	Dunnellon	2.7	H
	2 Holly Hammock Hiking Trail	Ocala	2.4	W
	3 Johnson Pond Trail	Citrus Springs	2.7	F
	4 Potts Preserve	Inverness	12.5	F
Central Highlands	5 Citrus Trail	Inverness	35	G
	6 Fort Cooper State Park	Inverness	5.5	H
	7 Chinsegut Hill WEA	Brooksville	5.6	W
	8 Flat Island Preserve	Leesburg	3.7	F
	9 Hidden Waters Preserve	Eustis	1	G
	10 Withlacoochee River Park Trail	Dade City	7.2	W
	11 Circle B Bar Reserve	Lakeland	4.4	F
	12 Silver River State Park	Silver Springs	8	G
	13 Bluffon Nature Trail	Volusia	1.2	H
	14 Wild Persimmon Trail	De Leon Springs	4.5	W
St. Johns River	15 St. Francis Hiking Trail	Deland	7.7	H
	16 Hontoon Island State Park	Deland	3.3	H
	17 Lower Wekiva River Preserve State Park	Sanford	2.1	F
	18 Spring Hammock Preserve	Winter Springs	3	F
	19 Geneva Wilderness Area	Geneva	1.8	H
	20 Lake Proctor Wilderness Area	Geneva	4	W
	21 Moccasin Island Trail	Melbourne	7.2	W
	22 Lake Lotus Park	Altamonte Springs	1.3	F
Orlando Metro	23 Split Oak Forest WEA	Narcoosee	6.4	W
	24 Hal Scott Regional Preserve	Bithlo	5	H
	25 Tibet-Butler Preserve	Lake Buena Vista	2.7	W
	26 Disney Wilderness Preserve	Poinciana	2.5	W

KIDS	CAMPING	NOTES
X	D	Enjoy scenic views of one of Florida's prettiest springs
X	B, D	Easy loop through shady hammocks along Ross Prairie
X		Restored sandhill bluebird habitat with rare rosemary scrub
	B	Giant cypress knees along the Withlacoochee River
	B, D	Rolling hills and caverns on Florida's longest backpacking loop
X		Old military roads run through this Second Seminole War site
X		Ancient stand of longleaf pine and a prairie for the birds
X	B	A botanist's delight, popular for beginning backpackers
X	B	Waters cascade down a steep descent into Eichelberger Sink
X	B, D	Deep forests on the edge of the Withlacoochee River
X		A trail system with a little something for everyone
X	D	Upland and river floodplain trails along the Silver River
X	D	Interpretive loop through an ancient riverside village
		Wild persimmons, a first-magnitude spring, and pancakes
	B	Century-old ghost town along the St. John's River
X	D	Rich archaeological history on an island in the St. Johns River
X		Superb showcase of Central Florida sandhill habitat
X		Ancient cypresses along the shores of Lake Jesup
X	B	Turpentine and railroad history around placid flatwoods ponds
X		A multitude of options on a very scenic trail system
	B	Floodplains and open marshes for birding along the River
X		Urban wilderness along the Little Wekiva River
	D	Sandhill crane habitat with an unusual old oak tree
	B	Pine flatwoods and prairie on the original ford of the Econ River
X		Interpretive trails in some of Central Florida's vanishing habitats
X		Pine flatwoods surrounding a pristine, undeveloped lake

KEY FEATURES: H = history, G = geology, W = wildlife, F = flora

50 Hikes in Central Florida at a Glance

	HIKE	LOCATION	MILES	KEY
Lake Wales Ridge	27 Crooked River Preserve	Clermont	1.7	F
	28 Catfish Creek Preserve State Park	Dundee	3.5	F
	29 Lake Kissimmee State Park	Lake Wales	15.4	W
	30 Crooked Lake Prairie	Frostproof	2	F
	31 Tiger Creek Preserve	Babson Park	8.4	F
Suncoast	32 James E Grey Preserve	New Port Richey	1.3	W
	33 Hillsborough River State Park	Thontonassa	8.4	G
	34 Lettuce Lake Park	Temple Terrace	1.8	F
	35 John Chesnut Sr. Park	Oldsmar	2.7	W
	36 Honeymoon Island State Park	Dunedin	2.5	W
	37 Caladesi Island State Park	Dunedin	3	F
	38 Eagle Lake Park	Largo	3	W
	39 Sawgrass Lake Park	Pinellas Park	1.9	W
	40 Fort De Soto Park	Tierra Verde	4.9	H
	41 Little Manatee River State Park	Sun City Center	6.5	G
	42 Alderman's Ford Preserve	Plant City	3.3	W
Atlantic Coast	43 Ponce Preserve	Ponce Inlet	2.4	H
	44 Lyonia Preserve	Deltona	2.1	W
	45 Smyrna Dunes Park	New Smyrna Beach	2	G
	46 Merritt Island National Wildlife Refuge	Titusville	8.9	W
	47 Enchanted Forest Sanctuary	Titusville	2.5	H
	48 Maritime Hammock Sanctuary	Melbourne Beach	2.8	F
	49 Turkey Creek Sanctuary	Palm Bay	1.6	W
	50 Oslo Riverfront Conservation Area	Vero Beach	3	W

KIDS	CAMPING	NOTES
X		Scrub and oak hammocks leading to Lake Louisa
		The most elevation change of any trail system in Florida
X	B, D	Wildlife sightings guaranteed in this historic park
X		Ancient scrub and wetlands along a large lake
		Highest concentration of endangered species in Florida
X		Beauty spot with boardwalks along the Pithlascotee River
X	B, D	Hike along Florida's rare rapids in the Hillsborough River
X		An observation tower and boardwalk through a cypress swamp
X		Boardwalks through cypress swamps along Lake Tarpon
X		Virgin slash pines house an osprey nesting ground
X		Fabulous oceanfront and piney woods history
X		An urban forest with fabulous birding
X		An elevated boardwalk through a red maple swamp
X	D	Several trails along Tampa Bay in the shadow of a historic fort
X	B, D	One of Florida's most beautiful hiking trails, with a don't-miss creek
		Lush forests and rapids along the Alafia River
X		Scramble over ancient middens on a high ridge near the ocean
X		Inland oak scrub habitat preserved for the Florida scrub-jay
X		Boardwalk with scenic ocean views over pristine sand dunes
X		The best birding in Central Florida and a view of NASA operations
X		Diverse habitats, unusual geology, and history in a compact park
		Variety of coastal habitats on a barrier island
X		Boardwalks and hiking trails along a tributary of the Sebastian River
X		Contrasting lush river hammocks with mangrove forest

KEY FEATURES: H = history, G = geology, W = wildlife, F = flora

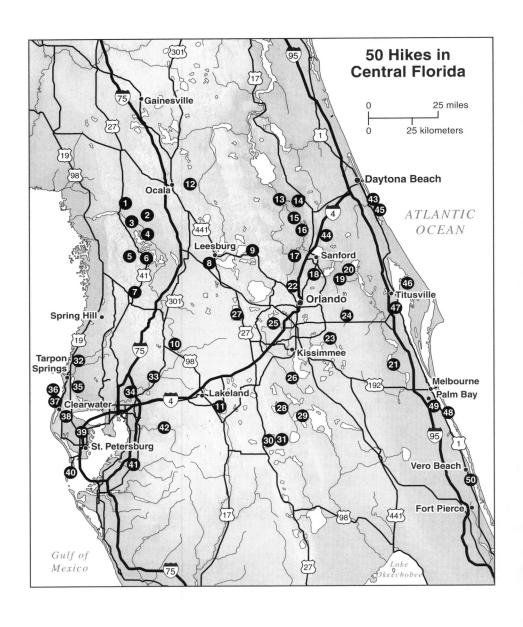

50 Hikes in
Central Florida

0   25 miles

0   25 kilometers

ATLANTIC
OCEAN

Gulf of
Mexico

Lake
Okeechobee

Contents

IV. LAKE WALES RIDGE

V. SUNCOAST

VI. ATLANTIC COAST

Acknowledgments

Thanks to the friends who headed into the woods with me for this second edition, including Brenda Anderson, Barbara Bowen, Niki Butcher, Morena Cameron, Joan Jarvis, Phyllis Malinski, Ellen Petersen, Jon Phipps, Mehmet Gulsen, Ruth Rogg, G. K. Sharman, and Rob Smith, Jr.

Special thanks to Barbara Bowen and Ruth Rogg for introducing me to new hikes I'd never experienced before and found interesting enough to add to this edition; to Vince Lamb, who chased down a missing GPS track for me at one of his favorite trails; to my mom, Linda Friend, who started adventuring with me after we lost the most important man in our lives; and to various friends, including Lori and Dan Burris and Sandy and Bill Huff, for opening their homes to me as I traveled to update this book. Instrumental, too, was Carlene Barrett at Florida State Parks, who advised me on which state parks were less busy and needed a few more hikers on their trails.

Special thanks, too, to Kevin Mims, without whom this project would have sat on a shelf for another hiking season. Kevin stepped in to assist after my Dad died, when life got too overwhelming for me to continue working on the book. For a busy couple of months, he rambled the region backpacking and updating the lengthier trails, filling in details to some of the new hikes I added to the book, and scoping out two new hikes recommended to me that I didn't have the time to explore myself—Circle B Bar Ranch and Moccasin Island. An outdoor writer and native Floridian, Kevin is a lifelong outdoor enthusiast and shares hiking videos at www.kevinmims.com.

Introduction

If you haven't hiked in Central Florida yet, you're truly missing out. It's a joy, more than a decade after I first started writing about hiking in Florida, to report that there are more trails—and more hikers out enjoying them—than ever. With our optimal hiking season coinciding with an influx of winter residents and major bird migrations through the state, we've become an outdoors mecca for America. In fact, American Trails named Florida the top trails state in the nation in 2009. Who cares if we don't have mountains? What we have that attracts outdoor enthusiasts is beauty.

The delights of Florida hiking are subtle, with some clear exceptions in Central Florida, where you scramble over some of the highest ridges in the peninsula or amble out into prairies that go on for miles. It's more likely you'll be focused on the little things. Shoestring ferns wrap the trunk of a cabbage palm in ribbons of green. Hooded pitcher plants cluster around a seep spring on a hillside. Sundews glisten with sticky jelly-like droplets. Spiderwebs glimmer in the afternoon sun. Sea oats sprout from windswept dunes. White ibises silently pick their way across the blackwater swamp of a cypress dome.

Botanical diversity thrives in Florida; our two time zones are home to 81 different natural native plant communities, ranging from temperate Appalachian-style forests of oak, maple, and hickory to tangled tropical jungles of gumbo-limbo. This spectrum of forests meets throughout the wilderness areas of Central Florida. Blessed with such biodiversity, hikers enjoy a broad range of habitats and wildlife that only Hawaii and California surpass. Trails pass through desert-like scrub islands, jungle-like hydric hammocks, and deep, dark bays where giant cypress trees rise out of inky water. Trails cross through salt marshes, river floodplains, and along coastal dunes and beaches with sparkling white sand. Each elevation gain or loss of only a few inches leads to an entirely new ecosystem. Central Florida is also home to delightful landforms of karst, from disappearing lakes and streams and yawning sinkholes lush with ferns to the world's largest concentration of first-magnitude springs, gushing forth billions of gallons of crystal-clear water from the Floridan Aquifer.

Between the massive conservation efforts mounted by the Florida Forever program, one of the nation's largest land acquisition programs; our many counties who established and are successful growing their own natural lands programs; and the Florida Department of Environmental Protection constantly adding new public lands to the Florida State Parks system, our options for exploring Florida's great outdoors have increased exponentially. This patchwork of preserved lands helps endangered species such as the Florida panther, the Florida black bear, the bald eagle, and the Florida scrub-jay to maintain or gain population.

When winter snows settle on northern trails, it's prime hiking season in Florida—although many hikers now head outdoors in the summer months, too. Between October and March, temperatures become comfortable, and the insect population declines, especially after the first freeze. Seasonally out of sync with most of the rest of the nation, Florida provides a perfect winter playground for the active hiker.

HOW TO USE THIS BOOK

As a longtime resident of Central Florida, I'm familiar with the abundance of regional names used to label our portion of the state, from "Horse Country" around Ocala to the "Space Coast" around Titusville. For purposes of this book, I've set my designation of Central Florida as the counties falling between SR 40 and SR 60. These include Brevard, Citrus, Hernando, Hillsborough, Indian River, Orange, Lake, Osceola, Pasco, Pinellas, Polk, Sumter, Volusia, and the southern half of Marion County. In terms of metro areas, this includes Orlando, Tampa, St. Petersburg, Clearwater, Daytona Beach, Cocoa Beach, Melbourne, and Vero Beach.

Hikes in this book vary from short interpretive boardwalks to multiday backpacking trips, with routes ranging from 1 mile to 35 miles. I generally avoid paved trails, except where urban alternatives are limited. I have also excluded hikes along the 1,400-mile Florida Trail, our National Scenic Trail in Florida, as I've previously written about them in a separate book.

In many of the parks, forests, and wilderness areas I visited, there are multiple alternatives for hikes. I show alternatives on the maps, but each discussion and mileage focuses on a particular preferred route. Each first-edition hike was originally measured using a surveyor's measuring wheel. For this update, we used a WAAS-enabled Garmin Oregon 400t GPS.

All attempts at habitat and plant identification are my own, using a variety of references. When there were multiple possibilities for a plant's name, I chose the one most commonly used in the local vernacular, such as "cabbage palm" for our state tree rather than the more regal "sabal palm" preferred by botanists.

KEY FEATURES

Each hike highlights a particular key feature—flora, geology, history, or wildlife.

Flora

Flora is perhaps what Florida is best known for—for both diversity and beauty. Of more than 4,000 types of plants found in Florida, 3,600 are native to the state. Only California and Texas surpass Florida in botanical diversity. Naturalists William Bartram, John James Audubon, and John Muir all expressed their delight at the variety of plants and flowers found in Florida. On the trail, every season coaxes forth color. Many trails are established to show off specific plant communities—boardwalks through cypress domes and over fragile coastal dunes, walks along mangrove swamps and through oak hammocks dense with bromeliads.

Geology

Florida's karst geology provides an interesting look at an unusual landscape. Karst is the name for any type of terrain where the bedrock dissolves easily. In Florida, limestone forms the "basement" of the state, often showing off fossils from millions of years ago. Since limestone dissolves easily, the landscape is full of cracks, crevices, and caves. Sinkholes form, allowing natural waterfalls to trickle down into their depths. Some trails focus on karst landforms, or lead you into reclaimed or historic mining operations, where bare rock is visible.

History

Many hikes focus on features of historic interest. Florida's human habitation dates back tens of thousands of years. Reminders of these settlements can be seen trailside, particularly middens—ancient trash heaps made up of shells—from long-dead cultures living along the St. Johns River and the Atlantic Coast. More recent events occurred over the past 500 years, from the waves of European settlements starting in 1565 to the many conflicts—the Seminole Wars, the Civil War, the Spanish-American War, and both World Wars. Fortresses, ghost towns, and living history demonstrations are just a few of the delights to be found along Florida's trails.

Wildlife

Florida's diversity of wildlife can be enjoyed on many trails through lands set aside specifically for wildlife preservation, such as Split Oak Forest, a sandhill crane habitat. Walk quietly, and you'll be rewarded with wildlife sightings—barred owls and pileated woodpeckers in the trees, bald eagles and red-shouldered hawks circling overhead, Atlantic bottlenose dolphins frolicking in the surf.

HABITATS

Since Florida's topography rarely lends clues as to where you are on a trail (Hike 28 being a notable exception), hike descriptions focus on the changes in habitat that occur as a trail gains or loses elevation. There are many variations in habitat across Central Florida, and different sources use different names for the same general habitat. The following summary explains the habitat designations used in this book.

Coastal Habitats

With more than 1,200 miles of coastline, Florida's habitats include many communities adapted to life along the sea, where wind and salt spray shape the environment. **Coastal dunes** are created by the wind and anchored by deep-rooted grasses such as sea oats. In the **maritime hammock**, windswept live oaks create a canopy above lush thickets of saw palmetto. Brittle grasses and succulent plants such as glasswort and sea purslane grow along the edges of **salt flats and salt marshes**, where herons, egrets, and ibises stride through the shallows. **Estuaries** and **coastal savannas** are extensive grassy salt marshes punctuated by islands of cabbage palms, typically found between barrier islands and the mainland. **Mangrove forests** grow around many barrier islands—or is it the other way around? The mangrove's dense roots form a trap for floating sediments, encouraging the buildup of new land.

Forests

Hardwood hammock is a catchall term for a forest of mixed hardwoods. The **oak hammock**, frequently dominated by live oak, is Florida's climax forest. **Pine flatwoods** are the state's largest natural community, covering nearly half of the land. With acidic, poorly drained soils supporting ferns, gallberry, saw palmetto, and a high canopy of tall pine trees, pine flatwoods feel very open. Historically dominated by longleaf pine, which has been logged out of most of Florida's forests, the pine canopy varies according to the soil drainage. Longleaf and loblolly pines prefer the high ground, while slash pine prefers some dampness. Pond pine tolerates seasonal flooding. A clay layer beneath the soil holds in rainfall, causing flatwoods to stay flooded for a few days after a rainstorm—expect the trail, the low spot, to be full of water. **Cabbage palm flatwoods** intersperse cabbage palms through a canopy of pond or slash pines, and occur in floodplain areas. **Scrubby flatwoods** have better drainage than most pine flatwoods, but the pines have more space between them, forming breaks in the canopy. **Upland hardwood forests** are a dense canopy of beech, elm, hickory, and southern magnolia, where azaleas and dogwoods may grow.

Prairies

Treeless and open, prairies are extensive dry grasslands that can be seasonally inundated with water. Wildflower enthusiasts seek out prairies for their unusual and colorful flowers, such as the pine lily, pale meadow beauty, and elephant's root. Prairies may contain islands of oak hammocks or cabbage palm flatwoods and are host to bayheads, cypress domes, and freshwater marshes. Less than 20 percent of Florida's prairies are under state protection; most have been converted to cattle ranches, sod farms, and citrus groves.

Sandhills

These gently rolling pine-topped hills of white to orange sand have suffered more than any other natural community from Florida's ongoing development because of their dryness. Prior to logging, longleaf pine was the dominant species; slash pine now provides most sandhill shade. Many varieties of oaks flourish in the dry, well-drained soil. Forming a protective layer over karst, sandhills allow rainfall to trickle through and recharge the Floridan Aquifer, the state's most crucial source of fresh water. A related habitat, **clayhills**, hosts the same types of plants on a base of thick red clay.

Scrub

Scrubs form on well-drained, loose "sugar sand" deposited along ancient shorelines. They are thought to be Florida's oldest plant communities, in existence for more than 20 million years. A limited number of plants tolerate the extreme dryness of the scrub environment. In a **sand pine scrub**, tall sand pines dominate the forest, with an understory of oak scrub, rosemary scrub, and saw or scrub palmetto. A **rosemary scrub** is an unusual place, where rosemary bushes up to 8 feet tall grow out of a white sand base; the ground may be covered in lichens. **Oak scrub** is dominated by sand live oak, wax myrtle, Chapman oak, and myrtle oak, with the highest diversity of scrub plant and animal life.

Swamp forests

Red maple, sweetgum, red bay, bay magnolia, loblolly bay, and water oak are common residents of the **floodplain forest**, created by rivers that seasonally overflow their banks, scouring adjoining channels higher than the normal river level. Thick with bald cypress, pond cypress, and cabbage palms, the low-lying **hydric hammock** occurs along river and lake floodplains, experiencing flooding whenever water levels are slightly above normal. **Palm hammocks** provide slight elevation over the surrounding marshes. A basin, or **bay**, is a swampy interior forest of cypress, bay, and mixed hardwoods. Looking like a dome from a distance, the **cypress dome** forms in a low depression in a prairie, fed by seeping water. Similarly, **bayheads** receive their watery base from seepage, encouraging dahoon holly, bay magnolia, and loblolly bay to grow. Unless a boardwalk is available, don't expect to keep your shoes dry when hiking through a swamp forest.

Wetlands

In addition to coastal marshes, mangrove swamps, and swamp forests, Florida's moist habitats include **freshwater marshes**, which form along lake and river drainages; **ephemeral ponds**, occurring in low spots during the rainy season; **flatwoods ponds**, created from the trickling runoff in the pine flatwoods; and **wetlands**, shallow grassy basins in pine flatwoods, scrub, and prairies. Rare **seepage slopes** happen primarily in scrub and sandhill, where an elevation change allows water to trickle slowly out of the side of a hill, nourishing moist meadows where carnivorous plants thrive.

ADVICE AND PRECAUTIONS

Alligators

Despite their place near the top of the food chain in Florida's wilds, alligators rarely cause problems for hikers. When you do have to be careful if is the alligator won't get out of your way. This generally means that someone has fed the alligator, and it has become habituated to human presence. Alligators are not smart enough to know the difference between a slice of bread and a hand. If an alligator fearlessly blocks the trail, do not approach it or try to walk around it. Make noise, stomp your feet, and let it move before you continue. Never feed or touch an alligator. Like most wildlife you will encounter, an alligator will typically turn tail and head the other way before you ever see it, startling you with an explosive splash as it jumps into the nearest body of water.

Bears

Consider yourself fortunate if you see a Florida black bear. Mostly active in the early morning hours, this elusive mammal teases you with scat and tracks left on hiking trails. A full-grown Florida black bear weighs no more than 350 pounds—although there have been notable exceptions of up to 700 pounds—and will quickly move out of your way if it sees you. No one has ever been attacked by a Florida black bear.

Camping

Tent camping (backpacking or car camping) in Florida is best enjoyed between October and March, when the muggy nights with high temperatures yield to a cool evening chill. Wildfires spark easily in Florida, so please refrain from building a campfire unless a fire ring is available—use a camp stove for cooking. Be sure to pack out all waste materials from your campsite. Where privies are available, use them; otherwise, dig a hole at least 400 feet from any campsite or water source. When camping in a primitive campsite, particularly an undeveloped site, follow Leave No Trace ethics. Leave the site as pristine as when you entered it. Eliminate any signs of a campfire unless there is an established fire ring. To protect your food supply, use a bear bag in bear territory, not only to foil the bears but also to outwit the wily raccoons that congregate near established campsites. Don't camp on the banks of a stream, lake, or pond—alligators do roam at night.

Deforestation

Even in protected areas such as state parks, state forests, and wilderness areas, a hiker is bound to come across gaping gaps in the forest—hammocks charred by wildfires, pine forests felled by loggers, and trees fallen like scattered matchsticks, victims of the Southern pine beetle. State and national forests issue permits to logging companies for regular harvesting of timber, and care is not always taken to leave a corridor of trees around a hiking trail. Sandhill and scrub habitats require wildfire to regenerate new growth. Logging frequently occurs to help restore these fragile habitats with fresh growth. Most insidious, however, is the spread of the southern pine beetle throughout Florida. These minute beetles primarily infest loblolly pine trees, exhibiting termite-like behavior as they tunnel through the soft inner tissue of the pines.

If you do come across an area where blazes are missing, use your best judgment in crossing an open area. Look carefully for telltale blazes on the distant tree line. If the trail has been following jeep roads, look for alternate routes around the clear-cut. Make sure that you know where you entered the open area in case you need to backtrack.

Heat and Dehydration

When hiking in Florida, it is very easy to become dehydrated without realizing it. The warm temperatures and sunshine will sometimes prompt you to drink, but not often enough. Dehydration and long exposure to the sun can lead to heat exhaustion, which starts with nausea, chills, and dizziness, and can lead to deadly heatstroke. If you feel any of these symptoms, stop hiking. Drink as much fluid as possible. Rest a while before attempting any further exertion. Always carry enough water for your hike. I carry a minimum of 1 liter per 4 miles, and twice that when temperatures are over 80° F.

Hunting

Florida's prime hiking season is also the state's prime hunting season, which can lead to conflicts on certain state lands, such as Wildlife Management Areas, Water Management District lands, state preserves, and state forests. During deer season, wear a lightweight blaze orange vest when hiking these lands. Hunting is not permitted in county parks or state parks. Backpackers should be aware that certain lands are closed to overnight camping during general gun season. For full details on hunting dates and restrictions in specific state lands, check the Florida Fish and Wildlife Conservation Commission's Web site at www.myfwc.com.

Insects

Thanks to our warm weather, Florida's insects enjoy longer lives than in most states. As a result, your hike will not be entirely insect-free until the first serious chill hits a region, usually by mid-November. Bug-free bliss continues through March. For the rest of the year, keep a long-lasting insect repellent in your pack. I've tried many over the years, and my current favorite is an organic repellent called 45°N 68°W, which has kept the mosquitoes

(and other flying insects) away on summer days.

To keep ticks and chiggers (also known as "red bugs") off you, spray your hiking clothing beforehand with permethrin. To minimize bug problems when you sit, carry a plastic garbage bag to sit on when you take your breaks.

Longtime Florida hikers recommend wearing long pants to beat the mosquitoes and dusting your socks with sulfur powder (available over the counter from a pharmacist, who has to grind it) to fend off chiggers. If your legs feel itchy after a hike, take a 15-minute plunge in a hot tub or a hot bath to ward off any further effects from chiggers, microscopic bugs that attach themselves to your skin to feed. Check yourself carefully for ticks.

Spiders can be annoying between March and November, as they build large webs across trails. Most commonly, you'll see the large golden orb spider in its sticky yellow web, and the crab spider, smaller but obvious because of the shell on its back. Be proactive. Pick up a stick (the stalk of a saw palmetto frond works well) and hold it tilted in front of you to catch any human-height webs. Try to duck under webs that you can see, as a spider's web is a masterpiece of nature—and the spider is helping to rid the forest of other pesky bugs.

Marine Life

Enjoying a barefoot hike along Florida's beaches means keeping your eyes open for the marine life that washes ashore, particularly clear, glassy blobs of jellyfish. Stepping on a jellyfish with bare feet means hours of intense pain. If you decide to enjoy a dip in the sea, bear in mind that Florida leads the world in shark attacks on bathers. Most attacks occur along the Atlantic Coast, with the highest concentration at New Smyrna Beach. Be particularly cautious about wading into the water at Smyrna Dunes Park. On the Gulf of Mexico, wading in the sea calls for the "stingray shuffle." Set each foot down on the ocean floor with a resounding stomp, which alerts the stingrays to stay clear.

MOUNTAIN BIKES AND EQUESTRIANS

On multiuse trails, mountain bikes and equestrians may share the trail. Allow them the right of way so they don't further tear up the edges of the footpath. You're more likely to see riders on horseback than bikers, since horse farms dominate the landscape of North Central Florida. Multiuse trails are indicated in the text.

PLANTS

No matter how far south you travel in the United States, there's no escaping poison ivy. Be particularly alert to the poison ivy vine that grows up trees along some boardwalk trails, since its large leaves mimic hickory leaves.

Tread softly, also known as stinging nettle, has a beautiful white flower atop a tall stem; its leaves are covered with tiny stinging nettles. Avoid brushing bare skin against it.

Many trails are not maintained between the months of April and September, since most hiking occurs in the fall and winter. An overgrown trail can be painful when burrs and nettles dig into your socks. Consider purchasing a pair of low gaiters to cover your socks and shoes, or do as the experienced hikers do—wear long lightweight pants when hiking, even in summer.

Proper Clothing and Equipment

Always carry rain gear! Storm clouds come up suddenly and unexpectedly and can easily put a damper on your hike if you're not prepared. Find a jacket that will fold down small enough to attach to a fanny pack or will fit inside your daypack. If you are hiking more than a couple of miles, carry some sort of small pack. At a minimum, your pack should contain water, a first-aid kit, a flashlight, a compass, and emergency food. To beat the heat, a sturdy fanny pack with water-bottle holsters is a good choice. A hat is essential to keep your head cool.

Because Florida's terrain is often sandy or wet, your footwear need not be the rugged mountain climbing gear you see at most outfitters. Avoid heavy leather boots and "waterproof" lined boots—your feet *will* sweat, and to minimize blisters, you need your feet to breathe. Look for a lightweight hiking shoe, a trail running shoe, or even comfortable running shoes. Some Florida hikers use sports sandals with socks. When your shoes get waterlogged, you want them to be able to dry.

Wear two layers of socks—a good hiking sock on the outside, and a thin polypropylene or silk/nylon sock on the inside. Instead of rubbing against your skin, the socks will rub against each other. Avoid cotton socks. When they get damp, they abrade your feet. If you do feel a hot spot or a blister coming on, treat it immediately. Cover it with a piece of moleskin (found in the foot care section of most drugstores) and apply a small piece of duct tape over the moleskin to keep it water- and sweat-proof.

Interested in backpacking? Many of the trails in this book feature backcountry campsites, some along relatively short trails. The Florida Trail Association offers several beginners' backpacking workshops each year, which is a great way to try out gear (and the whole concept of backpacking) before you spend any money on the hobby. While a hands-on workshop is your best bet, you may not have the time—so read one of the many excellent books on backpacking, including *Backpacking* (Adrienne Hall), *Backpacking: One Step at a Time* (Harvey Manning), *The*

Complete Walker III (Colin Fletcher), and *Hiking & Backpacking: A Complete Guide* (Karen Berger).

Snakes

Central Florida's poisonous snakes include the southern copperhead, the cottonmouth moccasin (sometimes called water moccasin), the eastern coral snake, and three types of rattlesnake—timber, eastern diamondback, and pygmy. Although nonpoisonous, the black racer can be aggressive. In areas where the trail is overgrown, be wary of where you set your feet. Never handle a snake.

Sun

When hiking under the bright Florida sun, use a high-strength sports sunblock lotion and wear a hat for the protection of your face. Depending on the habitats you'll be hiking through, you may want sunglasses as well.

Unattended Vehicles

Use common sense when leaving your vehicle at a trailhead. Don't leave valuables in plain sight, and lock the vehicle. If a permit was required to enter the land or to hike the trail, be sure the permit is showing inside the front windshield.

Water

Florida's trails run to extremes on water supplies—either they have plenty of it, or they have none. Because of drainage from citrus groves and cattle pastures into rivers and creeks, you cannot trust water sources to be pristine, with the exception of free-flowing artesian wells and springs along the trail. Even these can have an unpleasant taste due to a high sulfur or salt content, and may require filtering. Not all water sources can be easily reached—a flatwoods pond, for instance, may require some slogging through muck before you reach water. I mention water sources for backpackers, but suggest you carry your own supply whenever day hiking. Always use a water filter or chemical treatment such as iodine before drinking "wild" water. Do not drink the water in mine reclamation areas.

Weather

The frequency of afternoon thunderstorms in the summertime doesn't always keep a hiker off the trail. But darkening skies are no laughing matter. Violent thunderstorms can spawn fierce wind gusts and occasionally, tornadoes. Central Florida is well known as the lightning capital of the world. If you are caught out in the open during a storm, attempt to reach cover as quickly as possible.

FLORIDA STATE PARKS

With more than 160 state parks and 75 years of history, the Florida State Parks system is one of the finest in America. Most Florida State Parks require an entry fee, varying from location to location. Residents can save themselves some money by picking up a Florida State Parks Annual Pass ($60 individual, $120 family), covering entrance fees for a year. The family pass is good for up to eight people entering in a single vehicle. Florida State Parks are generally open 8 AM–sunset. Many provide camping facilities, which must be reserved in advance through ReserveAmerica.com. Walk-ins for campsites are never guaranteed but always possible, but you must check at the park entrance station the day you want to camp. For more information on the state park system, see www.floridastateparks.org or download my iPhone app, "Florida State Parks," from the iTunes store via www.floridahikes.com/apps/florida-state-parks.

FLORIDA TRAIL ASSOCIATION

Founded in 1966 to build a backpacking trail the length of the state, the statewide Florida Trail Association (FTA) encourages hikers to build, maintain, and enjoy Florida's trails. Volunteers from the FTA maintain many loop hikes across the state. Look for the FT sign at the trailhead for trails built and maintained by the Florida Trail Association. Local chapters hold monthly outdoors-focused meetings and sponsor frequent hiking, backpacking, and trail work activities to introduce Floridians and visitors alike to the great outdoors, Florida-style. For information on a chapter near you, contact the Florida Trail Association, 5415 Southwest 13th Street, Gainesville, FL 32608, call 877-HIKE-FLA, or visit their Web site at www.floridatrail.org

FLORIDA TRAILWALKER PROGRAM

The Florida Division of Forestry's Trailwalker Program encourages you to get out and hike designated trails in Florida State Forests. As you complete each hike, send in a postcard to the program. After 10 hikes, the state awards you a Trailwalker patch and certificate. There are additional rewards for each group of 10 trails hiked. For a Trailwalker application, visit any of the designated Trailwalker trailheads for a brochure, call 850-414-0871, or visit www.fl-dof.com.

FLORIDA HIKES!

Since February 2006, I've shared the adventure of discovering new trails—and revisiting old ones—at www.floridahikes.com. Stop in and join the hiker forums, share your trip reports, photos, and videos, and join special interest groups such as "Hiking with Dogs" and "Trailwalkers" to share tips and plan hikes together. Dig through the database for hundreds of places to hike throughout Florida, each including interactive Google maps and directions so you can find the trail and hike it. Subscribe to the blog to keep up with hiking and conservation news, too.

I. Central Highlands

Hiker dwarfed by virgin longleaf pine forest at Chinsegut Hill WEA

1

Rainbow Springs State Park

Total distance (2 circuits): 2.7 miles

Hiking time: 1.5 hours

Habitats: formal gardens, floodplain forest, oak hammock, hardwood hammock, pine flatwoods, sandhills

Trailhead coordinates (lat-lon): 29.100980, -82.433454

Maps: USGS 7½' Dunnellon; Rainbow Springs State Park map

Admission: $2 per person

Hours: 8 AM–sunset

A panorama of timeless beauty opens up as you step onto the terrace after entering Rainbow Springs State Park and look out at the Rainbow River flowing away in full force from the clear, chalky blue first-magnitude spring at the bottom of the hill. It's hard to imagine a day when this was a hillside ravaged by mining, but that's part of the legacy of Rainbow Springs. In the 1930s, private reclamation efforts turned the steep hills and deep pits into a stunning public garden with waterfalls, a rarity in Florida. Never mind they poured from pools created by water pumped uphill out of the river—it was the illusion that mattered.

Now a Florida State Park, Rainbow Springs offers a variety of activities for visitors to enjoy. Bring a picnic and settle down on a blanket on the hill above the springs. Jump into the constant 72°F water for a brisk swim, or don your fins and snorkel to stare at fish up close. Rent a canoe and paddle downstream to see dozens of tinier springs in hidden coves where cormorants rest on gnarled oak branches and green herons pick through the shallows. Or just come to ramble the park, as most visitors do. Your dog is welcome to join you.

THE GARDENS

Although the hiking trail at Rainbow Springs focuses on the natural habitats above the spring, to get there you must roam through the historic gardens. More than a century ago, the forests surrounding Rainbow Springs were a beehive of activity as miners dug pits in the limestone to find nuggets that

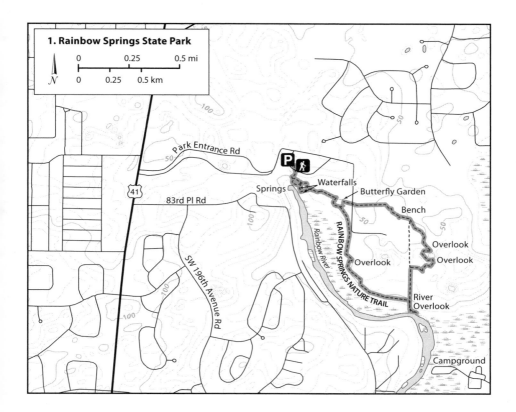

1. Rainbow Springs State Park

made the community of Dunnellon, emerging at the confluence of the Rainbow and Withlacoochee Rivers, a boomtown. It wasn't gold that shined a spotlight on this humble riverfront town, but phosphate. Phosphate is a mineral used in the production of hundreds of commercial products, most notably soap and fertilizer.

In those less enlightened times, the ravaged landscapes and pits left behind were left as is as the mining company moved on to excavate more ore from another landholding, as were hastily erected towns built to house the mining crews. The town of Juliette sprung up in these woods, where phosphate mining carved deep clefts in the hillsides and sandhill forests. Once abandoned by indus-

try, the beautiful spring was claimed by owners who wanted to make it a park to attract tourists. Planting thousands of azaleas and camellias on the mine-torn slopes and pumping water to generate several waterfalls, they created a garden paradise that became a destination for tourists headed south. A lodge was added to encourage people to stay, and later, a restaurant and gift shop.

From the terrace with its National Natural Landmark memorial, walk down the path to the right, and take the next left. This lower path provides a better view of the spring itself. First known as Blue Spring (there are many Blue Springs in Florida), it was later dubbed Rainbow Springs to sell the attraction, which had a giant rainbow out front. The park has been a part of my family history since I was old enough to walk. We came here to ride the submarine boats, which were a different spin on experiencing the crystalline waters. Unlike the glass-bottom boats at nearby Silver Springs, the submarine boats let you walk down a staircase and sit in a seat, staring out a porthole at the fish and turtles. As the boat slowly made its way downriver, the skipper told tales of the spring and chanted the names of the fish. The original boat dock was down below this point, and later shifted to where the swimming area is now, off to your right.

As the lower path joins into the larger path coming downhill, take a right. Arrive here in February or March for one of the showiest displays of azaleas and camellias in Florida. By the 1970s, a monorail called the Forest Flite drifted above this point, suspending four people inside a big leaf as it cruised silently above the plantings. The path leads to a four-way junction. Turn right to continue downhill. To the right, a cove bubbles with dozens of tiny springs that pour out into the river. Keep right at the fork to walk out between the cove and a glassy spring on your left, where you might see a young mud turtle propelling himself through the water. The path converges with the wide trail to bring you up to Seminole Falls, the first of the two waterfalls splashing down the steep hillside. Passing the pump house and he remains of old otter and turtle pens, take the next right down a long boardwalk. It ends at the mouth of a larger cove along the river, where the paddlewheel boat and river raft used to dock. These shallows are busy with birdlife—look for wading birds of all types amid the clumps of lance-leafed arrowhead.

Returning back along the boardwalk, turn right onto the main path. Now you can see the bubblers up close, here on the right. Stand and watch the tiny springs throw grains of sands up like fountains as striped fish swim through these miniature sandstorms. Well-shaded by the live oak canopy, it's a mesmerizing spot. As the path swings around to the left, you see Rainbow Falls, which looks like a scene out of Hawaii. Tropical plantings crowd the outflow from the falls, which tumble down a massive moss-covered limestone wall. There used to be a restaurant perched on the left next to the falls, and the zigzagging path to the right leads up through the old aviary, home of another waterfall.

The main path continues up the hill and swings around to the right beneath the oaks to enter the area that was once a small zoo. The former rodeo grounds lie just beyond it. The remains of the bleacher posts are here, as well as the foundation of the horse stalls. Walk out into the butterfly garden that was built in the area. Despite the natural environment and these man-made enhancements, it wasn't enough to keep the public interested in Rainbow Springs after Interstate 75—and Walt Disney World—arrived on the scene, and travelers started bypassing Dunnellon entirely. The Rainbow Springs attraction closed in 1974.

In my teen years, the land was sold to a developer who threatened to build houses above the spring. As you saw on the entrance road, the threat came close enough. It was through the major efforts of concerned citizens banding together as the Friends of Rainbow Springs that the springs and gardens were purchased as a county park. Much volunteer cleanup was required before it fully opened as a state park in 1995, the year my brother and his wife got married on the terrace above the springs.

SANDHILLS TRAIL

After you enter the butterfly garden, turn right and continue out to the old access road.

Along the Sandhills Nature Trail

There you'll find the "Nature Trail" trailhead with a large kiosk and map of the trail. The broad and well-trodden Sandhills Trail leads you through the pines to the edge of a man-made ravine reclaimed by the forest. This is the first of several former mining pits you'll see along this hike.

Emerging into an open meadow where cattle grazed once upon a time, the trail follows the edge of the meadow, sticking to the shade beneath the trees. At a well-marked trail intersection, three blaze colors are shown on the post: yellow, white, and blue.

To sneak your peek at the Rainbow River, head downhill along the blue blazes on a spur trail that reaches a spot with a bench at the river. The trail extends a little ways downriver through the cypresses for another glimpse. Returning along the blue trail, you see a white-blazed trail off to the right. That's the perimeter trail, which gives you a 2.1-mile

loop. It's a beautiful option in the fall, when the sandhill wildflowers are in bloom. Most times of year, however, you'll want to follow the yellow blazes for a more interesting historic hike. Keep heading up the hill.

The yellow blazes follow a forest road briefly and then take off into the forest on the right, leading past a cistern carved into the limestone, perhaps once the site of a homestead. Just down the trail, you hear a strong tapping at the top of a longleaf pine—a pileated woodpecker, Florida's largest, distinguished by its size and its bright red crown. Pine flatwoods are its domain, where it ranges over a wide area and announces its arrival by pounding on hollow trees.

As you head deeper into the forest, the trail undulates up and over mounds, and the forest grows on these mounds as well—they are leftover diggings from the phosphate pits. You soon encounter the extremely deep pits,

Rainbow Springs, the beginning of the Rainbow River

each with a fence along the edge, where the forest has filled in. Slash and loblolly pines reach for the sky, as tall above the pits as they are below.

Albertus Vogt, a gentleman who moved to Dunnellon from Charleston, where phosphate was first discovered in the Americas, struck it rich with a find of high-grade phosphate ore closer to the downtown area, near a small spring. Florida's mining boom was on. In 1889, the Marion Phosphate Company, followed by the Dunnellon Phosphate Company, grabbed all the available land in the area and used heavy manpower to dig deep pits to extract the ore. Within less than 10 years, there were more than 215 phosphate mining companies in the state of Florida. Hard rock mining was an expensive process, however, and as phosphate ore was later discovered in pebble form near Lakeland and

along the Peace River Valley south of Tampa, the mining industry slowly tapped out its resources near Dunnellon. The last mines in this region closed in 1965.

The yellow blazes once again intersect with the white blazes. Turn left and follow them across the meadow, where a bench sits in the shade of a large cedar tree. Plum trees show their bright white blooms in February. Entering a stand of regularly spaced planted pines, the trail crosses a park road and returns you to the butterfly garden, completing a 2-mile circuit.

To return to the park entrance, walk back through the gardens. This time, take the right fork before the path makes the steep descent down to the waterfall. This upper trail leads you around and over the pools of water that feed the two waterfalls. The pools are brilliantly awash in color in February and March as the azaleas come into fullness. After you cross the second bridge, follow the winding path down to the junction of pathways at the base of the hill below the terrace. Head back up to the terrace, where you'll find restrooms, a small snack bar and picnic tables, interpretive displays, and the gift shop. Be sure to browse on your way out!

In addition to the activities at the headspring, Rainbow Springs State Park also has a campground connected by the river but detached by road. Offering tent and trailer camping, it has full hookups, special spots set aside for fishing and swimming along the river, and a canoe rental. Just 1.4 miles south of the campground on the same side of the river is the destination for one of Dunnellon's most popular aquatic activities—tubing the Rainbow River. The park offers a two-hour loop trip. A local outfitter, Dragonfly Watersports, handles the shuttle upstream, providing you with a two-hour float back down to where you parked your car.

DIRECTIONS

From I-75 exit 352, Ocala, follow SR 40 for 19 miles to US 41 north of Dunnellon. Turn left and drive 0.8 mile. The park entrance is on the left. Follow the winding park road 0.8 mile back to the parking area. The campground is along Southwest 180th Avenue Road, 2 miles south of SR 40, on the east side of the river, and the tubing entrance is 1.4 miles south of the campground along Southwest 180th Avenue Road.

CONTACT

Rainbow Springs State Park
19158 Southwest 81st Place Road
Dunnellon, FL 34432
352-465-8555
www.floridastateparks.org/rainbowsprings

2

Holly Hammock Hiking Trail

Total distance (circuit): 2.4 miles

Hiking time: 1 hour, 20 minutes

Habitats: hardwood hammock, freshwater marsh, pine flatwoods, prairie, sandhills, scrub, scrubby flatwoods

Trailhead coordinates (lat-lon): 29.037983, -82.295851

Maps: USGS 7½' Dunnellon; Ross Prairie State Forest map; Trail map available at kiosk

Admission: Free. If you're planning to camp overnight, you must obtain a free permit in advance from the Florida Division of Forestry. Call 352-732-1201 for a permit.

Hours: Sunrise–sunset. If the gates to the Ross Prairie Trailhead are closed, park outside the Ross Prairie State Forest fence along the entrance road to the trailhead.

Several years after the first edition of this book was published, I was asked by renowned Florida Trail Association trail builder Kenneth Smith to join him on an expedition to flag a brand-new trail in a brand-new state forest adjoining the Cross Florida Greenway. I lived near the Greenway, and found the exercise of trail planning an eye-opener, as the three of us involved had different concepts of what hikers wanted along an easy trail. Full shade? Big trees? Camping? Open areas for birding? Destinations to hike to? In the end, we included them all. My favorite part about this trail is the extreme habitat diversity showcased in such an easy loop.

Although it shares the Ross Prairie Trailhead with the Cross Florida Greenway—which has a campground, restrooms, equestrian parking, and access to the statewide Florida Trail from a nearly adjacent trailhead—Holly Hammock attracts plenty of interest from folks who want a quiet walk in the woods (with or without their dog) in the early morning hours. It's a delight to introduce you to it.

Ross Prairie is a landform that folks driving from Ocala to the Gulf Coast zip right by and hardly notice, what with SR 200 posted at 55 mph and drivers moving through at 70. It's the only significant remaining natural prairie west of Ocala, draining toward the Withlacoochee River. In the wet seasons, the prairie teems with aquatic life, hosting ponds where American lotus bloom on the surface and purple pickerelweed creates natural bouquets. During the dry seasons—of which there are many—the prairie grasses grow tall and colorful, waving in sheets of golden and orange

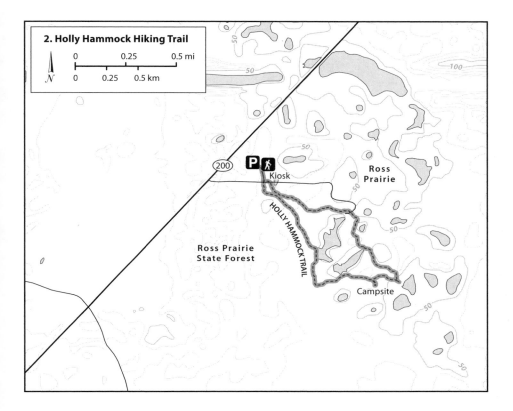

2. Holly Hammock Hiking Trail

hues. Ross Prairie State Forest is one of Florida's younger state forests, established in large part to protect more than 3,500 acres along the many arms of this sometimes freshwater marsh, sometimes dry prairie.

Start your hike at the sign near the parking area. It's well marked with a trailhead sign, so you shouldn't miss the gap in the fence that leads you into the deep shade of an old oak hammock. The narrow footpath emerges through another gap in a fence marking the boundary between the Cross Florida Greenway (where you're parked) and Ross Prairie State Forest. A kiosk on the left shows the trail map and may have trail brochures available. This trail is part of the statewide Florida State Forests Trailwalker program, so on your

way out don't forget to pick up a postcard to send in.

Cross the firebreak—which serves as part of the larger equestrian trail system on this forest—and follow the blue blazes into a very dense oak hammock. Per the name, American holly is a major component of this hammock, as is sparkleberry. Also known as farkleberry or huckleberry, this tall member of the blueberry family has crooked limbs and a distinctively smooth reddish-brown bark that always seems to be peeling.

A little elevation makes a big difference in habitat as the trail rises up into the sandhills, where young longleaf pines rise above a sea of wiregrass. The understory is very open, the better to showcase colorful wildflowers, crooks of their branches. Look closely, and in summer, you may notice greenfly orchids in bloom, hidden amid the profusion of resurrection ferns.

After a half mile, the trail emerges along what looks like a large retention pond, but is in fact an arm of Ross Prairie, with dikes built up along the edges by a rancher who once owned this land. In the early morning, you may see sandhill cranes or herons here. Turn right and follow the dike to the next HIKING TRAIL sign, which steers you back into the forest through a thick carpet of deer moss and reindeer lichen. Back in the shade, the trail passes more massive oaks with ferns and orchids. Look for fungi, too, growing in the leaf litter and on rotting logs. After making a sharp left turn at a bed of moss, the trail ambles around more large trees to emerge again along the prairie arm. It makes a right and passes a large sand pine that sits low to the ground, where you can clearly see its pinecones. Along the trail's edge, purple blooms of spiderwort delight the eye and attract the showy tiger swallowtail butterfly.

Turning right, the trail reenters the shady hammock. After 0.9 mile, a sign in the woods marks the side trail to the campsite. Lime green blazes lead to the right, snaking through a patch of deer moss to emerge in an open spot beneath the oaks. A picnic table and fire ring mark the center of the camping area, with places to pitch your tent scattered around in several directions. Returning to the main trail, turn right. You start to see light through the trees, as you're approaching one of the larger expanses of Ross Prairie. As the trail slips out into the open, you're greeted with a panorama of grassland and a distant tree line. Take a moment to walk out into the prairie to savor the view. American lotuses decorate a pond just down the slope. It's a beauty spot, but be cautious of alligators sunning along the water's edge. In Ross Prairie,

Side trail to the camping area

including pawpaw and blazing star, in spring and fall. In the winter, the winged sumac turns a bright crimson. As you descend back into the hammock, the elevation change is obvious, and you enter a mix of sandhills and scrub, where sand live oaks shade the trail and silk bay grows next to holly. Look for red blanket lichen on the holly trunks—it almost looks like blazes! Colorful lichens are a major component of this hammock. The sand live oaks get very large here, and typically have lush gardens of resurrection ferns in the they generally don't have many opportunities to find a body of water this big.

The trail returns to the shade of the hammock, meandering past more large oaks. As the footpath winds through the woods past sentinels of sand live oaks, it passes through an oak portal before emerging at the end of a prairie arm. The bright pink blooms of pale meadow beauty lend color to the landscape as you cross a firebreak and reenter the forest. It doesn't take long for the elevation to rise again, and you enter the sandhills, with longleaf pines all around. Delicate wildflowers peep out of the wiregrass. A glossy red and black snake slips out of sight quickly—a coral

Along the Holly Hammock Hiking Trail

snake, a relative of the cobra, and one of Florida's venomous snakes. Two harmless snakes mimic the colors of the coral snake— the scarlet kingsnake and the scarlet snake. To distinguish the snakes, look at the color bands. A coral snake's head is always black, with slim bands of yellow separating the thick bands of red and black. On a kingsnake, red touches black. Or as the child's rhyme goes, "red touch yellow, kill a fellow." The coral snake's toxic venom can only be injected when the snake chews on a soft part of the victim's skin. Although the coral snake lives in many Florida habitats, it prefers dry pine flatwoods and sandhills, with lots of leaf debris covering the forest floor.

Descending again, you're greeted with patches of saw palmetto along the sides of the trail and can see patches of prairie off to the right through the understory. The trail weaves its way around one patch to emerge into the sun within sight of a fence line. Turn left, and you'll see the kiosk up ahead to complete the loop. At the kiosk, turn right to exit.

DIRECTIONS

From Interstate 75 exit 350, Dunnellon/Hernando, follow SR 200 south from Ocala, crossing CR 484 after 9 miles. After another 1.5 miles, look for the Ross Prairie Trailhead on the left, and turn left. Follow the entrance road around to park near the restrooms. The trailhead offers an RV campground, access to equestrian trails, and another hiking trail, the 3.5-mile Ross Prairie Loop on the Cross Florida Greenway, which leads to the Florida Trail.

CONTACT

Ross Prairie State Forest
2735 Northeast Silver Springs Boulevard
Ocala, FL 34470
352-732-1201
www.fl-dof.com

3

Johnson Pond Trail

Total distance (circuit): 2.7 miles

Hiking time: 1.5 hours

Habitats: oak hammock, oak scrub, prairie, pine flatwoods, prairie, rosemary scrub, sandhill

Trailhead coordinates (lat-lon): 29.005133, -82.384067

Maps: USGS 7½' Dunnellon, USGS 7½' Holder, Withlacoochee State Forest map at kiosk

Admission: Free

Hours: Sunrise–sunset

Flowing northward toward the Gulf of Mexico, the Withlacoochee River defines the boundary between Citrus and Marion Counties. Just south of the river lies the Two Mile Prairie Tract of Withlacoochee State Forest, where the Johnson Pond Trail provides a walk through several stretches of Florida's least common scrub environment, the rosemary scrub.

Despite the predominance of scrub habitat along this hike, the Johnson Pond Trail is also a birder's delight. Designated as a bluebird habitat trail, nesting boxes were placed along the trail by Girl Scout Cadet troop 678 from nearby Dunnellon. Every two weeks, the scouts monitor the boxes for bluebird activity. It's not just bluebirds you'll see amid the sandhills and scrub. Watch for the yellow flash of the palm warbler, and listen for the languid warble of the warbling vireo. Great blue herons step gracefully through the shallow waters of Johnson Pond.

Starting at the kiosk, pass through the split-rail fence and follow the trail as it swings left onto a forest road into the sandhill habitat, where young longleaf pines rise to touch the sky. Eruptions of orange sand along the trail mark the underground paths of pocket gophers. Loblolly and sand pines intersperse with the longleaf pines; the scent of pine rises from the path on a damp day. Clumps of soft seafoam-colored deer moss hide beneath the turkey oaks.

After 0.5 mile, the trail makes a sharp right past a bench. Thickets of saw palmetto cluster under the turkey oaks. Watch for the first of many gopher tortoise burrows on the

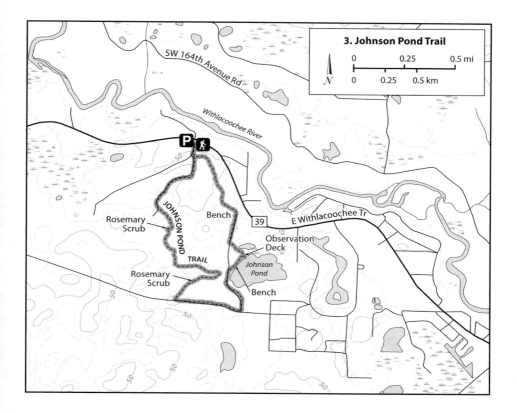

right. Sandhills are prime gopher tortoise habitat, and the scattered gopher apples and prickly pear cactus provide fuel for the tortoise's wanderings. Turning left, the trail passes through a stand of gnarled old sand live oaks, past a prairie edged by longleaf pines. By 0.7 mile, you reach Johnson Pond, a broad, marshy flatwoods pond. Lily pads float across the open water; pond cypresses crowd the edge of the marsh. An observation platform affords you a chance to watch for colorful water birds that frequent the pond—the purple gallinule, the green heron, and the great blue heron. The trail continues along the edge of the lake past a set of picnic benches.

Where a forest road comes in from the right, the trail makes a left through a stretch of bamboo-like maidencane, continuing to work its way along the edge of the pond. Another left leads you into an oak hammock behind the pond cypresses on the south side of the pond, as the trail leaves the forest road to follow a pine-needle-strewn path along the cypresses. Gray squirrels chatter in the trees. The trail emerges from the forest to follow a soft sand ridge, arcing to the right under the slash pines. Turn right onto a causeway built up over a natural channel into Johnson Pond, buttressed by large limestone and chert boulders. Keep walking straight up the forest road into an oak hammock, where the soft velvet of a buck's antlers clings to the furrowed bark of a sand live oak. A red-tailed hawk cries from a high perch in the tree. Songbirds flit across the trail, small blurs in motion.

A blue-blazed trail intersects from the left at 1.2 miles—one of the horse trails from the southern extreme of Two Mile Prairie. It shares the hiking trail for the next 0.2 mile, so expect the footpath to be rather rough going. Although the trail is *not* posted for bicycle use, don't be surprised to see fat-tire enthusiasts zipping past. In the soft sand along both sides of the road, look for sand pine whitlow-wort. These endangered wildflowers grow only in a limited region of Florida's sand pine scrub, and have dense square flower clusters of pale pink or white, blooming through the summer and in October.

Deer moss in the oak scrub

After you pass a barbed-wire fence on the left, the hiking trail turns away from the horse trail, to the right and downhill along the orange blazes, descending through a live oak hammock as you enter the rosemary scrub. Most rosemary scrubs are small patches of tall Florida rosemary growing atop bald patches of sugary white sand in the midst of a sand pine scrub or oak scrub. Here, the trail winds through a rosemary scrub for several hundred feet. The domed shrubs, some up to 10 feet tall, are reminiscent of sagebrush. Florida rosemary is not related to the edible herb rosemary, which is in the mint family. In an odd adaptation to its harsh, desert-like environment, the rosemary bush releases a natural herbicide into the sand to inhibit the growth of its seedlings and other plants, a process called allelopathy. Not until fire sweeps through the scrub does the chemical dissipate, allowing at least one seedling to take root and occupy the place of the parent, accounting for the near-perfect spacing between rosemary bushes in the scrub.

Several species of lichens carpet the sand between the rosemary bushes, including *Cladonia prostrata,* a crispy-looking silvery lichen. When this lichen becomes damp, the crispy edges unfurl like a miniature staghorn fern, exposing a greenish interior. The larger puffy lichens, such as pale greenish-gray *Cladina evansii* and yellowish *Cladina subtenuis* are lumped under the colloquial name of deer moss. Like the smaller lichens, these plants become brittle when dry, and soft and spongy when wet.

The trail parallels a dry streambed to the left, then veers left into the slash pines before rising up into an oak hammock, where bright pink red blanket lichen livens up the live oak trunks. Southern red cedars are scattered amid the oaks. A large Florida dogwood shows off its white blooms in spring, its red seeds the remainder of the year. An American

Rosemary scrub

holly shades a small limestone outcrop on the right, at 1.9 miles. A shaded bench sits at the upper end of a steep karst valley; the trail swings to the right, climbing up into another rosemary scrub set amid live oaks. As it continues to climb, the trail works its way back onto the sandhills, where turkey oak and longleaf pine dominate the canopy, and the grassy understory hosts a parade of fall wildflowers—blazing star, deer's tongue, and yellow buttons.

As you descend into a crowded forest of live oak and willow oak, a large hole is hidden under the pines—a fox den. Not native to Florida, foxes were introduced in the early 1900s to please the patrons of hunting clubs. With no predators and plenty of prey, they spread throughout Florida's forests. The gray fox prefers a heavily wooded habitat such as this oak hammock, while the red fox sticks to the open spaces, like sandhills and prairies. Both sport a reddish coat and can be heard howling and whining after dark, sometimes mistaken for the coyotes prevalent in this region. Gray foxes can climb trees—the only member of the dog family to do so.

The pines show burn scars as you climb a long uphill through turkey oaks, dressed in their fall colors of crimson and brown. More than any other Florida habitat, the sandhill shows the change of the season. Winged sumacs turn a deep, dark crimson, while the wiregrass fades to straw. Swinging left around a short stand of wax myrtle, the trail plunges downhill under the longleaf pines to complete the loop. Continue straight for another 0.1 mile to return to the parking area.

DIRECTIONS

Take Interstate 75 exit 350 Ocala (southbound) or exit 341, Belleview (northbound), heading west on either SR 200 or CR 484 for about 10 miles, where the two roads intersect. From the intersection, follow SR 200 west 6.2 miles to the Withlacoochee River bridge, turning right onto CR 39, between the two gas stations. Drive 2.6 miles to the trailhead on the left side of the road. The trail starts at a kiosk with a map of the trail, with a picnic bench alongside the parking area.

CONTACT

Withlacoochee State Forest
Recreation/Visitors Center
15003 Broad Street
Brooksville, FL 34601
352-754-689
www.fl-dof.com

4

Potts Preserve

Total distance (circuit): 12.3 miles

Hiking time: 7 hours or overnight

*Habitats: pine flatwoods, scrubby flat-
woods, oak scrub, meadow, floodplain forest, hydric hammock, oak hammock, hardwood hammock, prairie*

*Trailhead coordinates (lat-lon):
28.906472, -82.278834*

*Maps: USGS 7½' Stokes Ferry;
Southwest Florida Water Management
District map; Florida Trail Association Map
Central 1*

*Admission: Free. Free permit required for
camping.*

Hugging the eastern shore of Lake Tsala
Apopka and the western shore of the Withlacoochee River, the patchwork of habitats in
Potts Preserve present an unbroken wall of
wilderness on the edge of Citrus County.
From the maps of the preserve, you would assume the main trail would always be in sight
of water, but the majority of Potts Preserve is
upland habitats, including pine flatwoods and
scrub.

Two trails depart from the trailhead. The
orange-blazed trail marks the original outer
loop, and this narrative follows the orange
trail. Enter the preserve on a limerock road
through a hardwood hammock of hickory and
oak. After 0.2 mile it veers right off the road
through an open grassy area on a beeline toward the river for your first glimpse of the
Withlacoochee River. From this small bluff,
look for turtles sunning themselves on logs on
the far shore and wading birds stalking the
shallows. Veering back past a barbeque pavilion and picnic tables, the trail rejoins the limerock road for the next half-mile through a
hammock of tall live oak and southern magnolia up to the Oak Hammock Campground.
Canoeists, car campers, equestrians, and
backpackers can use this free campground,
but you must first contact the Southwest
Florida Water Management District for a free
permit. It's a large grassy area along the river,
primitive but popular.

Watch for the one high blaze on the lone
tree in the middle of the meadow. The trail
keeps toward the river, skirting around a live
oak with sprawling low branches before it
reaches a fence line. Turn right at the double

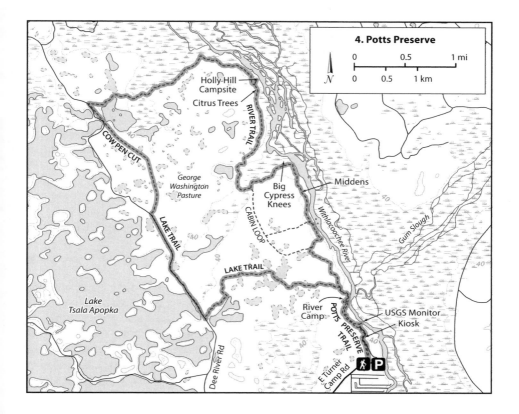

blaze into the woods, walking through dense cabbage palms within the river floodplain. Turn left, crossing a jeep road into a hammock of live oaks and cedar, with a crowded understory of young cabbage palms. A slight rise takes the trail into a more temperate forest, with water oak and loblolly pine. After 1 mile, you come to the junction of the River Trail and the Lake Trail. Turn left to start the big loop around Potts Preserve.

The forest is a mixture of older pine flatwoods and stands of young pine reforesting open meadows. Before acquisition by the state between 1988 and 1993, this was the Dee River Ranch. The many crisscrossing jeep trails and stretches of open meadow on the property attest to the changes brought by settlement. Originally pine flatwoods, this area was logged out, ranched, and replanted with pines, altering the look of the landscape. Only the many flatwoods ponds give an indication of the original habitat. The waving green flags of arrowroot signal the presence of water in many of the ponds, as do the strong melodies of frogs attracted to the dampness. The pines here are loblolly pine, a species that looks deceptively like slash pine, thanks to its short (5-inch) needles. However, the needle clusters are generally in groups of three, and slash pine clusters are groups of two. On the tree, the loblolly pine needles seem to reach toward the sun, while on slash pine, the needles hang downward.

The trail continues through pines and saw

palmettos. Continuing through the woods along the edge of a large prairie off to the left, you'll cross a jeep track in a deep ditch at 1.7 miles, entering a pine forest with an understory of tall deerberry bushes and tangled blackberries. Skirting another prairie, the trail continues under the canopy of loblolly pine before making a hard left into a dense forest of live oak and sweetgum. A cypress swamp encroaches on the right, and the number of saw palmettos increases. Turning away from the pines, the trail winds through tall oaks between two cypress swamps, making a sharp right turn as the trees become larger. An armadillo rustles under the saw palmetto. Oyster fungi advance up a rotting tree trunk. At 2.9 miles, the trail reaches a limerock road. Turn right.

Horses share the road, which follows the floodplain forest along Tsala Apopka Lake. The new orange blazes connect the old Lake Trail back to the River Trail; the blue blazes to the left connect to an alternate trailhead on Dee River Road, used primarily by equestrians. Following the orange blazes, the road rises up along an oak scrub, eventually coming to Pasture Road at 3.8 miles. A grassy parking area awaits horse trailers. You're walking through the open, sunny edge of the George Washington Pasture, a vast remainder from the Dee River Ranch. Flat-topped goldenrod stretches out to the distance. Continue on to the ruins of the Cow Pen, across from a large flatwoods pond. Make a right onto Cow Pen Cut, heading out into the open meadow. Songbirds flit in and out of the low shrubs as you approach. Follow this jeep road for the next mile, passing through one large blackberry patch on your way to the distant tree line. After crossing a jeep trail at the tree line, continue on the same road along the edge of an oak scrub. Deep soft sand chokes the jeep trail in places.

At 5.3 miles, continue straight along the same jeep trail as you finally meet up with the blessed shade of the oak hammocks after more than 2 miles in the sun. The trail crosses over a cattail-edged slough. The sand in the middle of the road becomes deep, so stick to the left edge as you approach the junction with Twin Pond Road. Turn right. Watch as small gray toads with black dots scatter at your approach. A creature of the pine flatwoods, the oak toad breeds in the small grassy puddles and pools that appear after a heavy rain. A bright white stripe down the toad's back makes it easy to find. More active in daytime than most toads, the oak toad peeps like a baby chicken.

Twin Pond Road ends at another equestrian parking area. Continue forward to a trail junction sign, at 5.9 miles. To the left is the old Lake Trail, now defunct; turn right to follow the River Trail back to Hooty Point. It's a joy to return to the shade of the oak hammocks. Make a left at a double blaze, turning onto a jeep track to cross a bridge over a slough filled with clay-colored water. Royal ferns grow along its banks. Pay careful attention here, as within 50 feet the trail abruptly turns off to the left after crossing the bridge; the wider jeep trail continues straight.

Passing some unusually high rocky mounds on the right, the trail turns, crossing a slough. You can tell you're approaching the river by the cypress floodplain swamps that start to appear. Unlike many Florida rivers, the Withlacoochee does not flaunt its charms—it hides behind floodplain forests, making it difficult for a hiker to actually reach the water's edge. As the trail crisscrosses many old jeep trails through this section, take care to always watch for the next orange blaze. After heading down through a narrow corridor of scrub live oak and tall loblolly pines, the trail emerges into hydric hammock, thick with cabbage palm and massive live oak trees.

Wildlife is more prevalent in this part of the

KEVIN MIMS

Blue loop at Potts Preserve

park, where the water supply is guaranteed. An armadillo roots up grubs, while a red-tailed hawk cries as it swoops after a gray squirrel. White-tailed deer come to the river to drink. A black racer pauses while crossing the trail, its scales shimmering in the sunlight. Half-hidden by the leaves, a barred owl perches in a tall branch.

Surface limestone appears, and the trail follows a small ridge. After passing by a loblolly pine that rises more than 100 feet high, the trail makes a sharp right turn, passing a comparably sized live oak on the left. The forest changes to hickory and sweetgum, tinged in shades of yellow and orange in the autumn months. Examine the trailside limestone boulders closely, and you'll see the fossil impressions of scallops and snails. You

catch your first glimpse of the river since the beginning of the hike, off to the left.

If you are backpacking this loop, start paying attention for your campsite when the trail becomes crowded between large American holly trees. This is Holly Hill, and the campsite is off to the left, down a blue-blazed trail at 7.6 miles. There isn't much to it, just a fire ring under the trees, and river access through the cypresses to gather water for cooking. A signpost indicates the side trail. It seems like a curious place for a campsite, but as you continue hiking along the river, you'll discover why. There aren't many dry spots, thanks to the floodplain forest. Be sure to clear your tent site of pointy holly leaves before you lay the ground cloth down.

Continuing past the campsite, you begin

Johnson Pond Trail

Green tree frog

to see scattered wild citrus trees amid the large live oaks. The land along the river was a homestead, and the landowner grew a small citrus grove. After passing through a stand of enormous southern magnolias—upward of 70 feet tall—the trail descends back into hydric hammock, passing more immense live oaks.

As the river vanishes from view, the patchwork of habitats continues, from hardwood forest to cypress swamp, to pine flatwoods and back to hydric hammock, changing with every twist and turn of the trail. One stand of knobby bald cypress surrounds you with cypress knees in every direction—some of them as tall as 3 feet! Watch the blazes as you exit this area, since the trail jumps on and off some of the narrow jeep trails as it winds its way through the forest, and it's easy to walk off in the wrong direction if you aren't watching for those orange blazes on the trees.

Reaching the RIVER LOOP sign at 9.1 miles, turn left. Although the orange blazes continue straight ahead, the River Loop provides a scenic blue-blazed day hiking loop, accessible by following the River Trail straight up the river from Hooty Point. You'll walk along the eastern part of the loop to follow the river. The trail soon turns right, heading south along the floodplain forest. Watch out for the many small cypress knees in the trail—it's easy to bang your feet into them. Marsh ferns cascade from a large limestone boulder. The trail turns right onto a causeway, then climbs up a rise into a grove of cedars, providing a nice view of the river through the trees. This hill isn't what it appears to be. It's a midden, a trash heap laced with earth, shell, and stone, left behind by the long-vanished Timacuan culture. There are a dozen large middens along this section of the river, which is why there are no campsites on these scenic hills—

Florida law protects these archaeological sites. At 10.3 miles, you reach the RIVER LOOP/CABIN LOOP sign, pointing to a blue-blazed cross-trail that is part of the day loop. Continue straight, and you'll pass a rustic tumbledown cabin on the left, the original pioneer homestead along this section of the river.

After the trail curves away from the river, it quickly meets up with the main trail. Turn left at the trail junction, following the orange blazes into hardwood hammock. You'll cross a high bridge over a deep ditch, entering a forest of oak and cabbage palm. A tall snag rises to the left, providing a home for shelf fungi. A green tree frog clings to a saw palmetto frond. The trail passes through wild citrus and southern red cedar before live oaks again dominate the forest. Roots and rocks break up the footpath as you edge along a cypress swamp, where duckweed coating the water's surface makes the swamp glow green. Southern magnolias tower overhead as you approach the end of the big loop, reaching the RIVER TRAIL/LAKE TRAIL sign. You've hiked 11.3 miles.

To return to your car, continue straight, retracing the first mile of your hike. Follow the orange blazes to the river and through the Oak Hammock campground on the way back to Hooty Point Road, completing your hike after 12.3 miles.

DIRECTIONS

From Interstate 75 southbound, take exit 350, Ocala, following SR 200 west to Hernando. From the intersection of SR 200 and US 41 at Hernando, drive 5.2 miles south to CR 581, inside the city limits. From Interstate 75 northbound, take exit 329, Wildwood, following SR 44 for 11 miles to Inverness. Follow US 41 northbound to CR 581. Follow CR 581 east for 6.8 miles to reach Hooty Point Road. Turn right. The trailhead is 0.3 mile ahead on the left.

CONTACT

Southwest Florida Water Management District
2379 Broad Street
Brooksville, FL 34604-6899
352-796-7211 or 800-423-1476 (Florida only)
www.swfwmd.state.fl.us/recreation

5

Citrus Trail

Total distance (circuit): 35 miles

Hiking time: 3 days

Habitats: caverns, freshwater marsh, hardwood hammock, oak hammock, oak scrub, prairie, rosemary scrub, sand pine scrub, scrubby flatwoods, sinkholes

Trailhead coordinates (lat-lon): 28.799305, -82.384676

Maps: USGS 7½' Lecanto, USGS 7½' Brooksville; Withlacoochee State Forest Citrus Hiking Trail map; Florida Trail Association Map Central 2

Admission: Free

Hours: 24 hours

With nearly 158,000 acres spread over four counties, Withlacoochee State Forest is Florida's third largest state forest, and arguably the most popular for outdoor recreation. Its largest tract, Citrus, contains the state's longest backpacking loop trail in a single contiguous forest—the Citrus Trail, four stacked loops containing more than 40 miles of trails. The Citrus Trail is Central Florida's most rugged backpacking trail, with aggressively rolling sandhills, steep descents into sinkholes, and rock-strewn footpaths, providing a stunning array of contrasting habitats and numerous opportunities for wildlife encounters. It is also a well-groomed trail, easily followed, with a clearly defined footpath and signposts at trail junctions. Orange blazes designate the outer loop, while blue blazes mark the cross-trails and side trails. This hike describes the outer loop of 35 miles, but you can easily stitch together the loops to come up with shorter or longer backpacking trips, as well.

Backpacking the Citrus Trail takes some logistical planning. There are no surface streams, so you must consider this a dry trail. Karst features—sinkholes and solution holes—seasonally retain some rainfall, as do flatwoods ponds. There are only four permanent water sources along the trail, so check the map first and determine beforehand if you need to cache water jugs at forest road crossings before you start hiking. The official primitive backpacker-only campsites (no water sources) are spaced far apart, making for long days to start. Camping is permitted anywhere you see white bands painted around trees. Since a network of sand roads

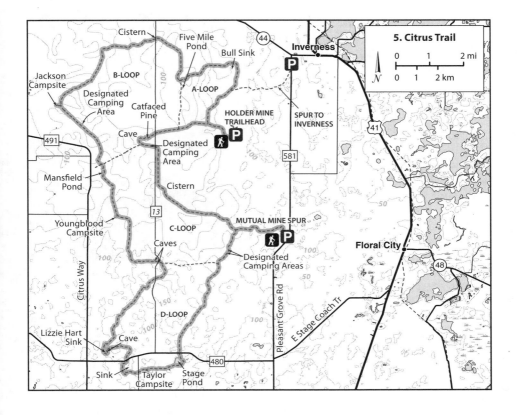

crisscrosses the forest, you can day hike certain portions of the trail. The shortest loop, Loop A, takes 8.5 miles to hike from Holder Mine Campground, and is part of the Florida State Parks Trailwalker program. With the exception of FR13 and FR10, forest roads require a high-clearance vehicle and/or four-wheel drive. No permits are required to hike or camp along this trail, but be sure to check your hiking schedule against the hunting dates posted by the Florida Fish and Wild-life Conservation Commission on their website. The Citrus Tract is one of the region's most popular deer hunting grounds, so hiking is **not** recommended during deer season. Always wear an orange safety vest if *any* type of hunting is going on along the Citrus Trail.

DAY ONE

Total distance (one-way): 11 miles
Hiking time: 6 hours

Start and end your backpacking trip at the Holder Mine Recreation Area, where you can fill up on potable water just outside the campground, along the entrance road. When you sign in at the kiosk, specify how long you plan to be on the trail. Walk over to the road and turn left, following the blue blazes until they veer right, into the forest. After you pass a low depression on the right, you cross two horse trails. The Citrus Tract has separate sets of trails for hikers, bikers, and equestrians. A color band around the trees designates horse trails. Florida rosemary bushes grow up to 8 feet tall, forming neat patches under the sand

---

pines. Reindeer lichen blankets the glittering white sand. As the trail ascends sharply, it enters a forest of turkey oaks and sand live oaks with scattered wiregrass, which gives way to oak scrub.

The blue-blazed connector trail ends after 1 mile, at the LOOP A sign. Turn right to begin the orange-blazed outer loop. Oak scrub gives way to sandhills. Be alert as the trail veers to the right after crossing a jeep trail, rising into a forest of longleaf, slash, and sand pines. Quail explode from the wiregrass. Gopher apple grows in shady spots. You pass a longleaf snag heavy with resin—lighter pine, the heartwood of a dead longleaf pine, a perfect fire-starter.

The open understory impresses upon you the size of this forest as the wiregrass fades into the distance, a taupe fog. You start a long, slow descent down the sandhill, passing by a tall wax myrtle where young bucks rub their antlers. When you reach FR 8 at 1.6 miles, you'll see trail signs on both sides of the road. Usually, these signs indicate on the back which road you're crossing, which makes it easy to find your place on the map. Descending under the longleaf pines, you enter a grove of sand live oaks, with their trunks and branches all swept toward the left. The orange eruptions of pocket gophers pockmark the footpath. As you climb up and down the sandhills, watch for gopher tortoise burrows and rounded armadillo holes. By 2.1 miles, you reach the Florida Trail spur leading to Inverness. The Florida Trail Association is in the process of moving its Western Corridor segment of trail off the Withlacoochee State Trail, a paved rail-trail through Inverness, and into the Citrus Tract to connect with other parts of Withacoochee State Forest farther south.

At 2.9 miles, you cross under a power line and over a paved road. After climbing up and over a ridge, the trail drops down and around

Camping out along the Citrus Hiking Trail

a prairie, which hosts an ephemeral pond. Jeep trails crisscross the trail as it winds through the dense shade of an oak hammock. The trail starts a long uphill, crossing FR 6 up into a longleaf forest, through a narrow corridor of dense sand live oak, until it emerges in a clearing along the bottom of a steep sandhill, nearly 100 feet high. Returning to the woods, the trail turns right and climbs up the sandhill, reaching an open forest of turkey oaks at the top. A summer tanager flits by in a blur of red. Oaks yield to pines as the trail descends, crossing FR 11 and continuing to descend through a hunt camp into an oak hammock, where Five Mile Pond lies off to the left, in the open prairie. It's another ephemeral pond, so don't count on it as a water source.

After 5 miles, you reach the A-B Loop junction. Turn right to remain on the outer loop. The trail makes a long slow uphill through the sandhill before crossing FR 6, rising into a mix of turkey oaks and longleaf pine. On the downhill, the trail passes tightly between two longleaf pines; the one on the right sports a catface from turpentining. Watch for scattered clay pots, relics of the days when men tapped the trees for their resin. Continuing up and down over the sandhills, the trail drops down through a longleaf forest, on a needle carpet so thick that it buries the wiregrass. At the bottom of the hill, the trail winds through an oak hammock, then rises back up into the sandhills, meeting FR 13 at 6.8 miles. FR 13 is the most accessible road through the forest, and the trail crosses it six times over the course of the loop—use it as your water drop point, if you opt to cache water. Just beyond FR 13 is the first permanent water source along the trail, a massive concrete cistern for watering horses. Because of its proximity to the road, it isn't a great water source—you'll see beer cans and cigarette butts floating in the water. But it is the only water source for the next 8 to 13 miles. Be sure to strain *and* filter the water.

The habitat changes from sandhills to sand pine scrub as the trail crosses FR 2 and enters an oak scrub, a restoration project to attract the Florida scrub-jay to this habitat. You're on the extreme northern edge of the property, and can hear some traffic noise from SR 44. A chuck-will's-widow bursts out of the wiregrass, flushed by your approach. After crossing the open oak scrub, you reenter a stand of tall sand pines, its understory dense with myrtle oaks. Just after crossing FR 2, white bands on the trees indicate a camping zone. Since these camping zones are open to hunters and equestrians, many of them have an inordinate amount of trash lying around. Unless you feel a need to stop now, continue on to the backpackers' campsite, another 3 miles ahead. The trail meanders through stands of saw palmetto under the longleaf pines, the habitat shifting to scrubby flatwoods as it crosses FR 4 and FR 4A in quick succession. Watch for an animal den in the ruins of a longleaf stump, right in front

of the trail—big enough to be a hobbit hole, but likely the home of a coyote or fox. Climbing up through the pines, the trail crosses FR 6 at 9.1 miles. Expect wildlife sightings in this remote corner of the forest, as you spy the white flags of two retreating white-tailed deer. Look for bobcat tracks along the footpath. FR 17 sits in a deep ditch, making the crossing a little tricky. The trail continues downhill under the longleaf pines into a dense corridor of sand live oaks, making a long, slow descent to FR 8. Just after you cross FR 8, start watching for the campsite sign, at 10.8 miles. Follow the blue blaze off to the right for 0.2 mile as it jogs through the forest to the Jackson Campsite, an open spot under a gnarled live oak. Set up your tent, pull up a log, and enjoy the serenity of an evening away from the sounds of civilization.

DAY TWO

Total distance (one-way): 11.5 miles
Hiking time: 7 hours

After packing up your gear, take care to find your way back to the blue blazes (look for the white rings on the trees) to return to the loop trail. At the campground sign, turn right, following the orange blazes. As the trail descends through scrubby flatwoods, blueberry bushes crowd the forest floor, a perfect feeding ground for bears or for your breakfast, if you hike through here in April or May. Where the understory opens up, yucca grows in scattered clumps between the wiregrass. Crossing FR 10A, the trail veers left to parallel the road briefly, passing through another white-ringed camping zone frequented by hunters. Climbing uphill, you cross two jeep trails in quick succession. As the trail heads downhill, notice the longleaf pines in their candle stage—like a bunch of spiky hairdos. After crossing FR 3, the trail veers left, reaching a power line, then FR 17 at 1.3 miles. Most of the older longleaf pines along this section of the trail bear the scars of catfaces, some embedded with metal shaped like a broad "V" to channel the resin into the turpentine cup. As the trail drifts west, you hear traffic on CR 491. The trail rises up a steep sand slope that has been degraded by horses. Despite the many POSTED signs and the many miles of horse trails available to equestrians, some visitors choose to ride their horses down the hiking trail, at risk of a stiff fine. At the top of the hill, take in the view of longleaf forest stretching off on both sides.

You reach the signpost for the B-C Loop junction at 2.6 miles, along with another camping zone. Continue straight through a stand of southern magnolias. Descending steeply into an oak hammock, the trail makes a sudden sharp left. Watch the blazes carefully through this section, as the trail zigzags through the forest, on and off jeep trails. A giant split oak sits off to the left, its trunk cleaved in three sections, sprawling across the ground, sending up limbs as thick as trunks themselves. You are skirting around Mansfield Pond, a flatwoods pond off to the left. Because of its size and low location, it's a reasonably reliable water source, but it can go dry. You'll likely need to slog through muck to get to the water. As the trail veers away from the pond, it passes under a canopy of tall live oaks, climbing back into the scrubby flatwoods. Watch for a railroad rail, strangely bent as if it were wrapped around a tree. In the early 1900s, several railroads crossed the forest, linking together newly opened phosphate mines with a port at Yankeetown, on the Gulf of Mexico.

Crossing FR 14, the trail continues past the Youngblood Campsite at 3.3 miles. Just beyond the turnoff for the campsite is a camping zone on both sides of the trail. When you approach the edge of the meadow, walk softly. It's an ideal place to watch for deer. The trail crosses FR 16 at 5 miles, paralleling an

area replanted with longleaf pines. Look carefully at those broad tracks in the trail–a Florida panther. Hikers report encountering these endangered mountain lion–sized felines in the Withlacoochee State Forest, but the panther quickly slinks away.

Two live oaks form a gateway into the pine forest, where maidencane grows tall in damp spots along the trail. The forest becomes a dense mix of oaks and pines as the trail twists and turns through a corridor of saw palmetto. When rocks begin to appear in the footpath, you've reached the rolling karst hills of the central forest. Limestone outcrops appear on the surface as small rocks and large boulders. Look off to the left for a dark pit, an entrance to a cave, where a cave mouse scurries between the boulders. Karst is a landscape shaped by the action of water on rock, where rainfall trickling through tannic oak leaves becomes an acidic solution that etches pathways through soft bedrock. Karst features in this forest include caverns and sinkholes, and rough exposed limestone along the trail. In karst, water flows down instead of out, so what few seasonal streams flow through the Withlacoochee State Forest are gobbled up into sinkholes.

You cross FR 13 at 6.3 miles, dropping down into a karst valley, which drains off to the right into a plugged-up cave entrance. Limestone-loving spleenwort grows in clusters on the bare rock. Climbing up into an oak hammock, the trail reaches the signpost for the C-D Loop junction. Turn right, climbing up through the scrubby flatwoods to cross FR 18A and FR 18 in quick succession. The trail merges on to a jeep road, veering off to the left through the flatwoods before rising up through an oak hammock to cross FR 13 again at 7 miles. As you cross an old railroad bed, two bald eagles break into an argument at the top of a tall live oak; one swoops down low under the canopy, winging its way deeper into the forest. Descending down a rocky slope, you're back in a karst valley. Sweetgum and American holly crowd the trail. Off to the right, there is an open area with a depression. If you leave the trail and walk to the left through the depressions, you'll come across a sinkhole that seasonally serves as a duckweed-choked pond, a potential water source.

Watch for a hard left and a hard right as the trail ascends back out of the valley into scrubby flatwoods. Mourning doves rise from the wiregrass as you pass. You continue uphill through a low oak understory, with bracken ferns spilling across the forest floor. After crossing FR 20 at 7.9 miles, a divided road with a power line, the trail drops downhill under the pines. The flowering plants with waxy green leaves and ivory blossoms are sandhill milkweed, attracting dozens of colorful butterflies, including the long-tailed skipper. In this section of the trail, you'll cross over numerous horse trails, each marked with a different-colored band. After the trail rises up through a stand of tall pines, it crosses FR 15, down in a deep ditch, at 8.2 miles. Pines yield to sandhills—in this part of the forest, many of the sandhills were planted over with

longleaf pines after the original forest was logged, so it's difficult to determine the habitat. When the trail drops down a steep grade into an older forest of pines, keep alert, as needles obscure the footpath, making it easy to miss where the trail veers to the right. Rocks come to the surface again in a cedar grove, where the trail passes through dense pines and oaks before reaching FR 22 at 8.8 miles. From here, the trail drops steeply downhill, past a deep gully on the left, into a mixed forest of elms, hickory, southern magnolias, and cedar. Just beyond, you can look over the rocky lip of Lizzie Hart Sink, a massive depression cradling numerous caves at 9.1 miles. Because of the rocky terrain, the footpath becomes indistinct. Follow the orange blazes carefully, watching your footing, and be respectful of the fragile, unusual terrain. As you pass through an old board fence, you can see the bottom of the sink, to the left. The trail twists and turns around obstacles, including a colossal swamp chestnut oak and the dark mouth of a cave. When the trail leaves Lizzie Hart Sink, keep alert for where it crosses a jeep trail, descending into a forest of oaks and sweetgum. At 10 miles, a swampy water-filled

Surface limestone along the Citrus Hiking Trail

KEVIN MIMS

sink hides behind the bushes off to the right, another potential water source. Clambering over a railroad bed, the trail rises steeply, reaching the CR 480 crossing at 10.4 miles. Carefully cross the highway, then head up into the rolling sandhills. The trail turns right along a dry streambed, then turns left to cross it. This seasonal stream flows a significant distance, cutting a deep ravine along the trail's edge until it plunges into a large sinkhole fed by several similar streams. At 10.9 miles, this is your last opportunity to gather water before reaching your campsite. You'll only need water for dinner, as another water source is less than a mile past the campsite. Stay right at the fork. At the top of the hill, the trail turns right, crossing FR 13 at 11.1 miles. You wind through a rocky forest of oaks and hickories to reach the campsite sign at 11.2 miles. Turn right and follow the blue blaze for 0.1 miles down to the open space between the white-ringed trees, and select your spot at the Taylor Campsite. After this interesting but tiring hike, it won't be long before you're sleeping soundly.

DAY THREE

Total distance (one-way): 12.8 miles
Hiking time: 6 hours

After packing up in the morning, return up the blue blaze to the main trail and turn right. Rocks poke out of the footpath. Descending into the sweetgum forest, the trail becomes a narrow track. A marsh lies off to the right, surrounded by dense forest. After crossing a jeep trail, a large open area looms on the left—Stage Pond, a permanent and reliable water source at 0.9 mile. Netted chain grows along its edge. The trail follows a jeep trail along the eastern edge of the lake, with two good access points for filtering water. After the trail turns right, it veers through an oak hammock to meet CR 480 at 1.4 miles. Cross the road and enter a forest of scattered sand pines,

longleaf pines, and scrub oaks. In the early morning, the sandhills are alive with the furious activities of birds darting between the trees—blue-gray gnatcatchers, yellow vireos, cedar waxwings, and downy woodpeckers. Crossing FR 22 at 1.9 miles, you pass between two live oaks, and the trail veers to the right, flanked by the profuse blooms of sandhill milkweed. Crossing FR 11, the trail drops down under sand live oaks, continuing on an undulating route over the sandhills. After you cross FR 20, keep alert for several sharp turns in the trail as it enters an extensive laurel oak forest. Emerging out into the sandhills, the trail jumps on and off jeep roads before reaching FR 18. Blue flag iris bloom in a damp area along a seepage slope. At 4.4 miles, you meet the sign for the C-D Loop cross-trail. Turn right, following the orange blazes. The landscape opens up, with scattered longleaf pines showing off old catfaces. Icicles of hardened amber resin drip from one catfaced pine, off to the left. Passing through a camping zone on a dry, windy hilltop, you soon cross FR 18A and discover another old railroad bed, this one still decorated with the ballast used under the rails. Beyond FR 9A, FR 16 runs in a deep ditch. Cross FR 7 and enter a stand of young longleaf pines, as the trail rises up to a bench and the sign for Mutual Mine, at 5.8 miles. This developed campground sits along the edge of one of the phosphate pits dug in these hills during the early 1900s, and offers potable water, picnic tables, restrooms, and grills. It's a pleasant place to camp, more so than Holder Mine, and you may want to adjust your hike to start and end here. Today's trek, however, continues on to finish the full Citrus Hiking Trail loop.

Rising up through a young longleaf forest on the sandhills, the trail traverses open grassland replanted with longleaf pines, crossing FR 7 at 6 miles. Past FR 9, prickly pear grows in the open spaces between myrtle oaks and

Chapman oaks. Watch for gopher tortoises as you approach a camping zone, at 6.7 miles. The habitat yields to a more mature forest on the sandhills, with wiregrass and scattered oaks underneath a tall canopy of longleaf pine. You cross FR 11, then FR 14, climbing up into the pine-forested sandhills. A male eastern fence lizard flashes its bright blue belly as it climbs up a snag in search of a warm spot. These gray-and-white lizards blend easily against oak tree trunks as they patiently sit and wait for ants, spiders, and other choice morsels to wander past.

You see your first saw palmettos of the day just before crossing FR 14A, where a square concrete block water cistern shimmers along the side of the trail, at 8.1 miles. This is the last water source you will encounter before returning to Holder Mine. Take a moment and sit on the broad wall, watching the birds in the surrounding oaks. An eastern bluebird streaks past. The trail continues on through large clumps of saw palmetto under a dense pine understory, with plenty of blueberry bushes lining the trail. Off to the left, you see an orange gash, a break in the trees—the trail parallels FR 13. Several deer look up, then bound away. Just after you cross FR 13 at 9.6 miles, there are two camping zones in rapid succession. Neither looks suitable for a tent. You reach the junction with the B-C Loop cross-trail at 9.9 miles. Continue straight along the orange blazes.

As the trail drops down into an oak hammock, the vegetation becomes lusher. At the bottom of the hill, take a look to the left—the biggest cave yet along this trail, with a walk-in opening flooded with sunlight. Drop your pack and take a few minutes to explore. Chinese ladder brake and spleenwort ferns decorate crevices in the limestone. As you continue down the trail, notice the tall southern wood fern growing out of a sinkhole on the right. Limestone breaks up the footpath.

The trail veers to the left, down into an oak hammock in a vast karst bowl. As it emerges from the bowl, look for a catface with metal strips on the right. Crossing FR 13 for the last time at 10.6 miles, the trail rises through a blueberry patch to meet the final loop junction, the A-B Loop cross-trail. Continue straight, walking through a scrubby hammock under the longleaf pines. After you cross FR 11 at 11.5 miles, the trail rises into scrub, with sugary white sand underfoot, tall rosemary bushes, and dense growths of reindeer moss. After you cross two horse trails, you enter a narrow path through a dense oak scrub. Watch for Florida scrub-jays here, as they prefer a habitat dense with these short myrtle oaks and Chapman oaks. At 12 miles, you reach the end of the loop at the LOOP A sign. Continue straight along the blue blaze for another mile to reach your car at Holder Mine Recreation Area, completing your 35-mile journey.

DIRECTIONS

From Interstate 75, take exit 329, Wildwood. Turn west on SR 44, driving 11 miles to Inverness. Continue west on SR 44 into Inverness to CR 581, located opposite Whispering Pines Park. Turn left. Drive 2.5 miles, passing the fire tower, to the sign for HOLDER MINE RECREATION AREA. Turn right. The road becomes sand after the first mile, and continues for another mile as FR10 into Holder Mine Recreation Area. Pass the hunt check station and campground. The trailhead is on the left, with an FT sign and kiosk.

CONTACT

Withlacoochee State Forest
Recreation/Visitors Center
15003 Broad Street
Brooksville, FL 34601
352-754-6896
www.fl-dof.com

6

Fort Cooper State Park

Total distance (3 circuits): 5.5 miles

Hiking time: 3 hours

Habitats: hardwood hammock, freshwater marsh, sandhill

Trailhead coordinates (lat-lon): 28.807342, -82.306062

Maps: USGS 7½' Inverness; Fort Cooper State Park map

Admission: $2 pedestrians/bicyclists, $3 per vehicle, $5 for primitive camping

Hours: 8 AM–sunset daily

With a picnic area and playground along Lake Holathlikaha, and gentle, well-groomed trails winding through the woods, Fort Cooper State Park is a great place for a family outing, but the reason for this state park isn't as blissful. The park preserves a chapter of Florida history from the Second Seminole War, when a bedraggled battalion of sick and injured soldiers walking to Tampa stopped to regroup and recuperate after a month-long battle at the Cove of the Withlacoochee. A hastily built log fort protected the men against continued attacks. Named for Major Mark Anthony Cooper, who was charged with protecting the soldiers, the fort was abandoned when the soldiers were able to continue their journey. Florida's original military road from Fort King in Ocala to Fort Brooke in Tampa passes through the park and is incorporated into one of the hiking trails.

FORT SITE TRAIL

Start your exploration at the paved Fort Site Trail, a connector that leads through the forest toward the old Fort King Trail. You'll see a rough-hewn wooden sign at the junction, marking the crossing of the old military trail between Fort King (Ocala) and Fort Brooke (Tampa), along with a large kiosk. Head straight ahead to follow the paved path as it rises into upland forest and reaches the back gate of the park at the Withlacoochee State Trail. This connector breathes new life into the park, enabling bicyclists to peel off the main track and come explore this little gem.

Backtrack a little to the paved apron on the right and follow the footpath into the

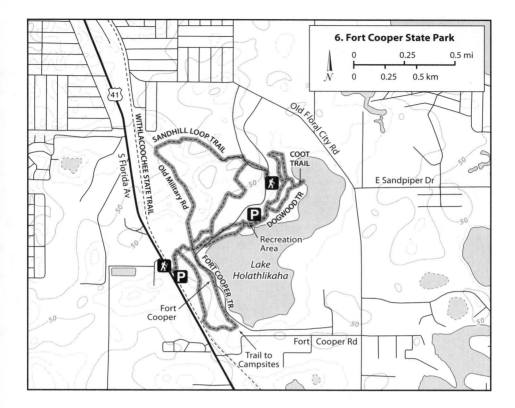

woods at 0.7 mile. Yellow footprint markers lead the way in the opposite direction. It's wonderfully shady here, with ancient live oaks furry with resurrection fern. You reach a loop that provides a shortcut back toward the trailhead. To stay on the outer loop, turn right and head deeper into the forest. The trail reaches a T intersection where you'll need to turn left. Continuing under ancient oaks, it rises up past a shaded bench to an open clearing in the forest, the site of Fort Cooper and of the annual reenactment of this skirmish during the Second Seminole War. When Cooper's battalion of 380 men stopped here in April 1836, the edge of spring-fed lake along the military road was an ideal place for the war-weary men to recuperate. Walking toward Tampa, bedraggled and ill, after a pitched battle at the Cove of the Withlacoochee, a battalion led by Major Mark Anthony Cooper built a log fort to protect the men against attacks from the Seminoles as the men recuperated. The fort was abandoned when the soldiers were able to continue their journey

After you walk past the kiosk, the trail continues in a straight line down the old Military Road where the soldiers marched en route to Fort Brooke. You'll pass the trail junction for the shortcut loop on the left, and soon reach the intersection with the rough-hewn sign, kiosk, and paved trail at 1.3 miles.

SANDHILL LOOP TRAIL

Continue straight ahead to start your walk on the newest trail at Fort Cooper State Park, the Sandhill Loop Trail. The trail is marked in

Passionflower

only one direction—counterclockwise—so turn right at the first footprint trail marker. This is an upland trail, focused on the highest, driest habitat in the park. Where you see a disturbance of sand—white and beige mixed together—follow it to the source. When a gopher tortoise creates a burrow, it pushes a tremendous amount of sand to the surface. This large gopher hole on the left is the first of many along the trail. A tortoise's burrow can be up to 40 feet long and 10 feet deep, and is just as wide as its creator. This isn't the gopher tortoise's only home, however—each adult tortoise creates up to nine different burrows across its territory, leaving plenty of time and space for other occupants to move in. The gopher tortoise is considered a cornerstone species of the sandhill habitat because its burrow, inhabited or not, provides a sort of apartment complex for the sandhill. In the dry conditions of the sandhills, the burrow stays cool and damp. More than 360 different species of animals will move into a gopher hole, including snakes, mice, opossums, quail, armadillo, burrowing owls, toads, and lizards. When wildfire rages through the sandhill, both predators and prey take cover in a gopher hole. Bound by some uneasy truce, all emerge intact after the danger has passed.

The trail sticks to the ecotone between sandhill and hardwood forest, offering a good bit of shade up until you get to the junction with the incoming trail from the trailhead on the main park road. Keep going straight, and you'll find yourself climbing uphill with a jog to the left. Wildlife is abundant here. Watch for gray squirrels leaping from tree to tree. A fox squirrel stands on a branch, surveying the trail. The fox squirrel is the largest of Florida's squirrels, as tall as 2 feet. Its distinctive black-and-white fur stands against the greenery of the forest.

The track is through rather soft sand, and there are deer tracks, fox tracks, and raccoon tracks to follow. In late spring, the gopher apple–a favorite of the gopher tortoise–is in bloom. The trail goes up and over gently undulating hills, rising into small patches of scrub habitat. When you complete the loop, you've done 1.8 miles on this trail and 3.1 miles overall. Follow the paved Fort Site Trail back to the parking area. Turn right and walk down through the recreation area to reach the trailhead for the final hiking loop, the Dogwood Trail.

DOGWOOD TRAIL

Starting on the east side of the recreation area, this easy interpretive loop shows off a mesic hammock, the climax community that takes over when pine flatwoods aren't subject to regular wildfires. Hardwood trees dominate the forest. Loblolly bay and southern magnolia compete for space, both showing off their glossy leaves. Although their coloration is similar, the leaf of a southern magnolia is broad and rounded, while that of the loblolly bay is long and narrow. The forest understory includes saw palmettos with unusually long trunks, young sour oranges, and deerberry.

Frequent benches allow for quiet moments of reflection along the trail. The first bench sits next to a four-way junction of trails. Take the first right, following the NATURE TRAIL sign. You'll soon come across an unusually undulating landscape–a reshaping of the forest by phosphate pits. Saw palmettos, sweetgum, and live oak cling to the misshapen hills. Florida's phosphate boom started in the late 1890s, just after a big freeze killed off the commercial citrus industry. Miners came from all over the south, digging small claim stake pits such as these or working in larger operations such as the ones at Rainbow Springs (Hike 1). Since most of the area's production

went overseas to Europe, the boom went bust with the advent of World War I. The industry later rebounded on a larger scale. Open-pit phosphate mining continues throughout Central Florida, ranking Florida as one of the nation's top states in terms of mining production.

At 0.3 mile, the Short Loop junction joins in from the left, providing a quick way to return to the start of your hike. Turn right, following the 0.2-mile Coot Trail spur toward the marshy shore of Lake Holathlikaha, winding through a forest of laurel oak past moss-covered limestone outcroppings. The trail ends along the edge of the marsh, where herons, coots, and gallinules browse through the grassy wetlands. Turn around and return to the trail junction. Turn right to continue on the Dogwood Trail. Four-inch-wide specimens of shelf fungus grow like steps along the trunks of some of the oak trees. Momentarily flashing its peacock-blue belly, a southern fence lizard scurries up the crinkled bark of a Chapman oak.

The trail veers left, turning back on itself to complete the loop. Fat round pignuts litter the forest floor. Fallen from the high canopy of hammock hickory trees (also known as the Florida pignut), these dark brown nuts provide food for squirrels and raccoons. Notice the many weathered stumps half-hidden by the undergrowth, the remains of a virgin oak forest that once covered these hills. These last oaks were cut by hand in the 1930s, after the phosphate boom subsided.

After passing beneath an 80-foot-tall longleaf pine, survivor of the logging days, the trail meets up with the Short Loop coming in from the left, 0.5 mile into the hike. A Florida dogwood marks the intersection of trails, with its distinctive broad heart-shaped leaves and fragrant white blooms in springtime. Continue straight through the oak forest past an unusual quirk of nature, two tree

Resting spot under the oaks

trunks that grew back together 5 feet above where they originally parted at the base of the tree. The trail veers left around a small solution sinkhole, a deep depression filled with leaves and saw palmetto. Arriving back at the original four-way junction of trails, you've hiked 0.9 mile around this loop and 4.7 miles overall. Continue back across the recreation area to the parking area, completing 5.5 miles of rambling around Fort Cooper State Park.

DIRECTIONS

From Interstate 75, take exit 329, Wildwood. Turn west on SR 44, driving 11 miles to In-verness. Take US 41 south to Old Floral City Road; turn left at the light. Cross the Withla-coochee State Trail, a popular biking trail. Turn right, following the signs 1.6 miles to the park entrance. After paying your Florida State Parks entrance fee, follow the winding road back into the woods. Start your walk from the second parking lot, at the Fort Site Trail.

CONTACT

Fort Cooper State Park
3100 South Old Floral City Road
Inverness, FL 34450
352-726-0315
www.floridastateparks.org/fortcooper

7

Chinsegut Hill WEA

Total distance (2 circuits): 5.6 miles

Hiking time: 3 hours, 30 minutes

Habitats: bayhead, cypress dome, oak hammock, pine flatwoods, prairie, scrub, sandhill

Trailhead coordinates (lat-lon)
Prairie-to-Pines Trailhead:
28.609866, 82.359268
Big Pine Trailhead:
28.599042, -82.377272

Maps: USGS 7½' Brooksville NW, FWC Chinsegut Hill maps

Admission: Free

Hours: Sunrise–sunset

A gentleman from South Carolina, Colonel Pearson, staked his claim to the high rolling hills north of what would become Brooksville in 1842 and built a fine manor house prior to the outbreak of the Civil War. By 1924, the manor and its lands passed into the hands of Colonel Raymond Robins, who dubbed it Chinsegut Hill after the Inuit word for "spirit of lost things," years after he returned from the Klondike with enough gold to settle down and live a life of ease. Mrs. Robins loved gardening, and she created extensive formal gardens around the house. A social economist, Colonel Robins moved in the upper echelons of politics and business and entertained folks such as Thomas Edison, J. C. Penney, and Harold Ickes at the mansion.

By 1932, the Robins family donated their land to the federal government as a wildlife refuge and agricultural experimental station. Among the treasures on the rolling hills were 400 acres of virgin longleaf pine, plus broad open prairies and dark hammocks. After Colonel Robins's death in 1954, the mansion passed on to the University of South Florida, which now uses it as a retreat and conference center. The surrounding tracts of land went to the uses for which they'd been bequeathed: agricultural and conservation, with portions going to Withlacoochee State Forest, the University of Florida, the USDA, and, most recently, the Florida Fish and Wildlife Conservation Commission (FWC). As one of their more unique public lands, the Chinsegut WEA is closed to hunting. With up to 8 miles of hiking across two

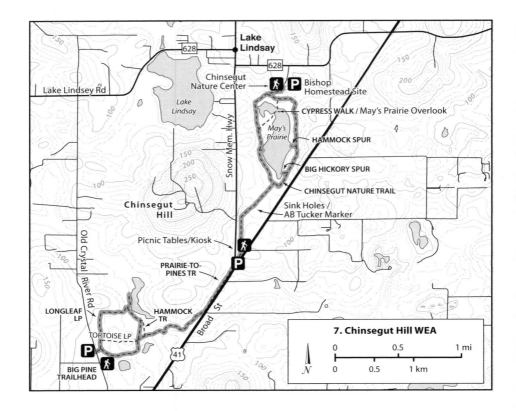

tracts with three trailheads, it's a great destination for Florida hikers and birders

The two major loop trails at this preserve—May's Prairie and Big Pine—are joined together by a linear trail, the 2-mile Prairie-to-Pines Trail. It passes through the primary trailhead at US 41 and Snow Memorial Highway, so it's possible to make one long day hike out of these two loops and the connector. However, the Prairie-to-Pines Trail is a fence line trail—out in the open with a lot of cows nearby—and gets into some serious wet areas as it connects with the Big Pine Loop. If you're bringing the whole family along, stick with doing each loop separately.

Just to mix things up more, the Chinsegut Hill Nature Center and its parking area are open on Friday and Saturday mornings, providing a shorter loop down to May's Prairie for small children and those who can't walk as far. The kids will love the terrariums and aquariums filled with native wildlife at the nature center.

PRAIRIE-TO-PINES TRAIL /CHINSEGUT NATURE TRAIL

Starting from the Prairie-to-Pines Trailhead parking corral, stop at the kiosk and pick up a trail map. Walking past the sign that points your way up the trail along this segment of the Prairie-to-Pines Trail, head up through the pine forest along the broad path through the baffle in the fence. The forest road is marked with posts with hiker markers. At a fork in the path, keep right and head up the grassy path. Passing a marker beneath the pines dedicated to A. B. Tucker, the trail continues up past a series of sinkholes at a half mile, shallow depressions beneath the forest canopy. When you reach the Chinsegut Nature Trail at 3/4 mile, turn left to walk clockwise along the loop. A white-tailed deer peers out from a thicket of young live oaks as you follow the forest road. Passing a maintenance shed, you come up to the first of several scenic spots along May's Prairie. At 1.1 miles, a boardwalk leads out to a wildlife blind on the prairie's rim, where you'll find yourself spending quite a bit of time watching the flocks of sandhill cranes that gather among the tall grasses. Nicely shaded, it's an excellent spot for photography.

Longleaf pines rise tall through the sandhill habitat as the terrain rises gently toward the Cypress Walk. When you reach the sign, turn right. A sinkhole sits off trail, pointed out by a small wooden sign. This footpath is much narrower than the forest road you've followed to this point, and winds through lush oak hammocks dense with saw palmetto and ferns. At a spot where you can see out across the prairie through the live oaks, an interpretive sign talks about one of the more interesting inhabitants of Chinsegut Hill, the tiger salamander. Growing 6 to 8 inches long, these "tiny tigers" live along the boggy edge of the prairie, feeding on earthworms, slugs, snails, and other invertebrates.

As you reach a narrow boardwalk, continue into a cypress dome along the edge of May's Prairie, zigzagging through the trees to turn right onto an overlook along the prairie's edge. Crickets and frogs add to the chorus of songbirds along the grassy fringe. Return to the main trail and turn right. The Cypress Walk emerges at the outer loop at a set of benches. Turn left. Continue up through the pine woods to the trail junction. Turn right

to walk uphill to the Nature Center, which you reach at 2 miles. It's a shame it's only open on weekends, because it's an interesting spot, with a loop around a historic site, the site of the old Bishop Homestead, and the nature center with its many native creatures.

After you finish checking out the homestead site, head back down the hill to the loop trail. Turn left and continue past the Cypress Walk. A maintenance shed peeks out of the forest on the left. The broad forest road continues through the pine woods down to another excellent view over May's Prairie from the Hammock Spur Trail, looking across to the wildlife blind. Watch the edge of the prairie for wading birds. Coming to the Big Hickory Spur after 2.9 miles, take a wander down this narrow path for a view across the American lotus, the cypress outlined against the far shore. Sandhill cranes clatter in the distance. As you leave, turn right. Head on down the broad forest road to complete the Nature Trail Loop at 3.2 miles, backtracking along the Prairie-to-Pines Trail back to the trailhead for a 4-mile hike.

BIG PINE TRAIL

A rare example of a virgin longleaf pine forest in Central Florida, the Big Pine Tract was preserved by the Robins family for future generations to visit. You'll thank their foresight as you walk the loop through this amazing pine forest. Starting at the kiosk, turn right to follow the Longleaf Loop. Although the hike, like the Nature Center Loop, is along forest roads with hiker signs, the trees make it worth the visit. Rather than a dark, dense forest, the Big Pine Tract is rather open, undergoing sandhill restoration as the understory is managed to cull out the thickets that cropped up from too many years without a prescribed burn. Walking counterclockwise, you pass a shed and enter the forest of giant trees after a quarter mile. Since the pines are extremely tall and skinny, it almost seems like they aren't as large as they actually are. Step back and look up. It helps to have a friend along to put it all in perspective. Many of the pines show signs of catfacing from the turpentine industry, but these are true giants, some growing with unusual curved trunks and spreading crowns.

As you continue along the loop, the scent of pine fills the air, compliments of the many small longleaf pines in their grass stage, distinguishable from wiregrass only by the deep green of their needles. These seedlings germinate in the winter. To cope with the frequent lightning-sparked fires that rage across sandhills and pine flatwoods, the longleaf pine has a thick, protected fire-resistant stem during the first five years of its life, while it concentrates on building up an extensive root system. In a sudden growth spurt of up to 3 feet in a single season, a longleaf pine reaches the candle stage, looking like a giant bottlebrush. Side limbs begin to form, making the young longleaf look like a furry mimic of a saguaro cactus. If the pine catches fire, the needles direct the flames away from the stem, burning quickly to ash. From its protected root system and stem, the pine regenerates anew. Longleaf pine is the most long-lived of Florida's pines and the most endangered. Due to the popularity of its tough heartwood, the longleaf was one of the first pines to be commercially logged in the United States; its slow growth led to other pines being planted in its place. Less than 2 percent of the origi-

May's Prairie Trailhead

KEVIN MIMS

nal longleaf forests of the southeastern United States remain.

Passing a sinkhole full of forest debris, you come up to an intersection with the Hammock Trail and the Tortoise Loop after a half mile. Turn right and take a short jog down the Hammock Trail. It connects with the Prairie-to-Pines Trail almost immediately along a bayhead. Turn left and follow the narrow path, which follows the ecotone between sandhills and hardwood hammock. After the Hammock Trail drops you back on the main Longleaf Loop, turn right and continue down to the Burns Prairie Spur, which heads down a shady path through grand old live oaks to the edge of a large sometimes-wet prairie. The trail becomes indistinct as you come to the overlook along the water, so turn around and retrace your steps. Returning to the Longleaf Loop, you've hiked a mile. Turn right, and make a sharp left at the next intersection so you don't wander off on a perimeter trail.

The remainder of the hike continues to loop through the pine forest—younger pines, not the old-growth ones at the beginning of the hike—with little change in landscape along the way. The understory is rather dense, but here and there you see colorful aster and phlox. At the next trail junction, make a sharp left and continue down a long straightaway, partially shaded by the pines. You pass a forest road off to the left. Continue past the incoming Tortoise Loop to complete the 1.6-mile hike at the trailhead kiosk.

DIRECTIONS

Both tracts of the Chinsegut Wildlife & Environmental Area lie between Floral City and Brooksville off US 41, south of the Withlacoochee State Forest headquarters and 7 miles north of Brooksville. To reach the main entrance to the Nature Center Tract, driving south on US 41, turn right onto CR 476. After a mile or so, the entrance will be on your left, and is only open Fri. and Sat. 8 AM–2 PM.

For the Prairie-to-Pines Trailhead, turn right off US 41 onto Snow Memorial Highway; the trailhead is immediately on the right. For the Big Pine Tract, turn a hard right (almost backward—this turn is more easily seen from the northbound lane) off US 41 just south of Snow Memorial Highway onto Old Crystal River Road and continue along this narrow, winding road for about 2 miles to the trailhead on the right.

CONTACT

Florida Fish and Wildlife Conservation Commission
Farris Bryant Building
620 South Meridian Street
Tallahassee, FL 32399-1600
850-488-4676
www.myfwc.com

8

Flat Island Preserve

Total distance (circuit): 3.7 miles

Hiking time: 2 hours

Habitats: hardwood forest, hydric hammock

Trailhead coordinates (lat-lon): 28.778544, -81.900365

Maps: USGS 7½' Leesburg West; Florida Trail Association Map Central 1; Preserve map at kiosk

Admission: Free

Hours: Sunrise–sunset

Surrounded by the vast Okahumpa Marsh, the hammocks of Flat Island shelter an interesting mix of flora—more than 110 species, including rare trees, unusual wildflowers, and colorful mushrooms. Dedicated to Rexford and Jean Daubenmire, botanists who retired to Leesburg and fought for the preservation of this land, the well-engineered trail follows a circuit around the edge of the island's high ground. Built and maintained by the Florida Trail Association, the trail is clearly blazed and signposted at every cross-trail.

Unless you're hiking after the first winter frost, apply your strongest insect repellent before setting out on the trail. Okahumpa Marsh is a breeding ground for insects, so clouds of mosquitoes will dog your steps most of the year. Starting your hike at the trail kiosk, sign in and follow the orange blazes. A large group campsite sits off to the right under the oaks, beyond the picnic table. Fresh water is available from a spigot behind the kiosk. Past the memorial to the Daubenmires, these trappings of civilization fall behind as you enter the deep shade of an oak hammock, walking beneath a tall canopy of oaks and cabbage palms. Monkeyflowers crowd the sides of the footpath. The trail turns into a causeway, up above the lapping tannic waters of the surrounding hydric hammock. Uttering a piercing cry, a red-shouldered hawk swoops past.

The Island Hammock Trail starts at Signpost A, where a stone memorial pays homage to the late John Weary, a tireless trail maintainer responsible for many of the Florida Trail Association's best efforts in Central Florida. Veer right, away from the service

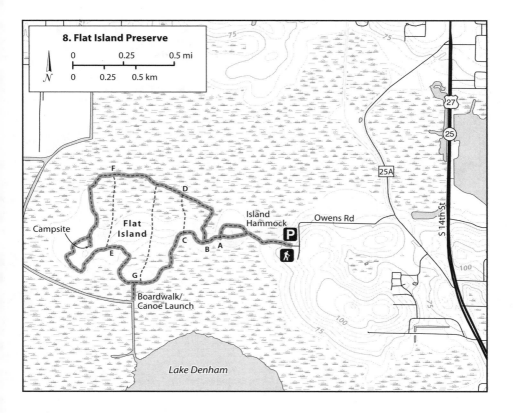

road, following the well-established treadway into a forest of southern magnolia and young laurel oaks. Look up *and* down—greenfly orchids cling to the trees, and collybia mushrooms grow in crowded groups, like miniature forests.

Crossing the service road, the trail continues through an area of younger oaks along the edge of a palm hammock. Roots break through the hard-packed dirt of the trail. At 0.5 mile, Signpost B marks the beginning of the outer loop. Continue straight ahead to walk the trail clockwise, passing under lofty live oaks. At Signpost C, pass the junction with the cross-trail and keep going straight as the oak forest yields to a hydric hammock. Around you, moss glows green on the trunks of cabbage palms. An earthy scent rises from the swamp as you first encounter the needle palm, which grows along the boundary between wetlands and uplands, as tall as 15 feet above the trail. Yellow-eyed grass and the bright purple berries of the American beautyberry lend a dash of contrast to the deep green landscape. A slight elevation rise returns the trail to the hardwood forest, with its sandy floor and tall oaks. The bark of a southern magnolia disappears under an array of air plants. The canopy opens up, allowing more sunlight to the forest floor and encouraging the understory to grow. Wild coffee, winged sumac, and greenbrier compete for the spaces between the saw palmettos.

After 1.1 miles, you'll reach a sign with a

Trailhead register at Flat Island Preserve

canoe symbol. Turn left and follow the board-walk into a cypress swamp. Interpretive signs point out many of the typical denizens of the swamp, including bald cypress, cinnamon ferns, and royal ferns. Pass the canoe rack. For avid canoeists who want to challenge the canoe trail—a series of narrow old canals through the Okahumpa Marsh—the Lake County Water Authority provides canoes. Pre-register at the caretaker's office next to the parking lot and plunk down a refundable deposit to pick up your paddles and safety gear before you start hiking to the canoes. The trail ends on the floating canoe launch above the dark waters of the canal, thick with the purple blooms of pickerelweed. Retrace your steps back to the main trail and turn left.

The trail continues through oak and palm hammocks, where downed palm fronds can sometimes obscure the footpath. Hundreds of tiny oak toads bounce away as they sense each footfall. At 1.6 miles, Signpost E marks the second cross-trail. Continue straight on into a thicket of needle palms, royal ferns, and marsh ferns. The trail is prone to flooding in this section, as the swamp creeps up close on both sides. After it reaches the western extent of Flat Island, the trail veers to the right. Mosses and lichens cover the trees, whose roots are frequently flooded. Notice the tall rotting stump covered with blue patches—the remains of a bluejack oak. Many of the water oaks and magnolias have bark covered with patches of white lichen and red blanket lichen. The trail continues to veer right, following the north edge of the island. Crossing a foot-wide ditch lined with cabbage palms, it returns to higher ground, carpeted with the fallen needles of tall slash pines. In the moist earth below, mushrooms abound—thick clusters of chanterelles and crowded families of glow-in-the-dark jack o'lantern mushrooms.

A metal enclosure sits alongside the trail at 2.1 miles, just before the turnoff to the primitive campground. To help new backpackers get their feet wet, the Florida Trail Association runs semiannual "beginners'" weekends at Flat Island Preserve. After a morning of learning the how-to of tent setup, camp stove operation, and packing a backpack, participants head down the trail to spend the evening at this primitive camping area. Sheltered by a canopy of oaks and magnolias, the campsite provides benches and a pitcher pump and is a great place to take the kids for a weekend outing. Free permits must be obtained in advance from the Lake County Water Authority.

As the trail elevation drops slightly, the scenery changes. As the sparse understory gives way to dense saw palmetto, the canopy shifts to cabbage palms and laurel oaks. Needle palms rise along both sides of the trail. At Signpost F, you pass the cross-trail from Signpost E. Continue straight ahead, entering an area of younger trees—live oaks, sweetgum, and southern magnolia. Their supple limbs braid into an arbor over the trail. A little farther along, hickory trees drop their bounty of nuts onto the trail. Each nut consists of two layers—a soft exterior skin and a tough, thick inner shell that hides the nutmeat.

When you reach Signpost D, you've hiked 2.9 miles. The cross-trail from Signpost C meets up with the main trail. Keep going straight ahead as the trail veers close to the edge of the island, skirting a broad expanse of swamp dense with bald cypress and cabbage palms. The trail crosses the service road, returning to the end of the loop at Signpost B. A blur of brown, a ground skink squirms through the leaf litter across the footpath. Turn left to retrace your steps back to the entrance, past Signpost A. Ending your 3.7-mile hike at the trail kiosk, be sure to sign the trail register before you leave.

Greenfly orchids bloom in summer

DIRECTIONS

To find the preserve, follow US 27 southbound from Leesburg. Turn right onto CR 25A. Follow it north 0.5 mile, then turn left onto Owens Road, a narrow dirt road. After 0.6 mile, you'll reach the preserve entrance and parking area, with its large trail kiosk and restrooms. A new addition to the trailhead is a small native plant garden in a field off to the left of the main trail.

CONTACT

Lake County Water Authority
107 North Lake Avenue
Tavares, FL 32778
352-343-3777
www.lcwa.org

9

Hidden Waters Preserve

Total distance (circuit): 1 mile

Hiking time: 30 minutes

Habitats: hardwood hammock, sandhill, freshwater marsh, sinkhole

Trailhead coordinates (lat-lon): 28.838570, -81.660787

Maps: USGS 7½' Eustis. Preserve map at kiosk

Admission: Free

Hours: Sunrise–sunset

Tucked away smack dab in the middle of the town of Eustis, Hidden Waters Preserve is one of those small but special places in Florida that inspire an "oh, wow!" upon its discovery. A network of short trails form a loop in and around the park's main feature—the Eichelberger Sink, an enormous sinkhole containing Lake Alfred. The "lake" (more properly a wetland area) can't flow out of the sinkhole, so it slowly seeps through the bottom of the sinkhole into the Floridan Aquifer. The Lake Alfred Trail, blazed blue, edges the freshwater marsh along the sinkhole lake. The Ravine Trail, blazed red, takes you around and down into the depths of the sinkhole itself, dropping more than 105 feet—a fun challenge for Florida hikers. Would-be long-distance hikers and runners looking to build up endurance often use this trail for training. The damp north slope of the sinkhole shelters an Appalachian-like forest, while the south slope hosts a drier sandhill environment, with abundant prickly pear cactus and the signs of a healthy gopher tortoise community.

Pick up a map at the trail kiosk, and sign in. Heading straight downhill along the trail, you'll come to the first intersection of the Lake Alfred Trail and the Ravine Trail. Stick to the left, following the red blazes downhill under tall laurel oaks. Orange and pink lantana grows in profusion. Before becoming a preserve in 1996, this property was a golf course in the 1950s and a citrus grove until the killer freezes of the 1980s. As a result, the natural forest community has been severely altered from its original state—a sandhill community dense with longleaf pine. Reforesta-

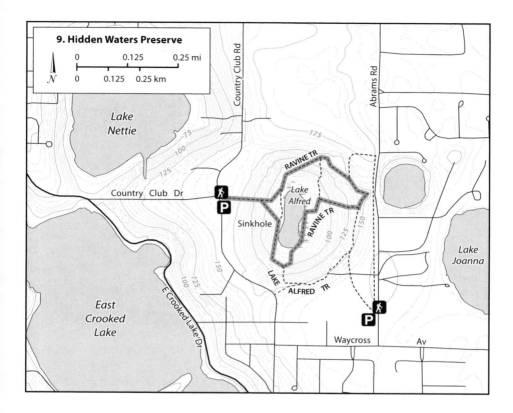

9. Hidden Waters Preserve

tion efforts by the Lake County Water Authority will eventually bring this preserve back to its natural state.

After crossing over some unusual dike-like structures, possibly related to the construction of the golf course, the trail swings up and around the edge of the deeply forested sinkhole, rising up the steep slope. You pass a trail off to the right. Tall sweetgum and laurel oak shade the trail until it emerges at the top of the hill. Here, it reaches a T intersection with a new set of trails in an open grassy area, perfect for local joggers. To stick to the interesting route, turn right and follow the trail around a fenced-off stormwater drainage area. The sound of running water begins to reach your ears.

At the junction with the Lake Alfred Trail, follow the Ravine Trail back downhill under the deep canopy of oaks and hickory trees. The trail makes a steep descent, with water splashing off to the right. Take the opportunity to walk out on a small side trail to the right to an overlook to see what the commotion is all about. No matter what time of year it is, no matter how long there has been a drought, water always flows down this ravine, cutting deeper and deeper channels through the sand. In the past decade since I first found this trail, the crevice has grown to a serious chasm. In sinkholes, seepage down the slopes occurs where water flows over a cap of denser materials (usually clay) near the normal surface of the ground. Where the sink-

Basin of Eichelberger Sink

hole intersects this layer, water seeps over the edge of the cap and down into the sinkhole. The water flowing into this sinkhole may come from such seepage from nearby higher-elevation lakes, but most certainly comes from stormwater drainage from above—a risky municipal move, since intentionally sluicing water into a sinkhole may make it grow faster.

The splashing waters are a delight for waterfall-starved Florida residents, as the steady, clear flow meanders down a series of deep ravines, edged by a dense growth of ferns. Sinkholes always provide a cooler environment for plants than the surrounding forest, encouraging a unique habitat. The broad leaves of elephant ears bow their heads over the water. As you descend into the sinkhole, thickets of sword fern give way to a mix of bracken, netted chain, and cinnamon fern. Royal fern and elderberries grow under a canopy of water oak.

As the elevation at the bottom of the sinkhole evens out, the splashing stream spreads out across the sand, accelerating downhill until it reaches the marshy edge of Lake Alfred. Perpetual dampness along the eastern edge of the lake encourages the sundew, a tiny carnivorous plant, to flourish. Home to a variety of turtles and small fish, the sinkhole wetlands attracts passing waterfowl, such as white herons, blue herons, and cattle egrets. The native Florida softshell turtle, a large and ungainly creature, inhabits the lake. With a flat, leathery shell more than a foot long, the turtle is distinctive due to its broad face and snorkel-like nose.

Reaching the next trail intersection at 0.7 mile, keep to the right along the lake and follow the blue blazes. The area opens up into grassland on the edge of the upland forest, where hawks and other raptors search for field mice and marsh rats. Local birders have

Stream flowing into sinkhole, step by tiny step

spotted a Cooper's hawk here, a threatened species in Florida. The Cooper's hawk has short wings and a long gray-and-white striped tail, with a reddish-brown breast and wingtips in black and white.

As you continue to loop around the lake, you return to the mixed forest of live oak, laurel oak, and open areas with prickly pear cactus. Watch for the red blazes off to the left, up the hill. Turn right and walk through the shady forest to emerge back out above the wetlands again. Your legs will notice the steep climb of more than 100 feet as you head back uphill to return to the trail kiosk, finishing the mile-long circuit. Sign out of the trail register before leaving the park.

DIRECTIONS

Hidden Waters Preserve is along Country Club Road in Eustis in the middle of a suburban neighborhood. From US 441 just south of Eustis, turn north on Donnelly Road (CR 44B). Turn at the first left, Waycross Road. Follow it until it ends; turn right. Watch for the grassy parking lot and distant trail kiosk on the right.

CONTACT

Lake County Water Authority
107 North Lake Avenue
Tavares, FL 32778
352-343-3777
www.lcwa.org

10

Withlacoochee River Park

Total distance (circuit): 6.9 miles

Hiking time: 3.5 hours

Habitats: river floodplain, hardwood swamp, pine flatwoods, oak hammock, sandhill, wet prairie, dry prairie, freshwater marsh

Trailhead coordinates (lat-lon): 28.344478, -82.120252

Maps: USGS 7½' Branchborough; Park map at entrance station; Florida Trail Association Map Central 3

Admission: Free. Primitive campsite $5, primitive cabin $10, campsite with electric $15.

Hours: Sunrise–sunset

At Withlacoochee River Park, dip a toe into one of Florida's largest and most important floodplains—the Green Swamp. It's the headwaters of four of Central Florida's largest rivers—the Hillsborough, the Ocklawaha, the Peace, and the Withlacoochee. The Green Swamp is no ordinary wetland. Instead of a vast sheet of water covering thousands of acres of floodplain forest, the Green Swamp is a patchwork of flatwoods, sandhills, and cypress domes, uplands and lowlands covering more than 860 square miles to the northeast of metropolitan Tampa.

Huddled up against the edge of the Withlacoochee River, Withlacoochee River Park trails lead out from within the park boundary into the vast Green Swamp. Inside the park, a yellow-blazed interpretive nature trail is perfect for families with small children. It rambles for 2.5 miles through sandhills, oak hammocks, and prairies, passing by a 1800s Florida history village and a 1700s Native American village, through picnic areas and a playground, over boardwalks and up to a 40-foot observation deck. A free primitive camping area with a rental cabin is just a half mile from the southern parking lot, providing families a chance to try "roughing it" with civilization close by. Older hikers and teens will appreciate the orange-blazed Florida Trail, which leads backpackers out of the park along a rugged but beautiful route to hidden campsites in the Green Swamp. Permits are required for all campsites, but can be obtained for free from Pasco County Parks. A canoe trail leads down the Withlacoochee River from the canoe landing, and a paved

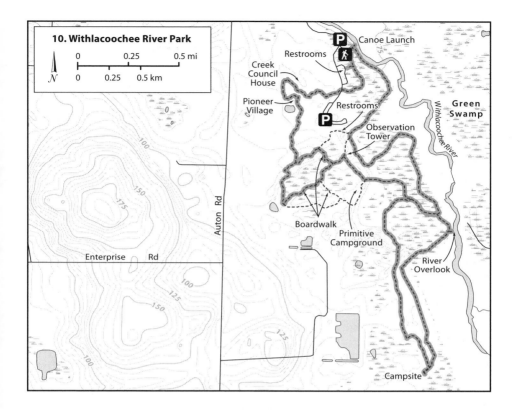

2-mile bike trail encourages freewheeling through the forest. Every February, the park plays host to the Mountain Man Festival, a gathering of folks who take the primitive arts seriously.

Pull into the first parking lot on the left to start your circuit hike, which combines both the Florida Trail and the nature trail to provide a diversity of habitats and terrain. Walk down to the canoe landing to take in the view of the Withlacoochee River. Dark waters swirl mysteriously around cypress knees as an ibis scouts the shallows for snails. The trailhead starts just to the right of the landing. Sign in at the register.

Follow the orange blazes upriver as you enjoy the river view. Interpretive signs appear along the first mile of trail, pointing out specific trees and shrubs. Live oaks dripping in resurrection fern arch overhead as the trail heads down a broad corridor through the saw palmetto. At 0.4 mile, you'll cross a sand road; the path jogs off slightly to the left and is a little obscured. Keep watching for the orange blazes! A prairie meadow stretches off to the left, a wide-open area sparkling with the lavender blooms of blazing star. The trail reaches a junction at 0.6 mile, with the southern parking lot and restrooms off to the left. Stay with the orange blazes as they veer left under a tangle of low live oak limbs and into a beautiful corridor of live oak hammock, a ribbon dividing the open sandhill habitat off to the right from the wet prairie down to the left.

Oak hammock at Withlacoochee River Park

Brilliant red and pink splotches of red blanket lichen cover the gnarled oak limbs that shelter the trail. Watch for telltale signs of armadillo: small holes dug into the sand at your feet. These shy armored creatures will jump more than a foot in the air if you startle them! They enjoy browsing down this corridor of live oak and saw palmetto.

The trail veers left at 0.8 mile, away from the tree line and into a low, open area of slash pine and damp ground, edging along the east side of the prairie. This starts the adventuresome portion of the hike. From this point on, the footpath is not always distinct. Always keep your eyes open for the next orange blaze, and head toward it. After crossing an area of tall grass, you emerge on a more distinct footpath—part of the nature trail—a mile into the hike. Turn left, crossing a sand road. The nature trail takes off to the left, but your route continues straight into the woods. Sweetgum trees share the forest with live oaks, laurel oaks, and dahoon holly. Vines drop down low, forcing you to duck. Passing under a series of spreading live oaks, the trail gains a little elevation, and the habitat changes to pine flatwoods, with part of the river floodplain—a cypress swamp—off to the left. Cross a sand track twice, meandering back into an oak hammock.

After 1.6 miles, you'll reach the junction of the loop trail. Turn right, crossing an open area and entering the forest just to the left of a large water oak into a pine hammock. For the next quarter mile, a wet prairie stretches off to the left. Sandhill cranes pick their way through the tall grass. The trail becomes rough underfoot in places, thanks to the feeding activities of feral hogs. Like armadillos, they root up the ground—but they do it in a *big* way. Crossing over a sand road and through an opening in the fence, you reenter the park. At 1.8 miles, a blue-blazed trail leads off to the right to the primitive camping area. Turn left and continue to follow the trail around the prairie, wandering past the knees of pond cypress trees that permanently depend on the moisture from this low area to survive. The trail enters a grove of tall slash pine, then turns abruptly left. Passing through the fence again to leave the park boundary, the trail crosses the sand road again and heads into an oak hammock. Black-eyed Susan lends a dash of color to the leaf-strewn forest floor. After crossing an open meadow, the trail veers to the left, along the tree line, meandering on a narrow dry strip between cypress swamp and wet prairie.

Crossing a sand track at 2.3 miles, you'll catch a glimpse of a large wet prairie off to the right; greenhouses climb the hill on its far shore. Back in the oak hammock, sword ferns cluster alongside chunks of rounded limestone. An open area with tall dog fennel provides a challenge—watch the footpath closely. It emerges into an area of tall laurel oak, where bracken fern grows in an open understory. At 2.9 miles, you reach the a blue-blazed trail to a primitive campsite. Turn left, following the orange blazes into the pine flatwoods, where tall goldenrod provides splashes of bright color. Crossing a sand track, the trail runs along the edge of a cypress swamp, veering right to follow the swamp—part of the Withlacoochee River floodplain. Crossing a sand road, the trail veers away from the cypress swamp. The first blaze on the far side of the road is a little tough to see as the trail dives into a narrow corridor of laurel oak paralleling the road. Veering right, the trail crosses the road again and meanders down the line of where the pine flatwoods and the cypress swamp meet. A grunting sow gives up her rooting in the soft black mud of the swamp and heads for the safety of the saw palmetto thicket, quickly followed by five squealing piglets. Black water stretches off to the right—a glimpse of the open river at 3.9 miles, with a Boy Scout cabin on the far shore.

The trail joins up with a sand road, then veers to the right to return to the beginning of the loop, 4 miles into the hike. Continue off to the right, retracing your route for the next mile back to the junction with the yellow-blazed trail. Follow the orange blazes across to the corridor of live oaks, and back to the trail junction near the southern parking lot and restrooms. From here, you can return to your car along the orange-blazed trail, completing a 5.6-mile hike. But there's plenty more to see and do if you turn left and follow the short blue-blazed trail through the fence to the yellow-blazed nature trail. Turn left and head past the restrooms, following the sign that says TOWER, CAMPING, NATURE TRAIL up into the sandhill habitat. The observation tower doesn't provide a view of the river (although you can plainly see the cypress trees that mark the river's course), but it does give a nice overview of the sandhills and prairies within the park, wide-open areas where herds of deer roam. Off to the south lies the main primitive camping area, accessed by a trail from the foot of the tower.

Hiking away from the tower, follow the yellow trail sign, descending off the sandhill and into a live oak hammock. Keep right at the fork into the shaded hammock. Low prairie stretches out from both sides of the hammock. Veer right at the next fork, passing a tall black cherry tree. Veer right at the next trail junction, crossing a boardwalk over the prairie. Several deer dash into the forest. A slight rise changes the habitat back to sandhill. Turn right at the trail junction, away from the camping area. The trail snakes along the edge of the prairie, under willow oaks and laurel oaks. Tiny green tree frogs hop across the sand.

At 5.8 miles, another trail joins in from the right. Continue straight downhill into an oak hammock, past an unusually tall specimen of gopher apple. The roots of this small shrub stabilize the sandhill, and its fruits are

Observation tower

delectable to the gopher tortoise. Rising back through sandhill, the trail veers right off the sand track and back into the forest. It circles around a low, broad sinkhole pond to enter a collection of original and replica buildings forming a 1800s Florida pioneer village. Contact the park for information about living history demonstrations here and at the adjoining Native American village across the field. Take a moment to wander off the path and experience the large, dark Creek winter lodge.

The yellow blazes veer off to the right into the woods between the two villages, passing through picnic areas and around a playground. At 6.4 miles, a sign points out the various activities in different directions. Your trail is headed toward the canoe landing, and it takes a sharp right after passing the sign. Crossing the paved road through the park, it rejoins the other branch of the yellow trail at 6.7 miles. Turn left. The last quarter-mile of trail passes by picnic pavilions and restrooms. On the right, take a moment to learn the difference between the Chapman oak

(concave and convex leathery leaves) and the sand post oak (scalloped leaves). The trail ends at the nature trail kiosk, completing your 6.9-mile hike.

DIRECTIONS

Follow US 301 south from FL 50 (I-75 exit 301, Brooksville, heading east) to the northern edge of Dade City. Turn left onto Truck Route US 301, making the immediate second left onto River Road. Follow the twisting, winding River Road 4.5 miles to its junction with Auton Road, just before the bridge. Turn right on Auton Road, then make the first left into the park. Stop at the kiosk at the park entrance for a trail map and an interpretive guide.

CONTACT

Withlacoochee River Park
12449 Withlacoochee Boulevard
Dade City, FL 33525
352-567-0264
www.swfwmd.state.fl.us

Central Highlands

11

Circle B Bar Reserve

Total distance (circuit): 4.4 miles

Hiking time: 3 hours

Habitats: oak hammock, prairie, freshwater marsh, impoundments, scrub

Trailhead coordinates (lat-lon): 27.989618, -81.857654

Maps: USGS 7½' Lakeland; Map at trailhead kiosk

Admission: Free

Hours: Reserve trails are open 5 AM–8:30 PM. Nature Discovery Center is open Tue–Sat 9 AM–4 PM and Sun 12 PM–4 PM.

A real gem of the Polk County Environmental Lands system, Circle B Bar Reserve was once a cattle ranch between Lakeland and Bartow. It's now home to the Polk Nature Discovery Center and one of the best places to go birding in the Lakeland area. Located along the shores of Lake Hancock, this former ranch has undergone extensive restoration to bring back the wetlands that originally filled the low-lying areas closest to the lake–this time, with trails atop berms so you can appreciate the diversity of wildlife that depends on the marshes for survival.

If the Nature Discovery Center is open when you arrive, stop in to acquaint yourself with the habitats and their inhabitants before you start your hike. The trail begins at the TRAIL STARTS HERE sign just past the kiosk, where you can pick up a trail map. Take a left to walk down a recycled-surface footpath to a T intersection with a sidewalk for the Shady Oak Trail. The sidewalk ends, but the trail continues, becoming a natural footpath near an interpretive sign about the wetlands. One of the more misunderstood habitats in Florida–or so it would seem given the general green light to destroy them for development–wetlands serve as natural filtration systems, with grasses and algae that can chemically break down substances like cow patties (or the outflow of a sewage treatment plant) and render them harmless, or at least less harmful.

In the early morning hours, the sun streams through live oaks draped in Spanish moss, the grass below making you feel like you're walking in a park rather than a forest. Such is the nature of reclaiming natural

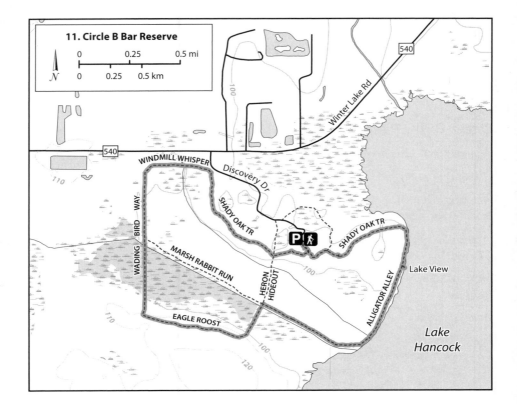

habitats. Past a connector with the Lost Trail on the left, there is a bench on the right and interpretive information about butterflies. Circle B Bar Reserve does an excellent job of education, from the markers you'll find along all the trails to the top-notch nature center, so this is a great destination for homeschoolers and families in general to gently immerse their children in Florida's native habitats. It's very much an outdoor classroom, as may be seen from the groupings of benches where a small field trip group can sit down and talk about what they see around them.

After you cross the footbridge, the trail intersects with a crushed-shell road and becomes Alligator Alley at a half mile. Paying homage through its name to one of the well-

known crossings of the Everglades, this footpath leads you through a shady tunnel of moss-laden oaks and red maples along the shore of Lake Hancock. Here there be gators, as well as measuring equipment to monitor the health and depth of the lake. A wooden walkway leads off to the left at ¾ mile to a canopied observation deck on the lake. Sit still and watch, and you'll be sure to see alligators cruising offshore. More benches provide places to pause and enjoy the view, most notably a very open spot at 1.2 miles next to a little cove.

As the trail leaves the lakeshore, it continues along restored marshes on a berm with a canal to the left. Lone cypress rise from the shallows to your right. A Florida cooter basks on a fallen log while a great egret spears a small fish. Moss-draped trees still provide patches of shade.

The trail comes up to a four-way intersection at 1.8 miles. Take a left to follow the Eagle Roost Trail. The open water around you is a prime birding spot. Look for purple gallinules and coots amid the grassy patches and wading birds along the edges. Passing a concrete water trough on the left, the trail continues into an open field under restoration to scrubby flatwoods. One eagle nest is clearly visible in the top of a tall longleaf pine. Circle B Bar Reserve has the distinction of having the most bald eagle nests on a single piece of land in Polk County—three at last count. It's the main reason for walking along this part of the loop, since the landscape around you is otherwise mostly barren as grasses and shrubs quietly reclaim this part of the cattle ranch.

Leaving the open area, the trail curves around past another concrete water trough and heads back out on a berm at 2.5 miles through the wetlands, again providing magnificent views across the open water along Wading Bird Way. A banded water snake slips along the grassy berm and back into the water. This colorful snake is often mistaken for the water moccasin, which as a pit viper has a pointed snout. The banded water snake does not. Unfortunately, most people assume that all snakes are harmful, especially water snakes. Not so. Snakes fill an important niche in the ecosystem, helping to keep rodent populations under control.

Passing the Marsh Rabbit Run trail coming in from the left, the Wading Bird Way continues along another stretch of wetlands. A cormorant rests on the shore, drying its wings in the morning sun to the delight of a flock of photographers. At 3.3 miles, you see an old windmill and reach the junction with the Windmill Whisper Trail. Turn right and walk

Observation point along the lake   KEVIN MIMS

down the oak-lined path through the uplands. The entrance road into the preserve is straight ahead when you reach the Shady Oak Trail. Make a right to walk beneath the shade of the live oaks, their curved limbs hosting thick jungles of resurrection fern. Reaching the junction with the Heron Hideout Trail, continue straight to return to the beginning of the loop, where the recycled-surface footpath comes in from the left. Turn left to exit and complete the 4.4-mile perimeter circuit of this preserve.

DIRECTIONS
From US 98, follow SR 540 (Winter Lake Road) west

CONTACT
Polk County Environmental Lands Program
4399 Winter Lake Road
Lakeland, FL 33803
863-534-7377

Sandhill crane pair at Lake Proctor

12

Silver River State Park

Total distance (3 circuits): 8 miles

Hiking time: 5 hours

Habitats: floodplain forest, hardwood hammock, hydric hammock, oak scrub, pine flatwoods, sandhill, sand pine scrub

Trailhead coordinates (lat-lon): 29.200774, -82.034845

Maps: USGS 7½' Ocala East; Silver River State Park map

Admission: $2 pedestrian/bicyclist, $4 individual driver, $6 per carload

Hours: 8 AM until sunset

Pouring forth from one of the world's largest springs, the transparent waters of the Silver River meander 7 miles through a jungle of hydric hammocks and floodplain forest to merge with the Ocklawaha, the largest tributary of the St. Johns River. Since the late 1800s, the Silver River has attracted tourists, with visitors climbing aboard glass-bottomed boats to oooh and ahhh at the swirls of fish attracted to the river's many springs.

Adjoining the private attraction, Silver River State Park conserves uplands and riverfront along the Silver River. With the park's focus on environmental education and preservation, its hiking trails are the star attraction, perhaps the busiest in the state. Silver River State Park is relatively easy to find, which adds to its popularity. A campground handles trailers, RVs, and tent campers, and has spacious new cabins as well. Mountain bikers can enjoy several loop trails in the southeastern portion of the park, behind the campground. But most people visit the park to hike, canoe, and savor the glassy waters of the Silver River.

When you pay your Florida State Parks entrance fee, ask the ranger for a map of the hiking trails. There are four distinct trails in the park, each short enough that young and old alike can delight in a walk in the woods. Although all four trails can be accessed from the trailhead at the main parking area, the Sandhill Nature Trail also has its own trailhead along the park road just past the ranger station, if you want to tackle it by itself. Many more miles of additional trails, such as the Ross Allen Trail, are open for use by hikers

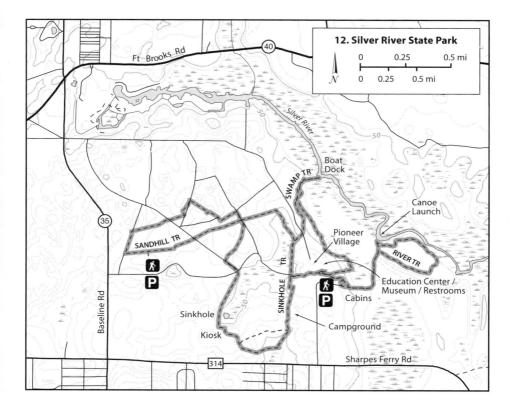

12. Silver River State Park

but are primarily in place for bicyclists.

Drive along the park road up to the main parking area, flanked by the Cracker Village, the Silver River Museum, the Environmental Education Center, and two arched trail-heads—Sinkhole Trail and River Trails. Open only on weekends, the museum (with an additional nominal charge) presents in-depth information on geology, paleontology, and the natural and human history of this region. Many important scientific finds have been made along the Silver River, from mastodon skeletons to artifacts from Florida's aboriginal cultures. The Cracker Village shows off the buildings found on an everyday 1800s Florida homestead and hosts living history demonstrations, especially fun during the park's signature event, Ocali Country Days, held each November.

SINKHOLE TRAIL, SANDHILL TRAIL, AND OLD FIELD LOOP

Begin your hike from the main parking area at the "Sinkhole Trail" archway adjoining the pioneer village, which is open on weekends. Hiking these three trails together, you experience all of the upland habitats found within Silver River State Park, en route to scouting the edge of the park's largest sinkhole. The trail markers are tipped with red, with silver arrows on red discs.

Follow the wood-chip path past the Cracker Village into a small sand pine scrub with scattered rosemary bushes. Grazing the

---

Silver River State Park

edge of the picnic area and playground, the trail turns right as it meets up with the park entrance road, turning onto an old jeep trail through a mature oak scrub. Deer moss creates a soft blanket under the oaks. After 0.3 mile, the trail makes a sharp left into the sand pine scrub, with the footpath ahead a blinding white as it leads you between the myrtle oak, Chapman oak, and sand live oaks in the understory. Sand pine forests are one of the more unusual natural communities in Florida, relying on fire to regenerate. The closed cones of a sand pine may become embedded and overgrown by bark rather than fall to the ground and sprout. When fire sweeps through the sand pines, it quickly climbs the pines' low dead branches. In the 1933 novel *South Moon Under*, Marjorie Kinnan Rawlings depicts the fury of a fire in the sand pine scrub— "dry pine-tops burst into flames with a roar. Balls of fire jumped 30 feet at a shot." Like popcorn, the cones burst in the flames and release their seeds, ensuring the regeneration of the forest.

At the junction of the Sinkhole and the Sandhill Trail, half a mile into the hike, there's a picnic bench with a kiosk just beyond it and a very large gopher tortoise burrow just beyond it. A very tiny gopher tortoise, sporting a yellowish shell, scurries into its proportionately compact burrow closer to the trail junction. Turn right at the kiosk to start the Sandhill Trail loop. Continue down the unmarked jeep road until you reach the yellow-tipped posts and yellow arrow markers that usher you to the left to walk through a young longleaf pine forest with a very open understory. There is a green glow throughout the forest, with longleaf pines in both grass and candle stages beneath the turkey oaks. Even in summer, the sandhills are full of subtle blooms. Gopher apple sports tiny white blossoms. American beautyberry has its little pink blooms, not as showy as the berries that dangle from its branches later in the year. Sandhill wireweed, with its spiky blooms, emerges from the wiregrass.

At the next T intersection, there is a yellow-tipped post and arrow. Turn left to follow a jeep track through a forest of planted pines. As you walk along, look closely at the tracks in the trail. Raccoon and deer tracks are common, but don't be surprised to see the wide impressions from the paws of a long, lean Florida black bear. Where the longleaf pines dominate the forest, notice the change in the understory. Blueberries take root in the acidic soil, as do winged sumac, which rises above the saw palmetto. A relative of the poison sumac, the winged sumac has the distinction of being one of Florida's most colorful shrubs in fall and winter, when its leaves turn to brilliant crimson and orange.

At 1.2 miles the trail turns right on a mowed path on the forest, away from the SERVICE ROAD sign. In early morning, birds flutter about—especially woodpeckers. Listen and watch for the pileated woodpecker, high up in a longleaf pine. Its large size—up to 19 inches tall—and distinctive red crest make it hard to miss. You'll more commonly see the red-bellied woodpecker, pecking at rotten wood. Although it is only 9 inches tall, its zebra-striped wings and red-crowned head make it easy to pick out amid the greenery.

Crossing a jeep track, the trail continues forward past an interpretive marker beneath the pines. Blackberries and blueberries are awaiting a rummaging bear or a hungry human. A six-lined racerunner dashes across the path, vanishing into a tangle of wiregrass. The trail comes up to a T and turns left on a park service road paralleling Baseline Road. You can see traffic through the open understory and hear the cars. Turning left again at 1.6 miles, you continue around the loop past tangled masses of grapevine, coming up to the exit out to the Sandhill Trail trailhead near

Boardwalk through a hydric hammock

the ranger station. Pass it by and continue past colorful clusters of milkweed with fiery orange flowers. A bumblebee clings for dear life to a roserush as the bloom sways in the breeze. At the Y junction, keep to the left. If you're as lucky as we were, you'll spot white-tailed deer using this broad trail.

After 2.3 miles, you return to the junction of the Sandhill and Sinkhole Trails, at the kiosk and picnic bench. Take a moment to relax and hydrate before continuing. Turn right. Soon after, the trail makes a sharp right, and a red-tipped post confirms you're on the right path. Passing through a confusing junction of unmarked trails, you emerge at the park entrance road at 2.6 miles. Cross the road and continue into the climax laurel oak forest on the other side. The trail reaches a T intersection, jogs to the right, and then to the left at the fence line. Deep shade is a welcome relief after walking through the open

scrub and sandhill habitats. Florida dogwood grows along this section of the trail; look for its white blooms in spring.

The trail starts to follow the edge of a large, forest-filled sinkhole, noticeable because of the long slope covered in saw palmettos dropping off on the left. Pignut hickories sprinkle hickory nuts and autumn leaves across the footpath. From here, you can look down into the forest in the sinkhole, a mix of red maples, sweetgum, and live oaks. A kiosk provides interpretive information about the sinkhole.

Turn right at 3 miles to follow the Old Field Loop, a side trail with an abundance of interpretive markers. Yellow-tipped markers lead the way. Winding through the turkey oaks, you pass a solution hole on the left, a sinkhole caused by gradual erosion. Sand pines and longleaf pines continue to reclaim the old field. An eastern fence lizard scurries up the side of a turkey oak trunk, blending in well with the bark. A gopher tortoise burrow provides a home for gopher frogs when the tortoise is away. Creamy gray with dark spots, these squat frogs forage at night, swallowing whatever they can find—including other frogs. The gopher frog is just one of more than 360 species of animals that make their home in a gopher tortoise's burrow.

As the trail swings left back into the oak hammock, it rounds a fallen live oak that continues to grow, sending up trunk-like branches from its prone trunk, thick with resurrection fern. It's a sudden, almost startling transition from the openness of the old field into the dark, mossy hammock. The trail drops down through a stand of loblolly pine and into a hammock of ancient live oaks, dense with ferns and lichens along the back fence of the campground, rejoining the Sinkhole Trail after 3.4 miles at a picnic bench. Follow the trail along the campground fence to reach the park entrance road again, crossing it to return to the beginning of the loop. Turn right, and walk between the picnic area (where the restrooms might be a welcome stop) and the Cracker Village to emerge under the SINKHOLE TRAIL sign after a 3.8-mile walk.

THE RIVER TRAILS

Directly across the parking area from the Sinkhole Trail, two trails branch off the trail leading under the "River Trails" arch. The more heavily used of the two is the Swamp Trail, a loop hike of 2.1 miles with a spur leading down through a floodplain forest to a boardwalk along the Silver River. The River Trail also remains popular, with a round-trip of 2.1 miles down to the river, with a loop trail at its end.

SWAMP TRAIL

Walk under the "River Trails" arch and turn left to follow the Swamp Trail. Rounding a yaupon holly hugging a laurel oak firm in its grip, notice the bat boxes up in the trees of this lofty hardwood hammock. Several species of bats live in Florida, including the Seminole bat, the evening bat, and the eastern yellow bat. The edge of a floodplain forest is the ideal roost for a bat colony, where its members can swoop out at night and eat their weight in flying insects, keeping down the moth and mosquito populations.

The trail turns left to follow the edge of the floodplain forest, a dense stand of cypresses leading off toward the river. You walk under tall southern magnolias and under hickory trees dense with clusters of wild pine. A swamp chestnut oak drops its enormous leaves on the trail. When you reach the T intersection, turn right (a left turn leads to the Environmental Center). The trail becomes crushed limerock underfoot, winding through live oaks, red bay, and tall slash pines, with cinnamon fern and gallberry in the understory. Where a trail comes in from the left, turn right. There are many trails leading off from the Environmental Center that join in with the swamp trail, affording Marion County schoolchildren a chance to investigate the forest as part of their environmental curriculum. The twists and turns may seem confusing, but as long as you stick to the limerock trail and follow the sporadic arrows, you'll make your way to the river.

After five more sets of turns through the pine flatwoods, the trail drops down into the floodplain forest, onto a boardwalk through the hydric hammock. After 1 mile, the boardwalk ends with frontage on the Silver River. A showy purple gallinule floats across the glassy surface. Anhingas roost in the trees, spreading their wings to dry. Stand and watch the three-dimensional world below, where bluegill hang in crystalline suspension and a mud turtle moves in slow motion across the river bottom, just a few feet offshore. Besides the headspring that pours out nearly 500 million gallons of crystal-clear water every day, the Silver River has dozens of smaller springs adding another 200 million gallons of water to the mix.

Turn around and head back up the boardwalk to the main trail. Turn left. Arrows will guide you on the return trip around the other side of the loop, which crosses the jeep road used to bring passengers down here to the dock. The loop enters a sandhill area and veers to the left through the scrub, descending to emerge around the edge of a Seminole chickee in the woods, used during living history events. As you enter the clearing, walk down to the Silver River Museum, stopping to visit the old schoolhouse along the way, and down the breezeway (where you'll find restrooms and water fountains) to get back to the River Trails arch.

RIVER TRAIL

At the "River Trail" arch, take the right fork. The trail wanders through hickories and oaks, past a low depression and over a grassy levee, emptying out onto a jeep road. Turn left, following the jeep road downhill into dense hardwood hammock. Make a left onto another jeep road at the bottom of the hill, following it through a cypress swamp. The trail rises into an open field with scattered sweetgum and then drops down into a hydric hammock, dense with cabbage palms and bald cypresses, before emerging in an open area along the Silver River at 0.6 mile. There is a shelter here and a landing to handle the heavy canoe traffic, as well as rental canoes right here for immediate launch into the river—no more pushing them down from the campground! A boardwalk offers a view of the river bend, where alligators drift through mats of pennywort, and ibises flutter up to the trees.

Turn back around and take the trail to the left, which makes a loop along the river through a cleared area, following the floodplain forest. Scattered cedars, cabbage palms, and groundsel bushes grow amid the tall grasses. Watch on the left for a broad game trail leading down to the floodplain forest, affording a view of the river from beneath the cypress trees. Return to the main trail. Shortly thereafter, you come to a bench with a river view, at 0.9 mile. The glittering blue bottom of the river hides more small springs. Purple asters cascade down the riverbanks. Long wisps of old man's beard dangle from a cabbage palm.

The trail loops back toward its beginning, through stands of tall wax myrtle, cedars, and cabbage palms, returning to the main trail. Turn left, following the jeep trail back through the forests, retracing your steps uphill to the entry trail, on the right. You pass a group of teenagers dragging canoes down to the river. Visitors are welcome to bring their own canoes or kayaks to the park, but you're on your own to get them down this trail to the river. Turn right, returning under the hickories and oaks to the parking area, to emerge under the archway after this 2.1-mile hike.

DIRECTIONS

From I-75 exit 352 (Ocala), follow SR 40 for 8.4 miles through the city of Ocala out to Silver Springs. Turn right on CR 35 and drive another 1.1 miles to the park entrance, on the left.

CONTACT

Silver River State Park
1425 Northeast 58th Avenue
Ocala, FL 34470
352-236-7148
www.floridastateparks.org/silverriver

13

Bluffton Nature Trail

Total distance (circuit): 1.2 miles

Hiking time: 1 hour

Habitats: floodplain forest, oak hammock, hydric hammock, freshwater marsh, oak scrub, sand pine scrub, bog

Trailhead coordinates (lat-lon): 29.125353, -81.503343

Maps: USGS 7½' Astor; Map at trailhead kiosk

Admission: $2 per person

South of Astor along the St. Johns River, the Bluffton Recreation Area in Lake George State Forest paints a picture of Florida's prehistoric past. As botanist William Bartram canoed the St. Johns River in 1773, he noted massive mounds of snail shells piled up on its shorelines. These middens, prehistoric garbage heaps, spoke to civilizations long gone who had plied the waters of the St. Johns for sustenance and travel. The Bluffton Mound was well known as a landmark along the river, thanks to its size, but like many middens along the St. Johns was carted away for roadfill in a less enlightened time in the twentieth century. Today, a visit to the Bluffton Nature Trail leads you into the past and through habitats common to the uplands along the St. Johns River.

Before your start your hike at the parking area, sign in at the kiosk. Walk along the shoreline for a glimpse of the St. Johns River at the canoe launch before you head south along a side channel of the river that runs along Bluffton Island; you have the opportunity to walk out on a floating wheelchair-accessible fishing pier and survey the scene. Cypresses rise tall on the far shore, where watermarks on their trunks tell the tale of just how high the St. Johns River can get at times. This is an excellent spot for birding, especially in the early morning. Gallinules drift across the shallows, and you might catch a glimpse of a limpkin picking its way beneath the Virginia willows along the shoreline.

Leaving the pier, turn right and walk between the Southern red cedars to the third sign-in spot for the forest, this time for the

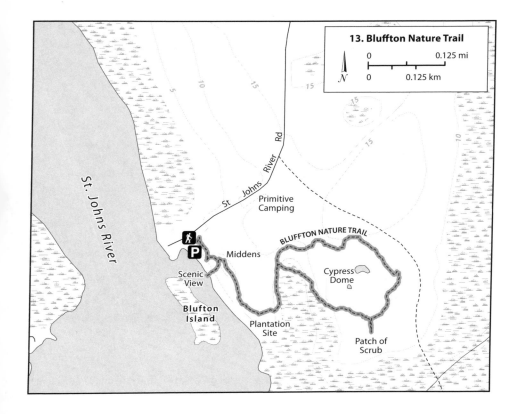

13. Bluffton Nature Trail

hiking trail itself. Here, you'll pay your entry fee. At the kiosk, pick up an interpretive guide, which has numbers corresponding to locations along the hike. An ancient village occupied at this spot, with a midden of freshwater snail shells that once rose up to 20 feet high across 35 acres of riverfront. The people who lived here enjoyed the bounty of the St. Johns River, not just in snails but fish, turtle, and manatee. Pottery and tools have been found in archaeological digs at this site. By the early 1900s, this site was known as Orange Bluff. Atop the midden, an orange grove flourished, and surrounding truck farms in the low-lying wetlands enabled the planters to ship oranges, tomatoes, and other vegetables from the dock at Bluffton

Landing. Some remains of the dock sit down along the water's edge.

As you start down the footpath, notice the tiny snail shells underfoot everywhere. These were all a part of the midden. The straight-line nature of the trail feels like a tramway, which probably was used to transport crops and cypress out to the river. A floating bridge sits forlornly at the bottom of a dry basin. A swallow-tailed kite swoops overhead in a flash of white and black against the blue sky.

Following lime-green blazes, the trail starts down a boardwalk and into a lush hardwood hammock, where citrus dangles from trees in the understory. Bamboo grows in profuse clusters. Passing an ironwood tree, you get into a dense stand of pignut hickory. As the

---

Bluffton Nature Trail

Path through the pines

forest canopy thickens, thanks to ancient live oaks and massive Southern magnolia trees, you reach the beginning of the loop at 0.3 mile. Turn right.

The trail leads through river bluff forest, the landscape undulating underfoot—perhaps due to river erosion, the removal of the midden materials, or furrows from truck farming. Sparkleberry rises overhead, notable for its peeling reddish bark and its berries. It's also known as huckleberry and is the tallest member of the blueberry family. As the landscape opens up a little, the habitat transitions into scrubby flatwoods. An unmarked spur trail at half a mile leads down to a patch of open scrub. Take a quick wander down there for a look. Low-bush blueberries spot blooms along the edges of the trail, which is fringed with Chapman oak and sand live oak. Returning to the main trail, turn right.

Back in the scrubby flatwoods, the line of cabbage palms in the distance indicates a flow of water through the landscape, along with tall cypress. Crossing another boardwalk, the trail continues past tall wax myrtles. Sphagnum moss and marsh ferns indicate the location of a bog, along with colorful wild bachelor's-button growing in the mushy spots. Poke around a little, and you might find hooded pitcher plants, according to the forest's list of native plants found here. A big puff of deer moss indicates another change in habitat as the landscape rises a little to accommodate gallberry, blueberry, and bracken fern, an island of sandhill surrounded by small boggy spots.

After Marker 11, the trail makes a sharp left past a stand of young sand pines. A sharp right leads you into the sand pine scrub. Signs of a bear's recent visit—trunks torn apart by long claws—are all along this section of the loop. This is a lush patch of sand pine scrub, with an understory of curvaceous branches of lyonia and sand live oak hosting colorful hanging gardens of lichens. The trail reaches a noticeable high spot, which might be part of the original midden. A Southern magnolia is swaddled in resurrection fern.

The loop ends soon after, at 0.9 miles. On the walk back through the hammock, enjoy the tall magnolias, live oaks, and cabbage palms as they cast long shadows across the trail. The trail turns right as it draws within sight of the river. Continue down the narrow boardwalk back out to the homestead site, and you'll soon emerge at the edge of the recreation area. Take a wander back down to the river to see if any new wading birds are poking around before you head back to your car, ending your 1.2-mile hike.

DIRECTIONS

From the junction of US 17 and SR 40 in Barberville, drive west 5.8 miles toward the town of Volusia at the Astor Bridge to the second sign for Lake George State Forest on the left. Turn south on St. Johns River Road. Drive 0.7 of a mile down this bumpy road to reach the state forest entrance. Stop at the kiosk and sign in. The road narrows sharply, although at the time I visited, it appeared they might be widening it so two cars could pass. After 2.7 miles you pass the entrance to a beautiful primitive camping area tucked in beneath ancient oaks, and after 3.4 miles the road ends at the trailhead and river access area. The entrance road may be a little tough on your vehicle but does not require four-wheel drive.

CONTACT

Lake George State Forest
5458 North US 17
De Leon Springs, FL 32130
386-985-7822
www.fl-dof.com

Mosses, lichens, and ferns on Southern magnolia

14

De Leon Springs State Park

Total distance (circuit): 4.5 miles

Hiking time: 2.5 hours

Habitats: hardwood hammock, floodplain forest, hydric hammock, meadow

Trailhead coordinates (lat-lon):
29.136952, -81.361309

Maps: USGS 7½' Lake Dias; Florida Trail Association Map North; Park map at ranger station

Admission: $2 pedestrians/bicyclists, $4 individual motorist, $6 carload

Hours: 8 AM–sunset

When Ponce De Leon sailed to Florida in 1513, he sought the fountain of youth. Exploring the St. Johns River, he wrote, "We ascended a large river, passing through two small rivers and three lakes, whence we came to a great boiling spring which the Indians call 'Healing Waters.'"

Pushing forth slightly sulfuric waters at a constant temperature of 72°F, the spring was a gathering ground for the Timucuan, as evidenced by an archaeological find of a dugout canoe more than 6,000 years old. In the 1780s, Spanish land grant settlers moved into the region after Britain, stung by the loss of its colonies, ceded the territory to Spain. The area became known as Spring Garden, a grand plantation with cotton, corn, and sugarcane, with the spring named for the Spanish explorer De Leon.

After Florida became a U.S. territory, the plantation passed into the hands of Colonel Orlando Rees, who built a waterwheel to grind his sugarcane. Although the plantation was sacked during the Second Seminole War and by Union forces in the Civil War, the waterwheel remains—an integral part of De Leon Springs State Recreation Area. Offering swimming in the now walled-in spring, canoeing down Spring Garden Run to Lake Woodruff, and hiking along the Wild Persimmon Trail, this is one of the busier state parks in the region. Not because of the activities, oddly enough, but because of the pancakes. That's right, pancakes. After you finish your hike, you'll find out why.

Since a great deal of the Wild Persimmon Trail winds through the hydric hammocks

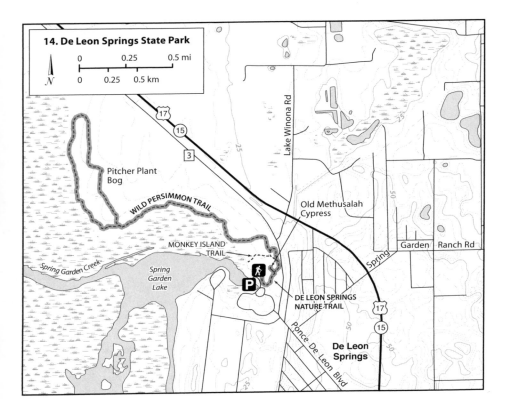

14. De Leon Springs State Park

Pitcher Plant Bog

WILD PERSIMMON TRAIL

Old Methusalah Cypress

MONKEY ISLAND TRAIL

Spring Garden Creek

Spring Garden Lake

DE LEON SPRINGS NATURE TRAIL

Lake Winona Rd

Garden Ranch Rd

De Leon Springs

Ponce De Leon Blvd

along Spring Garden Run, this is a trail best visited under an intense cloud of insect repellent, or better yet, in winter, when the mosquito population is bearable. Don't let the bugs deter you, however, as the trail is an enjoyable walk in the deep woods, where wildlife sightings are common. One word of warning—if the St. Johns River is high, many spots along the trail may be flooded, despite the bog bridges provided. If you're not prepared for what could turn into an adventuresome knee-deep wade through swamp forest, don't attempt this trail. To get to the Wild Persimmon Trail, you hike in on the park's paved interpretive nature trail. The nature trail has two trail-heads; start your hike from the one at the parking area behind the bathhouse

The nature trail meanders through an oak hammock, where immense live oaks tower overhead. You come to a boardwalk to the left. Follow it into the cypress swamp for a glimpse of "Old Methusalah," a bald cypress estimated to be nearly 500 years old. It's an amazing sight, rising more than 150 feet through the understory, and a sobering one—the forests along the St. Johns River were still populated with trees this immense just 200 years ago, before the advent of full-scale logging in the state. As you return along the boardwalk, notice the lush growth of netted chain and royal ferns along the swamp's edge. Turn left, continuing along the paved trail. You enter a small stand of giant longleaf pines, each more than 8 feet in circumference, the largest towering more than 150 feet. A red-tailed hawk swoops down, uttering a piercing cry.

When the paved trail forks, take a right. At 0.3 mile, you reach the Wild Persimmon Trail trailhead map and kiosk. Pick up a map (if you didn't already nab one from the park ranger) and turn right, into the woods. This is where the adventure begins. The trail is blazed with Florida Trail Association orange blazes, each the size of a dollar bill. Follow the blazes and signs carefully, and you won't get lost.

The hydric hammock closes in around you, dense and jungle-like, thick with cabbage palms, red bay, and southern magnolia. Oyster mushrooms grow out of the rotting trunk of a fallen cabbage palm as the trail quietly slips into a forgotten corner of Lake Woodruff National Wildlife Refuge. Longleaf pines rise around you, with tall cinnamon ferns growing at their bases. After 0.5 mile, the footpath becomes difficult underfoot, with mud puddles trapped between roots and "gatorbacks," the exposed trunks of saw palmetto. A boardwalk carries the trail over a permanent flow of tannic water through the hydric hammock. The

Spring Creek at DeLeon Springs

land rises slightly, the saw palmetto giving way to a grassy understory under the cabbage palms. When you reach the next bench, you get your first glimpse of an open meadow off to the right, an old pasture being reclaimed by the forest. You'll be walking through that meadow later on in the trip.

Several bog bridges provide stepping-stones across the lapping waters of the swamp. It's dark in the forest, even in the early morning light—the broad fronds of the cabbage palms serve well to block out the light, leaving only streamers of sunshine to filter through to the dark soil and tannic water. If the river is high, this area will be very flooded. Continue following the orange blazes if the footpath becomes indistinct. As you turn a corner past marker 7, rising up to walk along a corner of the meadow, you've walked 1 mile. The trail reenters the hydric hammock but soon emerges again, as a few inches of elevation changes the landscape—swamp yields to an oak hammock, with turkey oaks and laurel oaks. You pass the end of the loop trail (the back side of a sign with an arrow pointing in the direction from which you came) at 1.4 miles. Continue straight. The trail turns away from the meadow to stay in the oak hammock. The canopy overhead becomes increasingly high; saw palmetto makes up the understory. A pileated woodpecker dives past, flashing its distinctive red crown and black-and-white wings in flight.

At 1.8 miles, you pass a bench tucked in under the mix of live oaks and cabbage palms. Bromeliads—air plants—thrive in this humid hammock along the edge of the swamp; the cabbage palms sprout wild pine like hair. Long green plumes of goldfoot fern cascade from the soft thatch just below a cabbage palm's fronds. The understory opens up again as you skirt along the edge of the swamp—off to the left, water covers the forest floor.

Swinging to the right, the trail continues to meander through cabbage palms and live oaks until it loops around and emerges into the meadow, at 2.3 miles. A stand of wild persimmon trees grow right in front of where the trail enters the meadow. In spring, they're indistinct from the other trees, but in fall, when the foliage falls off, the persimmon trees drip with small orange fruits. Pucker up if you pop one in your mouth—wild persimmons are extremely astringent when first picked, but turn sweet when they are allowed to ripen. Raccoons and opossums make pilgrimages to this tiny grove for the ripened fruits fallen under the trees.

The trail becomes a grassy aisle, a mowed path through the meadow. Lone sweetgum trees show off red and purple leaves in the fall. A cool breeze sweeps across the open landscape. Look for a marker on the right pointing out a small pitcher-plant bog. After the trail jogs through a hammock of shady live oaks and longleaf pine, it turns to the right, passing through a fence line and next to a bench. Turn left at the tree line and follow the blazes into a picnic area (it looks like a campground, but no camping is permitted along this trail). Sit here a while, and you may be rewarded with the appearance of white-tailed deer in the clearing, or the hurried scampering of a flock of wild turkey into the underbrush. The remains of an old corral hide in the saw palmettos on the right. Leaving the picnic area, the trail swings off to the right, under a stand of live oaks. As you enter the tree line you reach the end of the loop, after 3 miles of hiking. Turn left. Retrace your steps along the orange blazes back to the trailhead, paying special attention to the interesting fungi growing at the bases of trees. Turn right and walk back along the paved trail to the parking lot, completing your 4.5-mile hike.

It's time for your reward. Take a walk to the other side of the spring past the ecotour boats and down to the old waterwheel. Here, you'll find the Old Spanish Sugar Mill Grill & Griddle House, where Floridians flock for its renowned pancake feast. Using batter made with grain stone-ground at the old mill, you pour out your own flapjacks on the center of your table, a hot griddle shared with the other people at the table. If bacon and eggs are more your style, you can cook them, too. Breakfast goes on all day, from 9 AM until 4 PM Monday through Friday, and 8 AM until 4 PM on weekends.

DIRECTIONS

The town of De Leon Springs is just north of Deland on US 17. From US 17 in De Leon Springs, turn west onto Ponce De Leon Boulevard. Follow it 0.8 mile. The entrance to De Leon Springs State Recreation Area is just after the railroad crossing. You can't miss it—it's an unusually grand entrance surrounded by ornate murals and a very kitschy roadside sign from the days when this was a tourist attraction. After you pay your Florida State Parks entrance fee, turn right at the T intersection to drive down to the parking area by the bathhouse. If the parking area is full, you'll have to park on the other side of the spring and walk across the bridge.

CONTACT

De Leon Springs State Park
601 Ponce de Leon Boulevard
De Leon Springs, FL 32130
386-985-4212
www.floridastateparks.org/deleonsprings

15

St. Francis Hiking Trail

Total distance (circuit): 7.7 miles

Hiking time: 4 hours

Habitats: floodplain forest, hydric hammock, oak hammock, bayhead, pine flatwoods

Maps: USGS 7½' Lake Woodruff, Florida Trail Association map NF-4

Trailhead coordinates (lat-lon): 29.012717, -81.392550

Admission: Free

Hours: Sunrise–sunset

Tucked away at the most southeastern point of the Ocala National Forest, the St. Francis Trail provides an interesting walk along the floodplain forest of several side channels of the St. Johns River. Two trails tempt, differing in distance and sights to be seen—a 2.8-mile loop out to a bubbling sulfur spring, or the full 7.7-mile loop out to the ghost town of St. Francis. Since this is a national forest, camping is permitted anywhere along the trail. Although there are no established campsites, the plant life and the terrain limits the number of optimal places to camp. Much of the hike is through river hammocks and floodplain forest, so slather on the mosquito repellent before you get out of the car.

No matter which of the two loops you choose to do, your hike starts at the trailhead kiosk. Take a moment to learn a little about this forgotten town along the St. Johns. St. Francis was a turn-of-the-century boomtown, built on cypress logging, citrus groves, and farming. As you start walking through the oak hammock, beaten paths lead off in many directions. Stick with the orange blazes as you walk though the forest of live oak and sweetgum. After the trail veers to the left, you cross the first of several bridges created by setting two long telephone poles side by side.

You'll quickly notice how unusual the ground is underfoot. The ups and downs of this section of the trail are due to furrows and ridges created when this forest was a plowed watermelon field in the late 1800s. The boomtown of St. Francis revolved around citrus, cypress, vegetables, and fruit. Now, deer moss and blueberries crowd the understory

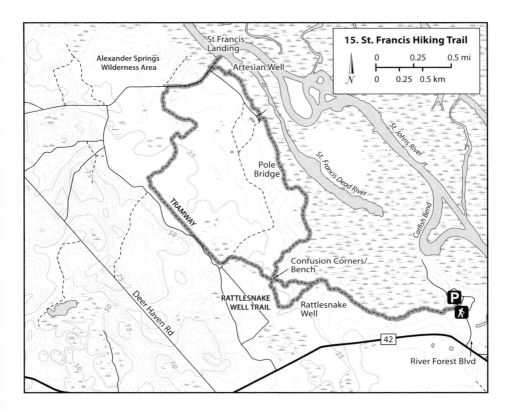

beneath-water oak, willow oak, and slash pine. Watch for the welcome mats—the trail maintainers laid down some industrial black mats in some of the soggier places, hoping to stave off erosion as the trail drops down into a floodplain forest of red maple, sweetgum, and pignut hickory.

After crossing a plank over a slimy puddle, you come to the first of many long board-walks on this trail, 0.5 mile into your hike. This one has some slip control built in—a fine mesh of hardware cloth provides traction. Board-walks in this humid environment become slip-pery quickly after a rain, especially in the summer months. The boardwalks keep you out of the dark mucky soil, allowing delicate ferns and fungus to take root. Watch off to

the left for the slender orange fingers of coral fungus. As you walk along the next few boardwalks, pay attention to the many ferns, including royal fern, netted chain, and spleen-worts. Tawny milkcap and violet cort mush-rooms rise from the muck on the right. The boardwalks bridge together tiny islands in the floodplain forest. Overhead, wild pine and other bromeliads grow in the trees. Shoelace fern drips down the trunk of a tall cabbage palm; farther up the tree, sunlight streams through a cluster of opaque gold foot fern. Whenever the trail leaves the boardwalk for dry land, the shiny leaves of dog-hobble dom-inate the understory.

There are an increasing number of roots in the trail as you walk between the cabbage palms. The dark earth is damp underfoot. After a mile, you cross a bridge over a small tributary flowing down toward the hidden St. Francis Dead River. As the forest canopy gets higher, it's possible to see the open sky indicating the river off to the right—but only in winter. This is a dense hydric hammock, shady and humid, the tree trunks covered with deep furry coats of sphagnum moss. After you pass an elbow in a stream, the water transparent to a sand bottom but tea-stained with the tannic residue of hickory and oak leaves, you cross a boardwalk through a bed of swamp lilies.

At 1.2 miles, you reach a trail junction with yellow blazes disappearing into the forest to the left. This is the Rattlesnake Well Trail, which provides the shorter of the two loop hikes. No matter whether you plan to hike the short loop or the long loop, continue straight ahead along the orange blazes, crossing a bridge over the stream that flows out of Rattlesnake Well. Immature fish glitter in the shallows. A grove of southern magnolia and its smaller cousin, the bay magnolia, crosses the trail, reflecting sunlight off large glossy leaves. The trail rises up a little, the footpath becoming needle-strewn under slash pines. You reach the next trail junction at 1.4 miles, where the sign says ST. FRANCIS LOOP. Here's your decision point. If you only want to hike the 2.8-mile loop, keep to the left, and make a left turn within a hundred feet onto the yellow-blazed trail at the bench. To hike the full 7.7-mile St. Francis Loop, turn right. Either way, take a look up at the tree behind the sign—an unusual double-trunked slash pine, rising more than 100 feet over the forest floor.

The trail turns down a corridor of saw palmetto under large live oaks, then drops down into a hydric hammock of tall cabbage palms. As it rises up again, it skirts the edge of a pine forest, continuing under a low canopy of oaks. On one snag on the right, a giant specimen of black shelf fungus perches, spanning more than a foot across—Nature's umbrella for the green anole pressed against the tree trunk. As the trail jogs off to the right, it enters a narrow corridor between saw palmettos, reentering the hydric hammock. You cross a bridge over a murky side stream, watching an oak toad disappear under the dried palm fronds. Veering left, the trail returns to the oak hammock, within sight of neatly planted rows of slash pine. Before this land became a national forest, citrus groves and vegetable fields once blossomed where most of these younger pine forests stand. As you wander through the pines, notice the slender stalks of bamboo growing along the trail.

At 2.4 miles, the trail crosses a sandy jeep trail in a deep ditch, then clambers up a bluff onto a levee. Built to allow farmers to flood the fields on the left to grow rice, this levee now provides high ground for the trail. A ditch

Artesian well

parallels the levee at its base. Cross a high bridge, where guy wires help you maintain your balance. Tannic water trickles below. As you come around a small bend in the levee, an unbroken expanse of saw palmetto stretches off to the right. Water flows across the trail in one mucky area, where it seeks to escape back to the river. You catch your first glimpses of cypress off to the right, the sluggish water around their bases thick with duckweed. During the dry season, consider the large flat spot on the right as a potential campsite, at 2.8 miles. The cypress swamp laps up close to this bed of oak leaves, providing nearby water—and the possibility of mucky ground under the leaves. This is not an ideal campsite, but it's the first flat spot along the trail that lends itself to pitching a tent.

White sand washes down the trail on the left from an intersection with an old sandy jeep trail. Turn left across the wash, then immediately right at the fork into the forest. Ahead of you are some poles made into a guardrail; the trail turns sharply right into the oak hammock before you reach the guardrail. You notice signs of disturbance to the land—the many jeep trails, some of which were once wagon roads, and the ditches to drain off water for farmland. You are now on the outskirts of St. Francis.

Where the trail widens and becomes dark underfoot at 3.2 miles, there are flat areas under the spreading live oaks that would make perfect campsites—especially perfect when you discover the artesian well, a free-flowing freshwater source piped out of the ground and flowing off toward the river. You can't miss the sound of gurgling water and the pipes off on the right. The trail veers to the left, turning sharply right at a large pond pine with two orange blazes. Needles grow directly out of the trunk, a characteristic feature of these bristly pines.

After you pass the sign that indicates you've walked 3.5 miles, the trail turns left onto a sand road. This is the old wagon road between the St. Johns River and Paisley, and the main street of St. Francis. There are no foundations left, no ruins to explore—the buildings, constructed of cypress boards, were recycled for their prize lumber, the remainders plundered by vandals. Imagine the old hotel over there in the opening between the trees, and the livery stable close to the road. A wagon stops at the general store to deliver dry goods. The post office opened in March 1888. Homes and cottages were scattered along the road and throughout the woods. If you'd turned in the opposite direction, the road ends down at the river, where the old dock used to be. Steamboats on the St. Johns came down from Palatka with supplies and headed back downstream loaded with fresh fruit and vegetables. But by 1894, deep freezes damaged the citrus groves. In 1886, the new railroad line from Jacksonville opened, coming down the opposite side of the river to miss St. Francis entirely. When the towns to the east started shipping their fruits and vegetables by rail, St. Francis was doomed. The steamboats stopped coming. A hurricane in the 1920s dealt the final blow. Most of the town suffered considerable damage from flooding.

The last resident of St. Francis left the woods in the 1940s. The land became part of the Ocala National Forest, and you may encounter the hunters and fishermen that use this road to access the river. You're walking along the southern boundary of the Alexander Springs Wilderness Area, an unbroken forest stretching more than 20 miles to the north. Unfortunately, this historic road sees more than its share of beer cans and bottles from visitors whose pickup trucks may force you to climb off the trail as they pass.

At 3.9 miles, the trail returns to the forest,

turning left into a hammock of cabbage palms and oaks. The landscape soon yields to tall straight rows of slash pines, planted to reclaim the land. Pine needles form a soft blanket underfoot. Blueberries and cinnamon ferns flourish in the acidic soil, as do scattered loblolly bay trees. Crossing a plank over a small murky creek, the trail meanders into a more open expanse of pine flatwoods, where saw palmettos form a solid understory. After you cross a jeep trail, the saw palmetto yields to dense thickets of gallberry. You see a hunter perched on top of his pickup. Use caution when hiking this trail in December and January, as the Ocala National Forest is popular with deer hunters. Check with the forest rangers for hunting dates, and wear a blaze orange vest when hiking here in the winter.

Bridge over a creek

KEVIN MIMS

You'll cross several jeep trails before entering a stand of loblolly bay, where the ground is soggy underfoot. Paralleling a jeep road, the trail reaches an old logging tramway at 5.6 miles. When the virgin pines and cypresses in these woods were logged, the logging companies built these slightly elevated grades to allow their railcars—first pulled by mules or oxen, then powered by steam—to reach the inner depths of the forest. Veer off to the right into the woods to avoid the large puddles in the tramway. Where the trail veers back out to the tramway, turn left to follow the old logging route, straight as an arrow, through the dense bayhead swamps. A murky duckweed-choked ditch parallels to the right. Thick sphagnum moss carpets the edge of the trail. Ducking under low branches, you must jump over several wet spots.

At 5.8 miles, turn left off the tramway for a brief walk amid the pines, as the trail soon emerges on a jeep road. Turn left, following the blazes a short distance down to where water tends to pool deeply in the road. Turn right into the bayhead, where the trail becomes a boardwalk through this frequently soggy ecosystem. Like the forest that paralleled the tramway, the bayhead is mostly made up of loblolly bay and slash pines. Crossing a jeep track, the trail wanders through into a planted forest of young slash pines, then veers to the right to parallel the jeep track. After crossing the jeep track again, you walk along a boardwalk through another relatively open bayhead. Cinnamon ferns rise up out of the tea-colored water. Soon after the trail turns left to enter the oak hammock, you end up at Confusion Corners—a trail junction for the two loops, at 6.3 miles. The bench here is your one chance to sit and relax before finishing up the remainder of the trail. Head straight down the orange blazes for the most direct route back if you're in a hurry; otherwise, take the time to turn down the yellow-blazed loop trail to Rattlesnake Well.

Turning left at a split-rail fence meant to block accidental meandering off the trail, the yellow-blazed trail leads you over some rough footing—gatorbacks, the stems of saw palmettos breaking up the footpath. A long boardwalk leads over a grassy area thick with ferns. After crossing two short bridges, you drop down a slope to cross a steeply eroded channel. The trail turns left to follow this small creek under a stand of southern magnolia, crossing numerous bridges as it meanders through oak hammocks to its main point of interest—Rattlesnake Well. The spring bursts forth out of the bottom of a small stream, a swirling hole of turquoise-blue with yellow streamers. A faint aroma of sulfur, like the tips of matches, wafts across the water.

Within a few hundred feet, the yellow-blazed trail rejoins the main orange-blazed trail. Turn right, retracing your steps across the boardwalks of the floodplain forest for the final 1.2 miles back to the parking lot, completing your 7.7-mile hike.

DIRECTIONS

From US 17 in Deland, follow SR 44 west over the St. Johns River drawbridge. Immediately turn right on CR 42. Drive 0.4 mile to the National Forest sign that says RIVER FOREST GROUP CAMP. Turn right on FR 542. After you pass the River Forest campground, the trailhead parking will be off to the left, 0.3 mile from CR 42.

CONTACT

Ocala National Forest
Seminole Ranger District
40929 State Road 19
Umatilla, FL 32784
352-669-3153
www.fs.usda.gov/ocala

16

Hontoon Island State Park

Total distance (round-trip): 3.3 miles

Hiking time: 1 hour, 45 minutes

Habitats: floodplain forest, pine flatwoods, hydric hammock, palm hammock, oak hammock

Trailhead coordinates (lat-lon): 28.974316, -81.357561

Maps: Maps: USGS 7½' Orange City; Map at trailhead kiosk

Admission: Free

Hours: 8 AM–sunset

Florida's state park system includes several island preserves, but Hontoon Island State Park is the only one surrounded by fresh water, and the only one to which the state provides a free ferry. From the park's parking lot on the shoreline of the St. Johns River, the island shimmers tantalizingly across the ribbon of water, just out of reach. Ibises walk the grassy shore as motorboats putter by. Eventually, the pontoon boat drifts across the current to meet you, and you're afloat, crossing the river to this unique preserve.

The Timucua lived here for more than 3,000 years, sharing the dark hammocks and bright pine flatwoods with the otter, the owl, and the deer. They carved totems to stand along the river, perhaps indicative of their clan names. In 1955, dredgers found a totem pole, a tall owl, buried in deep muck near the present-day parking lot for the park; in 1978, a pelican and otter. Totem poles are rare in North America; these were the only totem poles discovered outside the Pacific Northwest. Since the archaeological finds are now in museums, full-size replicas of the owl and the otter stand just off the ferryboat landing to the left, on the path to the picnic area.

In the 1560s, French artist Jacques Le Moyne recorded a wealth of information about the now-vanished Timucua culture on the upper St. Johns, near present-day Jacksonville. They lived in dome-shaped palm-thatched huts; grew maize, pumpkins, and beans; gathered wild nuts and berries; and hunted the many fish and mammals along the river, including the manatee. All along the river, the Timucua left their middens—refuse

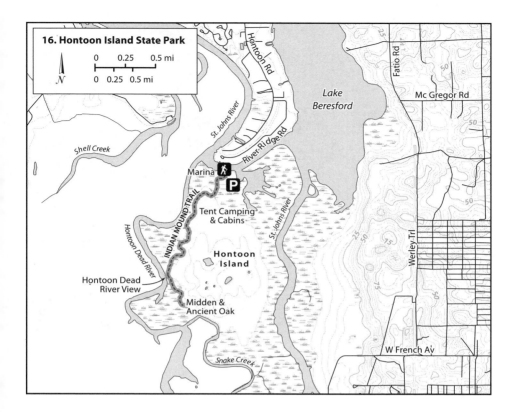

0   0.25   0.5 mi

0   0.25   0.5 mi

N

Hontoon Rd

Fatio Rd

Lake
Beresford

Mc Gregor Rd

Shell Creek

St. Johns River

River Ridge Rd

Marina

P

Tent Camping
& Cabins

St. Johns River

Hontoon Dead River

INDIAN MOUND TRAIL

Hontoon
Island

Werley Trl

Hontoon Dead
River View

Midden &
Ancient Oak

W French Av

Snake Creek

heaps of shells and other materials. Most were unceremoniously scraped up and used as roadbed fill for Florida's earliest roads, before archaeologists ever knew of the culture's existence. Today, the Museum of Science and Industry in Jacksonville presents one of the few comprehensive exhibits in the state about the Timucua along the St. Johns River.

Hidden in deep forest off a side channel of the river, one large midden survived on Hontoon Island and is the focus of the island's sole hiking trail, the Indian Mound Trail. To start your hike, turn right as you exit the ferryboat landing, passing in front of a large building containing the Island Store, the park museum, the ranger station, and restrooms. Walk along the water's edge up to the 48-slip

marina, where visitors are welcome to tie up their boats and stop for the day or to arrange an overnight stay.

The trail heads up a jeep road that parallels the river briefly before swinging into an extensive floodplain forest of live oak, cabbage palm, and sweetgum. Look for fragments of freshwater snail shells spilling out of the bluff into the road, remains of the middens that once lined the shoreline. Red cedars cling to the dry land at the edge of the road. The road leads to the park's campground, which caters to visitors who enjoy tent camping or who are fortunate enough to nab one of the park's few cabins.

Turn right off the road at a trail kiosk, following a series of bog bridges into a hydric

---

Ancient forest on Hontoon Island

hammock of tall cabbage palms. The trail rises slightly into a palm hammock, with spreading live oaks that branch up to 50 feet tall, their branches thickly covered with resurrection fern. This is an interpretive trail, so watch for the occasional markers as the trail winds through the saw palmetto understory. Sunlight filters through the tall cathedral of cabbage palms. Watch for plentiful shoelace fern, the dark green grass-like growths dangling like ribbons from some of the cabbage palm trunks. The palms look ancient and undisturbed, as though the Timucua walked here just yesterday. Shaggy patches of deep green sphagnum moss and mustard-colored lichens cover their lower extremities. A smoky blue-gray gnatcatcher flits past, landing on a saw palmetto frond.

A soft carpet of pine needles covers the trail as it rises into a forest of slash pine, then drops back down into the hydric hammock. Bog bridges cross water the color of midnight. On the right, you'll catch your first glimpse of bald cypress along this walk, with their telltale knobby knees. The dominant tree of the floodplain forest along the Hontoon Dead River (which parallels the trail through the forest), bald cypresses are healthiest when their roots are underwater most of the time. A bronze frog, small and dark, crouches at the base of a cabbage palm. As the trail rises into another slash pine forest, the footpath becomes mossy. Blueberry bushes crowd under the pines, flourishing in the acidic soil that results from the breakdown of pine needles. Pine flatwoods stretch off into the distance on the left as you spy a bench along the trail at 0.8 mile. When you pass a particularly large sand post oak on the right, keep alert, as the trail swings abruptly left, and the turn is easy to miss. You know you're on the right track when you see the interpretive marker for a slash pine on the left.

The footpath becomes a little mushy underfoot as you pass dozens of small hollows filled with water, river remainders from the last flood. Dropping farther into a palm hammock, you walk down a corridor of cabbage palms, interspersed with massive live oaks. Spiderwebs glisten in the bright sun. Clusters of sphagnum moss send up flowery shoots at the bases of saw palmettos. Dinner-plate-sized blossoms draw your attention to the tall southern magnolia on the right. Leaving the palms behind, the trail rises into an oak forest thick with deerberry and yaupon holly, crossing another bog bridge. Fallen white petals of magnolia blooms float on the bog's dark waters. The trail rises back into a canopy of cabbage palm, with marsh ferns and grasses between the saw palmettos on the forest floor. Sixty feet above, live oak branches sway in the wind, thick with resurrection fern, wild pine, and Spanish moss.

A fallen oak across the trail requires a duck-under or walk-around. It plays host to a variety of lichens and fungi, including shelf-like protrusions of 6-inch-wide mustard-yellow polypore. Overhead, the oak canopy remains 40 to 60 feet tall, densely coated with wild pine. After you pass under some low cabbage palm fronds, the trail opens into a clearing with a bench, at 1.3 miles. It's a short walk down to the Hontoon Dead River, off to the right. The St. Johns has many "dead" rivers, labeled so not because of their health but for navigational purposes—they are side channels that go nowhere. Look for the 1935 Geodesic Survey marker, near the bench. Two trails leave the clearing; head straight, following the route you came in on. A river cooter turtle strolls down the trail, coming inland to search for a suitable dry, sandy spot to lay eggs. The most common turtle you'll

see basking on logs along rivers and lakes, the cooter is one of Florida's largest freshwater turtles, up to a foot long or more. Its dark, rounded shell often becomes coated with green algae from the river.

Jump across the small stream that flows through the trail as it continues to follow the edge of the floodplain forest on the right. Off on the left, the far horizon opens up into pine flatwoods. At a yellow arrow and FVA sign (Florida Volkswalkers, a recreational power-walking club, whose signs you'll see along many state park trails), continue straight. The trail rises up onto the midden on a bed of small, bleached-white river snail shells. A red-tailed hawk swoops through the cypress canopy, perching in a sweetgum tree.

The trail jogs to the left to skirt a large fallen oak coated with a fine growth of violet-toothed polypore, shelf mushrooms with jagged violet tips and fuzzy black tops. Swinging up a steep grade, the trail becomes rough—plenty of roots underfoot as it dips in and out of small hollows along the edge of the midden. Snail shells spill out beneath roots underfoot. Watch for colorful and unusual forms of fungi on rotting logs and tree branches. As the trail becomes indistinct, keep to the dry mound. The trail ends at a bench beneath one of the largest live oaks you'll ever see, after 1.6 miles. This is a high spot on the westernmost edge of the midden. Sit down and take in the sweep of the scene—the ancient oak, the mass of fossilized snail shells, the floodplain forest stretching down to the Dead River.

Turn around and retrace your steps. As the trail descends the shell mound, watch for a coontie on the left side—a low, dark green, palm-like plant. Although they are popular ornamental plants, it's rare to see them in the wild. A member of the ancient cycad family, this was once a very common plant in Florida. Also known as arrowroot, coontie was a

Cypress knees on the Hontoon Dead River

mainstay of the diet of the Timucua, the Creeks, and later, the Seminoles. Although the raw stem of the plant is poisonous, it was put through a process to make it edible for bread—crushed into a powder, washed and strained, and set out to dry to become a flour.

Passing through the clearing by the Hontoon Dead River, be sure to head straight along the main trail. The side trail off to the right leads out into the pine flatwoods. If you stay on the island, be sure to pick up a park map that shows the unmarked jeep trails across the island, where you can do additional walking or bicycling. Where the main trail ends on the jeep road, turn left to return to the marina and the ferryboat dock, completing your 3.3-mile hike. Ferries run hourly, so take the time to check out the replica totems and the park museum while you wait, and take advantage of the picnic grove as a shady spot to watch white ibis, great blue herons, and limpkins wading the shallows along the river.

DIRECTIONS

From Interstate 4 exit 114, Orange City, take SR 472 north toward Orange City, follow the highway 3 miles to the off-ramp for US 17/92 north. Within the next mile, turn left on CR 15A (Business US 17/92). Several lights down, turn left on SR 44. Watch for the park sign and turn left on Old New York Avenue. Signs direct you along the rest of the 7.2-mile route to the park. Bear right onto Berensford Road (CR 4110), then left on Old New York Road, paralleling the river. Turn left on Hontoon Road, then right on River Ridge Road, which leads to the state park's parking lot along the river, on the left.

CONTACT

Hontoon Island State Park
2309 River Ridge Road
Deland, FL 32720
386-736-5309
www.floridastateparks.org/hontoonisland

17

Lower Wekiva River Preserve State Park

Total distance (circuit): 2.1 miles

Hiking time: 1.5 hours

Habitats: bayhead, oak scrub, sandhills, sand pine scrub, sinkhole

Trailhead coordinates (lat-lon): 28.815005, -81.405699

Maps: USGS 7½' Sanford SW; Lower Wekiva River Preserve State Park map

Admission: Free

Hours: 8 AM–sunset

Most drivers headed west from Sanford on SR 46 register this state park as a blip as they speed on by to cross the Wekiva River. What they see, however, is just the tip of the iceberg. Lower Wekiva River Preserve State Park encompasses more than 18,000 acres protecting the floodplain where the spring-fed Wekiva River meets the St. Johns River. With more than 10 miles of riverfront, it's long been a favorite of paddlers, who can rejoice that the old Katie's Landing has reopened as an official trailhead and launch spot within the park along the Wekiva River. More than 18 miles of wilderness trails are accessible from the north end of the preserve, requiring map and compass or GPS for navigation.

If you slow down at this easy-to-access trailhead and take an hour to explore one small corner of this state park on the Sandhills Nature Trail, it may leave you wanting to go adventuring more deeply into the preserve on your next visit.

The Sandhills Nature Trail starts at a kiosk immediately adjacent to the trailhead. Grab a map for the two stacked loops that make up this trail, named "Loop 1" and "Loop 2." Using these loops, you can hike a figure-8 on the trail system. The kiosk draws your attention to bear activity in the area. As part of more than part of more than 70,000 acres of public lands protected in the Wekiva River Basin, these are the stomping grounds of the endangered Florida black bear, a small subspecies of the black bear, with grown males typically weighing no more than 350 pounds—although there have been notable exceptions discovered of late.

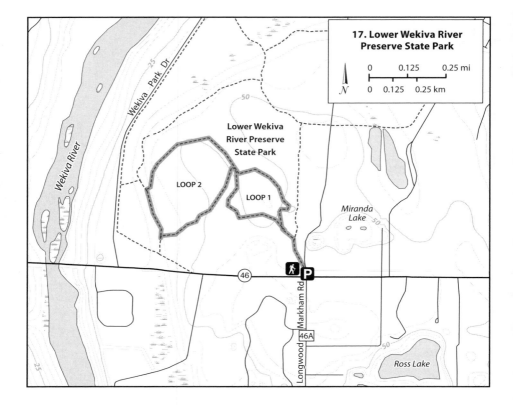

Starting down the trail, you see saw palmettos with trunks lifted well up in the air. Walking beneath a stand of oaks, you emerge into a classic sandhill habitat, with towering longleaf pines, young turkey oaks, an open understory with plenty of saw palmetto, and a forest floor carpeted in wiregrass. Blazed in both orange and white—the orange blazes indicating a segment of our statewide National Scenic Trail, the Florida Trail through this preserve—the trail passes interpretive markers keyed to the "Loop 1" brochure at the kiosk. It's a comfortable walk down a corridor of pine duff. At 0.1 mile you reach the top of the loop. Keep left.

Sandhill wireweed, spiderwort, and green-eyes lend color to the understory. Grass-stage longleaf pine blends in nicely with the surrounding tufts of wiregrass, forming a nursery of young pines. Passing a sinkhole on the left, a depression filled with saw palmetto, the trail continues through open flatwoods. All times of year, wildflowers bloom in profusion throughout this forest, among them dayflower, tickseed, and pawpaw. You see the scratch marks of a bear having torn open a fallen log in search of insects. No matter the time of year, you may encounter signs of bear—Florida black bears don't hibernate, although they can go into a state of torpor during chilly weather. Your chances of seeing a bear increase in the morning, as they lope through the flatwoods feeding on berries, insects, and the hearts of saw palmettos. They wade the Wekiva River, roaming from adjacent Seminole State Forest into this preserve, which touches more closely to suburbia.

A substantial-sized snag has massive woodpecker holes near the top of it, likely created by a pileated woodpecker. The habitat transitions into young sand pines and gatherings of sand live oaks, the scrub and sandhills seeping into each other as the elevation drops slightly. Low-bush blueberry grows along the footpath in large patches, another reason the bears love this habitat. You reach the blue-blazed connector trail. Turn right. Where the blue-blazed trail meets the white-blazed trail again at 0.5 mile, a thicket of blueberries crowds the junction. Butterfly weed raises colorful orange blooms well above the blueberry bushes, attracting a zebra swallowtail and many smaller insects seeking nectar.

Follow the white blazes to start Loop 2. Longleaf pine surrounds you in every stage of its life cycle, from grass to candle to tall trees old enough to attract red-cockaded woodpeckers, who require longleaf pines 70 years old or more in which to drill their nest holes. There is a meadow amid the longleaf pine forest, a perfect place to spot white-tailed deer. Morning glory spills over the underbrush. Passing through a series of very large blueberry patches, the trail continues to wind through the open understory, offering fabulous views in every direction.

As the trail closes in on the far end of the loop, older sand pines loom overhead. The understory oaks are crowding in, narrowing the pathway so as to herd you along—myrtle oaks with rounded leaves, Chapman oaks with points along the edges on the leaves, and sand live oaks with leaves that look like little canoes if you flip them over. The trail drops noticeably downhill toward the Wekiva River. You never see the river from this trail,

Young longleaf pines

however; you'll have to visit the canoe launch for a glimpse.

At a roughed-up firebreak, a wall of saw palmetto with a bayhead behind it is straight ahead. There are no blazes to guide you here, but look to the left and you'll see a well-beaten path paralleling the firebreak. Follow it, walking through large bracken ferns, and in a few moments you find a white blaze on a pine. In early summer, you'll catch both tarflower and loblolly bay with white blooms, an unusual juxtaposition of the dry scrub and wet bayhead habitats. The trail dumps down onto the firebreak. Be cautious of the broad sunny spots where pygmy rattlers may be sunning.

Leaving the firebreak after a prominent double blaze, the trail heads back into the forest, on the return loop along a shaded narrow corridor. The trail twists and winds as it heads uphill. Cicadas kick up a persistent chorus. Grand longleaf pines tower over the soft-needled young sand pines and canopies of sand live oak decorated with ball moss. Past a large opening in the forest, young longleaf

In a blueberry patch

sively in this preserve. These small rodents spend virtually all of their lives underground, building networks of tunnels up to 500 feet long. Living off tubers and roots it finds as it digs, the pocket gopher lives alone, meeting up with others of its kind only to breed.

Orange blazes join the white blazes as the Florida Trail enters in from the right at 1.9 miles. The habitats are truly intermingled throughout this stretch of trail, with both the oaks of the scrub and turkey oaks amid longleaf pine and sand pine. The footpath is a comfortable pine duff, transitioning to hardpacked sand through each sandhill patch. Look for the draping ivory blooms of pawpaw in spring. Entering a thicker and more mature forest, you reach the end of Loop 1 at 2.1 miles. Continue straight ahead to emerge at the trailhead after 2.2 miles.

pines, bottlebrush-shaped, stand sentinel along the footpath. You reach the end of Loop 2 at the blue blazes after 1.7 miles.

Walk the brief connector between loops, making a right. At the next right, you'll head back along the opposite side of Loop 1. The longleaf pines here are of moderate age, with a nice understory of blueberry bushes on the forest floor. You pass through another thicket of scrub oaks. A splash of orange sand indicates the presence of southeastern pocket gophers, which have been studied exten-

DIRECTIONS

From Interstate 4 exit 101, Sanford, follow SR 46 west for 4.2 miles to the trailhead on the right.

CONTACT

Lower Wekiva River Preserve State Park
State Road 46
Sanford, FL 32771
407-884-2008
www.floridastateparks.org/lowerwekivariver

18

Spring Hammock Preserve

Total distance: 3 miles (round-trip and circuit)

Hiking time: 2.5 hours

Habitats: cypress swamp, hydric hammock, pine flatwoods, scrub

Trailhead coordinates (lat-lon): 28.721406, -81.307319

Maps: USGS 7½' Casselberry; Trail map available at Environmental Center

Admission: Free

Hours: Sunrise–sunset

In the midst of primordial swamps fringing the edge of one of the larger lakes in the St. Johns River chain of lakes, Lake Jesup, Spring Hammock Preserve in Winter Springs is the land of the giants. Here, bald cypresses grow to incredible heights, recalling the redwood forests of the Pacific in their sheer majesty. It's no surprise that the Senator, the "Big Tree" of Big Tree Park, the oldest cypress in the Southeast, is a part of this preserve, and by far its most well-known inhabitant. For most visitors, a stop at Big Tree Park is all they ever experience of this dense preserve—unless they're a parent, student, or teacher involved in the robust environmental education program held here, the highlight of which is the "Mud Walk" through the floodplain forest along Lake Jesup. This is a fabulous playground for environmental education, with so many different ways to explore the trail system that you can come back dozens of times and never take the same hike twice.

BIG TREE PARK

Older than the preserve itself but now a part of it, Big Tree Park is a small park showcasing some mighty large inhabitants—the Senator and Lady Liberty, two of the largest bald cypresses in America. Follow the short boardwalk back from the parking area. As you walk the 0.3 mile round-trip, notice how large all of the trees are here in this floodplain forest. Both the Senator and Lady Liberty are large enough that only a panoramic camera can capture their stature—and you'll be craning your neck to see the tops of the trees. Named

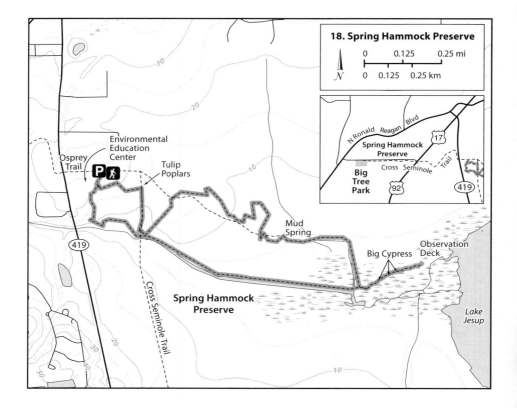

18. Spring Hammock Preserve

for Senator M. O. Overstreet, who left this massive cypress and the land around it to the people of Seminole County after his death in 1927, the Senator once rose over 200 feet tall, serving as a landmark for travelers through the region. In 1925, a hurricane lopped off the top third of the tree, but the Senator still stands, a glorious reminder of the ancient grandeur of Florida's cypress forests before European settlement.

The first European painter to record scenes of Florida, Jacques Le Moyne, lived in a French colony in 1564 close to the mouth of the St. Johns River near present-day Jacksonville. Fleeing a Spanish attack on the colony, he was one of the few survivors of the massacre. In engravings published in 1591, he portrays a Florida populated by the Timucua. As incidental backgrounds to his sketches of these now-vanished people, Le Moyne depicts cypress trees that rival the ancient trees of the forests of the Northwest, cypresses with such girth that their bases would blot out a present-day one-bedroom apartment.

These two trees are the easiest to visit, but are just the tip of the iceberg of the grand giants that await within the floodplain forests of Spring Hammock Preserve.

SPRING HAMMOCK PRESERVE
The wild fringe of this 1,500-acre suburban preserve is along the floodplain of Lake Jesup at the Seminole County Environmental Stud-

ies Center. Serving school groups on weekdays—when you'll find the restrooms and interpretive displays open and an attendant on hand to provide a trail map—the center (but not the trails) is closed on weekends. Start your hike at the Raccoon Pavilion just outside the center. Walk straight ahead past the Pine Woods Trail entrance. At the FLORIDA TRAIL sign, turn left past a picnic pavilion, heading down the path less traveled at a three-way fork. Trails branch off everywhere, which is why this preserve is so much fun and a bit tricky to navigate.

At the PRIMARY TRAIL sign, continue down the trail as it narrows through a stretch of ferns—cinnamon, netted chain, and Southern

Ancient cypress towers over the forest

woods fern adding textures to the understory beneath the palms and oaks. As you reach the banks of Soldier Creek, a shallow, sand-bottomed stream, turn left to follow the creek downstream. A bench overlooks the creek in the shade of an enormous slash pine. Its roots are undercut deeply by stream erosion.

The trail swings out to a picturesque spot on the creek where water pools and pours through a rotted log, creating a small rapid. There's a trail junction at a quarter-mile, where an "air potato collection bucket" encourages you to pick up and drop off these invasive tubers as you walk. The trail passes through a portal between two massive slash pines and winds its way through a wild orange grove, some in bloom, some dripping with fruit. You can hear water rushing through another cut in the creek ahead as you emerge at the paved Cross-Seminole Trail, which now intersects the preserve. Cross over it and head downhill, continuing along the route paralleling Soldier Creek. At the LIMPKIN TRAIL sign, keep to the right. The trail transitions onto a boardwalk beneath the maples and sweetgum. A boardwalk leads off to the left at an observation deck. True to the name of the trail, a limpkin dips its bill into the crystalline waters of the creek.

Continue straight along the earthen footpath, rounding the base of an enormous cypress. Two pileated woodpeckers flit back and forth among the thick branches below the broad crown spread. Crossing a pretty sheetflow stream, there are stumps of ancient cypresses off to the left. Florida's incredible cypress stands stood until settlers realized their economic value. The heartwood of a cypress, which takes 50 years or more to develop, resists termites and other wood-boring insects. The amount of board feet encompassed in the ancient trees meant the grand giants were the first to go. After the Civil War ended, cypress logging became a large-scale

Spring Hammock Preserve

Boardwalk to the Mud Walk

industry in Florida. Lumber companies built tramways for narrow-gauge railroads to deep into Florida's cypress swamps, to make it easier to drag out the massive trees. One 1936 Florida State Archives photo shows more than a dozen men riding atop a 3,000-year-old cypress tree that would soon be chopped up to make shingles, barrels, and paneling. Since cypress heartwood both repelled insects and didn't rot, it was considered ideal housing and packaging material.

The cypress knees here rise up to 3 feet from the forest floor. Notice the watermarks on the trees? Fed by the floodplain forest and local drainage, Soldier's Creek fills up quickly after a big rain, with waters rising high enough to swamp all of the trails in this part of the preserve beyond the Cross-Seminole Trail.

Passing a giant sweetgum and another enormous cypress, with knees in the footpath that are a couple of feet tall, take a moment to peek around the back of the cypress to see the deep cavity inside. Just beyond a bench, the trail rises up onto another boardwalk and series of bog bridges. Another massive cypress rises from a small trickling tributary into Soldier's Creek. Beyond the interpretive sign for alligators, the trail crosses a couple more bridges as it heads toward an opening on the forest, with another huge cypress next to a bench.

As you emerge into an open area at 1 mile, a canal meets Soldier's Creek, which flows off to the right toward Lake Jesup. Look straight ahead and off to the right a little to see one of the largest cypresses in Florida. The tree's crown rises well over the surrounding forest canopy, and a large cavity is noticeable near the top of the tree. Turn left. Turn right to cross the boardwalk over the canal. You enter a very lush floodplain forest. The boardwalk zigzags through a forest of awe-inspiring cypresses, enormous not just

at their bases but well up in the canopy as well. One cypress is so huge that its growing girth swallowed up the bases of two adjoining trees. Some of the cypresses have knees rising 5 feet tall and more from the tannic waters, making you feel Lilliputian. Throughout this part of the forest, numerous huge cypress stumps attest to the amount of logging that occurred over the past two centuries. The enormous cypresses you see today were spared only because they were flawed. If a logger saw a cavity in the bottom of a cypress, he would light a fire in it to see if smoke came out higher up in the tree. If it did, he considered the tree too rotten to be logged. Thank goodness. The cypress trees at Spring Hammock Preserve are some of the oldest and largest remaining in the Southeast.

The boardwalk once ended with a sweeping view of Lake Jesup, but it stops short of the view now due to reconstruction needed at the very end. Turn around and retrace your steps, taking in the ancient cypresses and listening to osprey overhead. Once you return to the trail junction at the canal, turn right. A red-shouldered hawk perches on a cypress branch. More massive cypresses surround you in the floodplain forests on both sides. The air is filled with birdsong as you pass a bench at 1.4 miles.

One of the most beautiful habitats in Florida is the hydric hammock, a swamp forest of cabbage palms, which now surrounds the trail. A hint of sulfur in the air draws your attention to the milky teal pool hidden between the palms on the right, a natural spring bubbling up to feed the forest. Steps lead down to its edge, where a sign calls it question pond.

The scent of orange blossoms is in the air as you walk along the canopied forest road in the cool shade, passing another air potato collection box. A boardwalk off to the left leads to another ancient cypress. You are in the presence of greatness. Lean back and stare up, tracing its trunk toward the sky. It has such a massive cavity near the top a whole family of bears could den in it, if they could climb that high. Benches provide a place to hang out and watch the birds. A sign, OLD BALD CYPRESS TREE, estimates the age of the tree to be between 2,000 and 2,500 years old. There is a large osprey nest atop this giant of the forest.

Returning to the main route, turn left. A boardwalk off to the right leads into the Hydric Hammock loop, which leads you along an accessible boardwalk into the dense forest of tall cabbage palms. Flagged cross-trails with mushy footprints vanishing down mucky corridors are part of the Mud Walk, the most popular field trip for kids going to school in Seminole County. The deep green palms in the understory are not saw palmetto, but needle palms, distinguished from saw palmetto by their more delicate fronds that do not join together like a fan at the stem. An uncommon species found in five southern states, the needle palm prefers floodplain forests, ravine slopes, and areas with surface limestone. These palms grow very slowly, and it can take up to two years for a seed to germinate. Needle palms are thought to be one of the world's most cold-hardy palms, surviving brief temperature drops down to -20°F.

Oranges dangle from the surrounding citrus trees and roll down the boardwalk past a bench. Big-leaved vines of poison ivy clamber up and over fallen logs and tree trunks. Delicate maiden fern nods in the breeze. The needle palms create a very jungle-like feel throughout the understory of this hydric hammock. Stumps of cabbage palms make natural planters for a profusion of sword ferns. At the exit to the loop, at 1.9 miles, you encounter the staging area for the Mud Walk, where the kids get oriented beforehand and

hosed off afterward. An interpretive marker explains the canal and how it changed the hydrology of the swamp.

Leading off to the left, a boardwalk passes interpretive information about elderberries. Slipping between two tributaries, the walkway ends up at a fork. Go straight ahead past more creaking trees. At the next intersection, keep going straight. Now you're following a part of the Mud Walk. Continue straight. A sign behind you says WET TRAIL. The understory smells like fresh-mown hay. Netted chain fern and Virginia creeper sprawl across the dark earth. A giant of a loblolly pine tree, a good 6 feet in circumference at its base, makes you stop and take pause.

As the trail reaches a boardwalk bridge, cross over to the old forest road along the canal. Continue straight ahead on a forest road perpendicular to the canal. It's another old tramway used by loggers, edged by a channel that accumulates water and keeps the trail dry. The air is awash in the aroma of orange blossoms as you return to the Limpkin Trail junction at 2.2 miles. Turn right and clamber up to the Cross Seminole Trail. Turn right to follow it past a bench near patches of spiderwort and terrible thistle. Within sight of a turnabout along the bike path, turn left to follow another interpretive trail, this one marked as "Florida Trail." You immediately see a marker for a tulip poplar on the left. It's a common tree in the Appalachians, but not so common in Florida. This is one of the southernmost spots where tulip poplars grow in the wild.

Shiny lyonia and rusty lyonia grow next to each other, enabling you to compare them as the elevation increases a little and the trail transitions into a patch of oak scrub. A maze of short trails winds through this pine forest as you approach the Environmental Studies Center. You can exit by following the Cinnamon Fern Trail to the right, the Rusty Lyonia

Trail to the left, and walking beneath the picnic pavilion. Take the first left after that, which meanders past picnic tables before reaching a boardwalk. Returning to the Raccoon Pavilion near the Environmental Studies Center, you've walked 2.6 miles. Near the restrooms, another series of very short interpretive trails traverse a patch of scrub forest. Take a few minutes to explore another tenth of a mile of trails—where you might see a gopher tortoise—before you exit.

DIRECTIONS

From Interstate 4 exit 98, Lake Mary /Heathrow, drive east on Lake Mary Boulevard for 1.6 miles to Longwood–Lake Mary Road. Turn right and continue 2.5 miles to where it ends at Ronald Reagan Boulevard. Turn left, and make the first right onto General Hutchinson Parkway. The entrance to Big Tree Park is on your right—a stop there is a must to see the Senator and Lady Liberty. Continue down General Hutchinson Parkway through the preserve to the traffic light at US 17-92. Turn left. After 0.8 mile, make a right at the light onto SR 419. Drive 0.6 miles to the preserve entrance, on the left across from the ball fields at Osprey Trail. Enter the gates and park on the right. The gates close at dusk.

CONTACT

Seminole County Greenways and Natural Lands
Ed Yarborough Nature Center
3485 North CR 426
Geneva, FL 32732
407-349-0959
www.seminolecountyfl.gov

19

Geneva Wilderness Area

Total distance (circuit): 1.8 miles (with optional 2.8-mile round-trip side trip)

Hiking time: 1 hour

Habitats: pine flatwoods, hardwood swamp, oak scrub

Trailhead coordinates (lat-lon): 28.708800, -81.123967

Maps: USGS 7½' Geneva; Preserve map at kiosk

Admission: Free

Hours: Sunrise–sunset

One of Seminole County's many wilderness preserves, Geneva Wilderness Area encompasses 180 acres just outside the suburban creep of Oviedo. Two main trails wind their way through the park. Red diamonds designate the Loop Trail, which runs along the edges of the park's many ponds and through a stand of pine forest that once was part of a thriving turpentine camp. The yellow diamonds provide a connection to the Flagler Trail, a north-south trail through the adjoining Little Big Econ State Forest.

Start your hike at the informational kiosk. Sign the register, and pick up a trail map. The trail starts off in a forest in miniature—gnarled sand live oak, scarcely tall enough to shade the trail. Dense clumps of foamy turquoise deer moss carpet the forest floor. At the first distinct junction of trails, turn left. At 0.3 mile, the trail leads up to a clearing with a restroom. It is here that the Loop Trail starts and ends.

Turn left and walk along the Loop Trail, staying right at the next fork to follow along the edge of the two largest flatwoods ponds in Geneva Wilderness. Although both ponds fade to mud during drought, they serve as magnets for wildlife when the waters return. Deer meander to the water's edge, unafraid. An osprey dips overhead, scanning for fish and small rodents.

Rounding the second pond, the trail forks again. Turn right and follow the trail paralleling the shoreline. Walk out to the water's edge and look carefully for the many small and delicate sundew plants along the shore. These unassuming plants look like blobs of strawberry jam, but are in fact carnivorous plants,

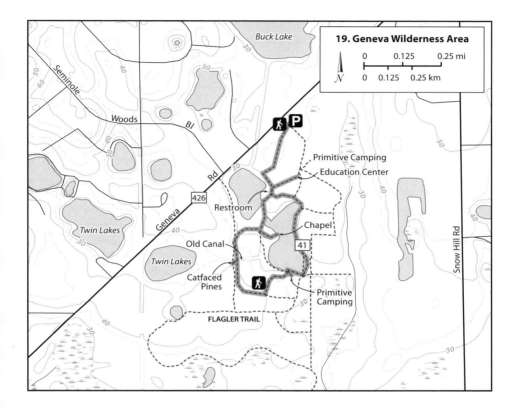

their red hue coming from leaves covered with thousands of tiny hairs coated with a sticky fluid. When an insect touches down, the hairs fold in like small hands, holding the insect down. Each leaf acts like both a trap and a stomach—glands in the hairs drown the insect in sticky fluid, then pour out digestive juices to consume it.

After 0.7 mile, you'll walk along the edge of the South Camp. The Geneva Wilderness has two group campsites, ideally suited for scouting groups and beginning backpackers. Situated beneath spreading live oak trees, the South Camp is the more pleasant of the two. Chopped wood fuels campfires, when conditions permit, and potable water and restrooms are an easy walk from the

campsite. When you reach the sign for SPIGOT #8, turn left and follow the narrow service trail up through the pine forest. Pause to enjoy spring blueberries and blackberries before you pass the restrooms. You'll soon come to a T intersection with the loop trail.

Although this circuit hike follows the Loop Trail to the right, you can extend the length of your hike an extra 2.8 miles by turning left, then right, following the route of the Flagler Trail. A round-trip walk to the Econlockhatchee River and back will take at least two hours. The Flagler Trail is blazed with yellow diamonds within Geneva Wilderness, but the blazes turn to blue rectangles painted on the trees once you enter the adjoining Little Big Econ State Forest. The Flagler Trail follows the former route of a branch of the Florida East Coast Railroad, founded by railroad magnate Henry Flagler. Completed in 1914, the railroad's Kissimmee Valley Extension ran down this route from Titusville, crossing the Econlockhatchee River into Chuluota, proceeding to Kenansville and down to Okeechobee. Loved and reviled as Florida's most extensive developer, Flagler is most well known for his connections with the Standard Oil Company and his grand hotels along the Atlantic Coast. He also made vast purchases of land in Florida's undeveloped interior, using his railroads to lure homesteaders into the barely inhabitable wilderness. Established in 1912, his Chuluota Land Company attempted to sell off 11,000 acres of land in this area, but met with little success. After this railroad line ceased operations, the state bought the right of way to build a highway that was never completed.

Geneva Wilderness Park is the former site of one of Florida's many turpentine camps. The Loop Trail soon crosses a narrow but deep cut through the forest, one of the few remaining canals from the turpentine era. Turn left for a quick side trip along the canal to see several of the longleaf pines that were once regularly tapped for turpentine. Sailors relied on the sap of pine trees for naval stores—tar, pitch, rosin, and turpentine. These products sealed and protected wooden sailing ships from the harsh effects of salt water. At the canal's end, near the property fence, notice one tall pine tree with a deep gash running more than 6 feet up the tree from its base. Beyond the fence lie several more tall pines with similar gashes. Called catfaces, these gashes provided the turpentine collector a means of "bleeding" the tree for its resin. A clay cup hung below metal strips set into the gash enabled the resin to pool into a collection basin, which would be emptied into larger containers for transport. Hikers sometimes stumble across these clay cups, scattered throughout the woods. If you find one, please admire it and leave it be. It's an integral part of Florida's history, best left undisturbed for the next visitor to enjoy.

Walk back along the canal to the Loop Trail, and turn left. The Loop Trail soon rejoins the shoreline trail in front of the entrance to the Chapel. Take a moment to walk the 0.2-mile trail down through the dense pine ham-

Flatwoods pond

Tarflower

mock to the Chapel. Built on a peninsula out into the pond, the Chapel provides scout groups and others with a nondenominational outdoors site for worship.

Returning to the Loop Trail, turn right. The trail squeezes between two flatwoods ponds on its way back around the loop. At least one pair of bald eagles nests nearby, providing hikers a chance to see these regal birds in flight over the open space of the ponds. At 1.4 miles, the Loop Trail has completed its full loop back to the first restroom. Turn left, and watch for a trail leading off to the right to the Ed Yarborough Educational Center. Used mainly for field trips and scout outings, this building is open the first Saturday of each month between 9 AM and noon for public workshops; check the kiosk for details. Once you reach the front of the building, take a look at the native plant garden. The North Campsite is a little ways up the entrance road near the caretaker's home, but it's more pleasant to walk back behind the building and head

back along the trail to the main trail. Turn right, and right again to exit through the tiny scrub forest, ending up back at the parking area after 1.8 miles.

DIRECTIONS

From Interstate 4, take exit 94, Longwood. Follow SR 434 for 13 miles east through Longwood and Winter Springs into downtown Oviedo. Turn left at the light, then immediately left on SR 426, following it 6.1 miles west, past the Little Big Econ State Forest trailhead at Barr Street, to the entrance to Geneva Wilderness, on the right.

LAND MANAGER

Seminole County Greenways and Natural Lands
Ed Yarborough Nature Center
3485 North CR 426
Geneva, FL 32732
407-349-0959
www.seminolecountyfl.gov

20

Lake Proctor Wilderness Area

Total distance (circuit): 4 miles

Hiking time: 2 hours

Habitats: bayhead, ephemeral pond, hardwood hammock, oak scrub, pine flatwoods, sand pine scrub, sandhills, scrubby flatwoods, wet prairie

Trailhead coordinates (lat-lon): 28.726609, -81.099136

Maps: USGS 7½' Geneva; Park map available at kiosk

Admission: Free

Hours: Sunrise–sunset

You hear them well before you see them— the haunting cries of sandhill cranes rattle across the open marshes and through the forests surrounding Lake Proctor, a meandering shallow wet prairie where sandhill cranes gather to eat, mate, and raise their young. Protecting 475 acres near historic village of Geneva—where the Fourth of July Parade is a slice of Americana that you just shouldn't miss—Lake Proctor Wilderness Area is one of the best places in Central Florida to watch these graceful birds from the shaded shore of the lake.

Before you start down this network of trails, it's smart to grab a trail map from the kiosk near the parking lot entrance. Several large loops and many small loops are possible along this trail system; this hike primarily follows the perimeter. Each loop is blazed using colored markers with arrows. Starting off on the red-blazed trail, it's a pleasant walk down a broad corridor flanked by saw palmetto and shaded by a hammock of sand live oaks with colorful gardens of lichens growing on their trunks and limbs. You come to a fork very quickly with an orange blazed trail. Keep right. Sphagnum moss carpets gatorbacks—the jagged trunks of saw palmetto— that protrude from the footpath. At sunrise, the air is filled with birdsong.

Making a slight left turn, the trail passes under tall longleaf pines within a sea of saw palmetto. One live oak shows off a bounty of resurrection fern, plump and green after the prior evening's rain. This is a narrow corridor of oak scrub, transitioning into sand pine

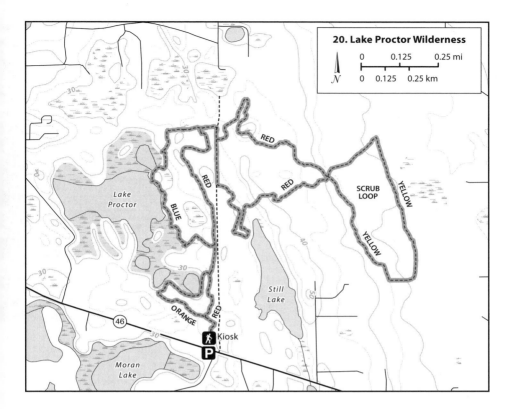

20. Lake Proctor Wilderness

Lake
Proctor

Still
Lake

Moran
Lake

46

Kiosk

ORANGE

RED

BLUE

RED

RED

RED

SCRUB
LOOP

YELLOW

YELLOW

0   0.125   0.25 mi

0   0.125   0.25 km

N

scrub with tall sand pines. Coming to a junction with the orange trail at 0.3 mile, continue straight ahead on the red trail. The habitat is now firmly sand pine scrub, with myrtle oak and Chapman oak in the understory. At the junction with the blue trail, continue straight as the trail loses its shady canopy to the open nature of the scrub. The trail heads down a very long corridor with lots of crunchy myrtle oak leaves underfoot.

As the trail narrows, it's surrounded by young sand pine, soft and fluffy but not tall enough to cast much shade. Emerging into a stand of longleaf pines, you face a very old sand live oak with limbs reaching out in all directions. The rattling cries of the sandhill cranes echo across the marshes. At what looks like a junction, a marker urges you left. Raccoon footprints lead down the white sand path.

Down a scrub corridor, the trail makes a sharp left and reaches a T intersection, the junction of blue and red trails, at an interpretive marker at 0.9 mile. Turn right. There is active restoration work going on, manual chopping of the understory in lieu of the use of fire to restore the scrub habitat to a younger phase where it is more suitable for hosting families of Florida scrub-jays. Emerging under a power line, follow the red marker to the right down this utility easement. At 1 mile, the trail quickly turns left and goes back into an oak scrub. The air traffic you hear overhead is from the Sanford International Airport, which is not far as the sandhill crane flies.

Crossing an unmarked trail, continue along the path outlined by the red trail markers. Entering a pretty patch of hardwood hammock, you notice the air cool down almost immediately. A female cardinal alights on a live oak branch. As you exit back into the scrub, you can hear the peeps and chirps of frogs as the trail works its way toward a depression marsh at 1.3 miles. It's a beauty spot, edged by saw palmetto.

Scrambling up a slight bluff, the broad trail emerges back into the scrub. Off to the left there is a corner of a fence line. The trail continues to the right, past a naturally aromatherapeutic silk bay. Stop and crush a leaf and breathe in the relaxing scent, reminiscent of eucalyptus but without the bite. This section of the red trail may be a little tricky to follow, since the majority of scrub restoration took place throughout this part of the forest. Keep alert to the red markers, especially wherever you encounter intersections. A seafoam-colored lichen, old man's beard, dangles from the crooked limbs of a rusty lyonia like stiff, dyed streamers of Spanish moss. You reach a covered rain shelter with a map (complete with "You Are Here") at 1.5 miles. Get your bearings here. Despite the temptation to follow the narrow trail, continue along the red trail, which follows the jeep road away from the shelter. The red trail comes up to a fork along the road; take the left fork to return into the forest.

At the next junction, the yellow-blazed Scrub Loop heads off to the left toward a bayhead, a marshy area with loblolly bay trees. This trail is an optional add-on for a perimeter hike. While it immerses you into even more of the scrub habitat, a large portion of its length is spent following the prop-

Oak scrub

erty line along a fence, which isn't particularly scenic but may be worthwhile for birding.

Continuing along the red blazes, you enter scrubby flatwoods. At the second junction of red and yellow blazes, turn right. Winding through the diminutive scrub, the trail crosses an access road. The scrub is regenerating through this area, and new interpretive signs have been put in place. Continuing uphill over an access road, there's a nice view of a wet prairie, where sandhill cranes may be wading. A bench sits within sight of a stand of bleached tree trunks, memorializing pines that lost their battle to pine bark beetles.

Paralleling the power line, the red blazes finally meander beneath it to a marker that ushers you to the left. The red blazes lead back to the parking area. However, the highlight of this trail system is the walk along Lake Proctor, and it's in the opposite direction. Turn right and walk up the power line, past the red trail to the right and up to the junction on the left. Continue left, headed back to the main trail junction at 2.6 miles. Continue straight, following the blue markers as the trail drops down toward the lake through the pine forest. At the next rain shelter, the crossroad of many unmarked trails, follow the blue markers to the left.

You have your first glimpse of Lake Proctor through the trees as the trail gently descends to the edge of this large, shallow wetland, more wet prairie than lake. A side trail leads right down to the edge, where leopard frogs sing in the shallows. What you see is just one little arm of the lake, which the trail now rambles along, beneath the longleaf pines and Southern magnolia, which release sweet scents from their dinner-plate-sized blooms each May.

At 2.9 miles, the trail swings right to work its way around a tall wall of saw palmetto, and you soon have the lake in your sights again. Lily pads drift across the placid surface. Faded yellow blossoms of Carolina jessamine are like fallen stars across the footpath. Meandering past a depression marsh, the trail makes its way back to the lakeshore at a spot with an interpretive sign and bench. Saw palmetto rises up on its trunks, stretching up above the trail, as you hear sandhill cranes kicking up a fuss not far ahead.

After a short jaunt along the lakeshore beneath loblolly bay trees, the trail emerges at another marshy arm of the lake. A pair of sandhill cranes works its way through the grasses, and you see a bundle of yellow move with them—a sandhill crane chick (or "colt"), scarcely a month old, being guarded and herded carefully by its doting parents, who are plucking choice morsels for their baby's delight while staying close enough to protect the bundle of fussing feathers. Mating

for life, sandhill cranes raise only one or two chicks per year.

Leaving the lakeshore past an ephemeral pond, the blue trail meets the red trail at 3.3 miles. Turn right. At the picturesque oak just a little ways down the trail, bear right to walk along the orange trail, the shortest of the loops. It makes its way quickly down to the marsh edge, where a sign marked EAST-BROOK WETLANDS claims the spot for a local school. A tall slash pine has a deep slash in its trunk, a catface speaking to the turpentine industry that was once an important part of the local economy. At 3.7 miles, a bench provides a beautiful view of this long arm of Lake Proctor. The trail makes a sharp left. The sound of traffic increases and the forest grows denser as you draw closer to the trailhead, walking uphill through an oak hammock. Keep to the right as you return to the red trail, and you emerge at the trailhead after 4 miles.

DIRECTIONS

Lake Proctor Wilderness is just east of the intersection of SR 426 and SR 46, east of Geneva. From Interstate 4 exit 101, Sanford, drive east on SR 46 for 4 miles to downtown Sanford. Turn right, following SR 46 along US 17/92 (South French Avenue) for 1.7 miles. SR 46 turns left. Continue another 12.1 miles, past the traffic light in Geneva to the trailhead entrance on the left.

CONTACT

Seminole County Greenways and Natural Lands
Ed Yarborough Nature Center
3485 North CR 426
Geneva, FL 32732
407-349-0959
www.seminolecountyfl.gov

21

Moccasin Island Trail

Total distance (circuit): 7.2 miles

Hiking time: 4 hours

Habitats: freshwater marsh, oak hammocks, pine flatwoods, prairie, ranchland

Trailhead coordinates (lat-lon): 28.230111, -80.811168

Maps: USGS 7½' Eau Gallie; St. Johns River Water Management District Recreation Guide to District Lands

Admission: Free

Hours: Sunrise–sunset

A birder's delight, the Moccasin Island Tract of River Lakes Conservation Area added more than 14,000 acres to a linear network of conservation lands protecting the floodplain of the St. Johns River as it rises from marshes near Yeehaw Junction and meanders north to Jacksonville. Much of the upland area within this preserve is still a cattle ranch, but as work on the wetlands continues, these grassy fields will vanish under a few inches of sheet flow as the floodplain is restored.

Most of the trail system is out in full sun along dikes en route to the loop on Moccasin Island. Slather on the sunscreen, pop on a hat, and bring plenty of water—especially if you plan to spend the night at the campsite on the island, open to backpackers. With all the cattle around, there's a lot of runoff that you probably don't want to sip in your drinking water, even when filtered.

Start your hike at the kiosk just past the parking area, where you should find a map of the trail to take along. Cross through the gate at the large concrete bridge over the canal, where alligators may be sunning on the shoreline below. Walk straight out along the dike, which is paralleled by small ditches. The tree line is well off in the distance up ahead.

Many of Florida's conservation lands are acquired as easements atop agricultural lands such as these. Cattle ranching has deep roots in Florida's frontier past, starting with the Seminoles rounding up and herding scrub cattle that wandered wild through the woods, descendents of cattle brought by Spanish explorers in the 1600s. When

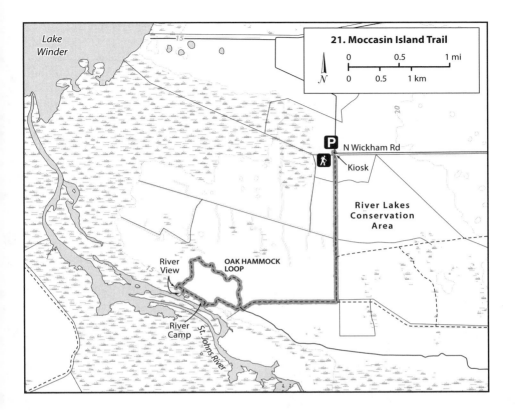

Florida opened up for homesteading in the early 1800s, ranching became a way of life and the cornerstone of Florida's economy through the Civil War.

After 0.3 mile, a slender canal snakes through the landscape, edged by spoil banks where invasive Brazilian pepper holds sway. Water pools in swales to both sides of the dike. As you continue along through the open ranchlands, this is the ideal time to keep alert for the crested caracara, which likes to perch on fence posts. These unusual raptors are members of the falcon family, but their heads look very parrot-like—a red face and a thick curved bill offset their black-and-white plumage. Although they will eat insects, rep-

tiles, and fish, they won't turn their beaks up at carrion if it's easily available. The crested caracara is Mexico's national bird. They prefer open, grassy rangelands, and are only found in Florida between Lake Okeechobee and Lake Kissimmee, living mostly on cattle ranches such as these.

Picturesque stands of cabbage palms break up the otherwise expansive landscape. As the elevation drops a little, there is a stand of cabbage palms and pines creating a small island along the rim of a newly re-created marsh, the beginning of an archipelago that parallels the trail to the east. Sandhill cranes browse through the tall grasses. At 0.9 mile, a canal provides a place for cattle to cool down in the hot sun. Cabbage palms line the eastern side of the trail as you continue walking in the open sun. The prairie opens up again after a bit, with scattered cabbage palms and a cypress dome off in the distance. Across another slender canal, there's a cattle feeding station. Expect to see the herd gathering around this area. At the next canal, the trail makes a sharp right. Continue through the cattle gate—and be sure to shut it behind you—at 1.5 miles, paralleling the canal. During the winter migratory months, you may see snipes along the footpath, hunting frogs that splash in and out of the canal. The snipe has an unusually long thin black bill and light brown stripes running down its back.

Bend in the St. Johns River

KEVIN MIMS

Where canals meet, you're cheered by the appearance of trees close to the trail—sand live oaks and cabbage palms. Cabbage palms grow thickly along the north side of the fence line. While the sweeping views are incredible, it's a relief to see the tall longleaf pines looming ahead above a thick cluster of forest spilling out across the trail. You've reached the tree line at 2.2 miles, blissful to reach the shade. Don't let the little open stretch through the dog fennel fool you—this hammock stretches to the river's edge.

After 2.5 miles, you reach the junction of the yellow- and red-blazed trails that make up the Oak Hammock Loop on Moccasin Island. Turn right and cross over the canal. Continue straight, following the red diamonds. The trail jogs along the edge of the hammock, providing both patches of shade and wide-open views amid the cabbage palms, but it's much more pleasant when the trail finally swings into the deep shade of the hammock and stays there for significant stretches.

The trail turns left, offering excellent views of the St. Johns River for the next half mile. A beaten path leads off to the right to the edge of the marsh. A limpkin browses along the grassy edge. Chestnut-brown with white spots, the limpkin has a curved beak much like that of an ibis. It is one of Florida's more rare birds, and has been listed on the protected species list. Its diet consists mostly of the apple snail, although it will also eat freshwater mussels, insects, small frogs, and crustaceans. Hunting of limpkins for their plumage brought the species to near-extinction, but several decades of protection from hunting helped bring back this unusual bird. It is still threatened by the draining and damming of Florida's wetlands, since it relies on shallow wetlands for its meals.

Meandering through beautiful palm hammocks, you come to the Moccasin Island

Walking through ranchland at Moccassin Island

campsite at 4.3 miles. If you're backpacking in, be aware that this is not a pristine spot. Airboaters—who often explore the marshes after dark, with the echo of airplane engines across the water—can easily access this campsite. There are broken bottles and litter beneath the trees.

You soon reach the junction with the yellow trail. Turn right and enjoy the rest of the shady walk through the oak hammock, which is over all too soon as you reach the end of the loop at 4.7 miles. Turn right and retrace your walk back through the open pastures to the trailhead, completing a 7.2-mile hike.

DIRECTIONS

From Interstate 95 north of Melbourne, take exit 191, North Wickham Road, and drive west for 5.9 miles. The road ends at the trailhead entrance.

LAND MANAGER

St. Johns Water Management District
Palm Bay Service Center
525 Community College Parkway,
Southeast
Palm Bay, FL 32909
321-984-4940
www.sjrwmd.com

Marshes along Lake Tibet

22

Lake Lotus Park

Total distance (circuit): 1.3 miles

Hiking time: 1 hour

Habitats: bayheads, floodplain forest, freshwater marsh, pine flatwoods

Trailhead coordinates (lat-lon): 28.644075, -81.425531

Maps: USGS 7½' Forest City; City of Altamonte Springs park map

Admission: Free

Park Hours: 8:30 AM–5:30 PM Wed. through Sun. Closed Mon. and Tues.

An unexpected slice of wilderness in a very urban setting, Lake Lotus Park preserves more than 150 acres of floodplain habitats fed by the Little Wekiva River. It's in the most improbable of places, surrounded by highways, apartments, and shopping centers where Altamonte Springs and Maitland, very close to Interstate 4 and right along Maitland Boulevard where it crosses SR 434. The trail system, primarily on boardwalks, provides a great respite from surrounding suburbia, immersing you in the sights and sounds of nature amid the buzz of humanity. Interpretive markers throughout the park include detailed descriptions and sketches of the flora and fauna, so you'll learn a lot just walking around and reading them all. This is a passive park, ideal for families, with a playground, plenty of picnic tables, and a designated fishing area. Pets are not permitted.

Whether you've been dropped off by a tram or parked over near the playground, follow the entrance road around to the boardwalk that starts to the far right of the picnic pavilions as the park road loops around the playground and restrooms. Your walk begins beneath tall red maples and sweetgum trees with large royal ferns crowning their roots. Passing two benches and a side trail leading to a picnic spot, you start paralleling the clear but tannic-tinged waters of the narrow-channeled Little Wekiva River, which forms Lake Lotus on its way to meet the Wekiva River. A warning sign alerts you to the presence of alligators, which do indeed live in Florida's suburban parks, too.

As the boardwalk extends out over a

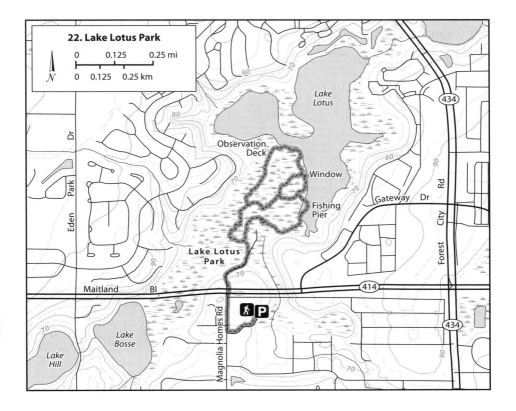

marsh, a Louisiana heron, resplendent in its blue-and-white plumage, lifts up a fish to swallow it. The marsh is in a cove to the left of where the Little Wekiva River pours into the lake, forming a delta. On the far shore, to the right of the apartment complex, look for an osprey nest high up in a longleaf pine tree. You may hear the osprey well before you see it. This lake is an important feeding and breeding ground for wildlife otherwise compressed into disconnected backyard habitats throughout this very urbanized area.

Crossing a fishing platform—which is optimized for wheelchair access and provides quite a few benches for just looking over the lake—the hike continues along the boardwalk over open water and then the lake's marshy edge. As the boardwalk reaches a T intersection, turn left. You know this is an urban park when you encounter your first emergency phone along the trail, and there are far too many benches along the boardwalk to mention. Surrounded by royal ferns, the boardwalk is a place to listen for birds. The trills of songbirds echo between the tall cypress and oaks, a perpetual symphony that transports you away from the cacophony of the outside world.

After 0.4 mile, turn right onto another boardwalk. Laurel oaks provide the high canopy, with royal fern and cinnamon fern soaking their roots beneath the boardwalk. Bald cypress and their attendant knees rise from the muck of the floodplain. An uprooted

---

Lake Lotus Park

Entrance to Lake Lotus Park

tree exposes a large root ball with a pool of water beneath, where frogs gather. A touch of fall color paints the sweetgum trees in hues of tangerine and mustard. Bright bursts of glob-ular blooms decorate the buttonbushes. As you come to a T intersection, you've returned to the lakeshore. Take a side trip to the right for a visit to the "Window on the Lake," a hexagonal structure with picture windows for birding. It turns into a hothouse inside on a warm day, but it's a virtual blind for watching the birds and other creatures out on the lake. Interpretive information inside helps you iden-tify what you see.

Turn right as you leave the Window on the Lake, and right again at the trail intersection. Continue straight, walking on the boardwalk inside the floodplain forest along the lakeshore. At a couple of benches and a broad spot in the boardwalk, it makes a jog to the left to follow the edge of a lotus-choked channel connecting two segments of the lake. The blooms are especially colorful and full-bodied each summer. They grow so densely together across this arm of the lake that it looks like you could walk across their shiny leaves to the far shore. Dahoon holly arcs over the water, with red holly berries swaying in the breeze.

Several waterways drain out through the floodplain forest into this part of the lake. They're shallow and sinuous, meandering through the ferns, but their source isn't obvi-ous—tiny springs? Residential drainage? As feeder streams, they add to the flow headed down the Wekiva River basin. Ignominiously, Lake Lotus, as the Little Wekiva River, drains out of the lake and heads toward the basin

Stroll along the lakeside boardwalk

through a culvert under a series of shopping centers.

Meandering away from the lake, the boardwalk enters a tangled jumble of vines and young trees. A grove of bald cypresses sway around you, tall and gray-barked. There is a broad deck here with benches, big enough to bring friends in for a picnic. Most of the benches along the boardwalk are indented into the flow of the walk so they don't get in your way. As the boardwalk winds through a willow marsh where the poison ivy grows very large as it creeps up tree branches, a cypress-lined shoreline looms ahead atop the mild bluff marking the floodplain's edge. Past another set of benches, there's an interpretive marker about the bald cypress. At the next trail junction, turn right.

When the boardwalk ends, the trail becomes a bark-chip path under a tall canopy of laurel oak, water oak, and pines. Sword ferns crowd together under the saw palmetto on the right. Grapevines attempt to smother the understory. On the left, there are netted chain ferns; on the right, cinnamon ferns. You reach a trail junction with a map after a mile.

Turn right and cross the bridge. The forest around you crowds close and dark. Rays of sunlight filter through the dense canopy. Cypress knees poke out of the rolling terrain that the trail now follows. The rich black soil is lush with ferns and strewn with tangled knots of roots snaking away from magnolia trees. Following the edge of a bayhead, the trail draws close to loblolly bay trees that bloom in summer, including one with roots exposed and sprawling like the arms of an octopus. The earth is squishy underfoot, with tiny puddles here and there. Spreading mats of smooth water hyssop grow across the middle of the trail, with plump succulent leaves and tiny star-shaped white flowers, so it's a clue that this trail dips underwater at certain times of year.

Rising uphill under tall pines, the trail reaches another junction at 1.1 miles. Continue straight ahead, and you emerge along the park road west of the loop around the playground and butterfly garden. If you're parked by the playground and restrooms, turn left and walk 0.2 mile up the park road to return to your car. If you're visiting on a weekend and need to return to your car at the parking area on the other side of Maitland Boulevard, you can turn right and walk out to your car—another 0.6 miles of walking—or turn left and head back to the beginning of the hike to wait for the tram to come around and pick you up.

DIRECTIONS

From Interstate 4, follow SR 414 (Maitland Boulevard) west past Maitland Center and the SR 434 interchange. The very next traffic light leads you into Lake Lotus Park (on the right) or to access via Magnolia Homes Road the overflow parking area for Lake Lotus Park (on the left)—you must park here on weekends and walk over or take the tram.

LAND MANAGER

Lake Lotus Park
1153 Lake Lotus Park Road
Altamonte Springs, FL 32714
407-293-8885
www.altamonte.org

23

Split Oak Forest WEA

Total distance (circuit): 6.4 or 7.8 miles

Hiking time: 3.5 hours

Habitats: pine flatwoods, oak hammock, freshwater marsh, oak scrub, prairie, bayheads, cypress domes

Trailhead coordinates (lat-lon): 28.353440, -81.211083

Maps: USGS 7½' Narcoossee; Preserve map at kiosk; Florida Trail Association Map Central 5

Admission: Free

Hours: Sunrise–sunset

It is a haunting cry, the call of the sandhill crane, as the bird glides overhead, casting giant shadows across the prairie. It is an unmistakable cry, a mournful, raspy rattle, naturally amplified through the nostrils of the crane's massive bill. Standing up to 4 feet tall, with a wingspan of up to 7 feet, the sandhill crane is a bird that quickly captures your attention, whether it is soaring overhead or striding through tall grasses. Migrating from the grasslands of Nebraska to the vanishing open prairies of Florida each winter, greater sandhill cranes look for open prairie with wetlands to shelter them from the cold for the season. Split Oak Forest WEA is managed as a sandhill crane habitat for these seasonal visitors as well as a less common subspecies, the Florida sandhill crane, which spends all year in the Sunshine State. The South Loop trail circles their habitat, while the northerly loop trails wind along forests, lakeshores, scrub, and marshes.

A sad irony of this preserve is that it was set up as a mitigation bank, a program allowing developers to pay the state to preserve habitat in exchange for a green light to destroy similar habitat. In the years that have passed since my first visit to the preserve, the thousands of acres of open prairie and ranchlands that surrounded it have become densely packed housing developments. Since the people who live in the houses don't want airplanes flying over their heads, a major approach to Orlando International Airport is now right over the preserve, with planes drowning out the song of the sandhill cranes.

Start your hike at the kiosk by picking up

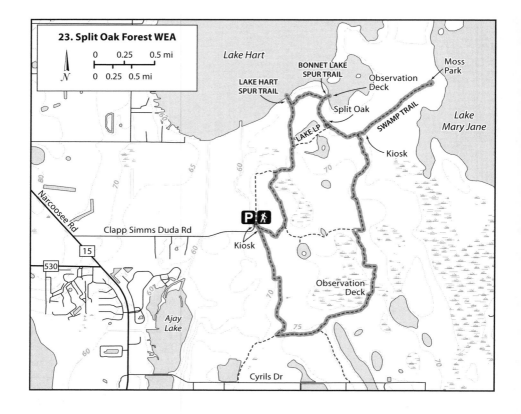

23. Split Oak Forest WEA

Lake Hart

BONNET LAKE SPUR TRAIL

LAKE HART SPUR TRAIL

Observation Deck

Moss Park

Split Oak

SWAMP TRAIL

LAKE LP

Lake Mary Jane

Kiosk

Narcoosee Rd

Clapp Simms Duda Rd

Kiosk

15

530

Observation Deck

Ajay Lake

Cyrils Dr

a trail map. Each trail has its own distinct blazes, but trail markings here can be confusing. Carrying a map and compass is a good idea. Since the centerpiece of the park is the Split Oak, you'll want to hike the northerly trails first.

Numbered green markers lead around the perimeter of the preserve. Walk from the trailhead into the shade of the live oaks, and turn left to follow the North Loop. Moss-draped live oaks yield to turkey oaks as you emerge on the edge of an open scrub, regenerating after restoration. Turn left and follow the firebreak—footing can be difficult in places, as the trail is multiuse, frequented by equestrians. Gallberry and saw palmetto predominate, with rusty lyonia growing along the

firebreak. The purple blooms of deer's tongue and blazing star add color to the scrub. Watch for tarflower, a fragrant white flower with pink stamens, on the taller shrubs. Although it is not a carnivorous plant, insects get caught on its sticky blossoms.

After a left turn, the trail enters a forest of tall longleaf pines and laurel oaks, where cinnamon ferns rise from the thick cover of needles on the forest floor. Bald cypresses emerge from a cypress dome. You pass a solution hole on the left, lush with ferns. After 1.2 miles, you reach the Lake Loop, which is blazed blue. Turn left into the pine forest, passing a massive saw palmetto. Deer moss and reindeer lichen cluster under the turkey oaks. An unusual forked longleaf pine sprouts equal-sized thick trunks. The trail winds between saw palmettos into a stand of laurel and live oaks

You reach the Lake Hart Spur at 1.6 miles. Continue straight, following the white aster markers through the cinnamon ferns and down to the marshy edge of Lake Hart, where wild irises line the trail as it vanishes into the sparkling blue water. An earthy smell rises from the mud. Turn around and return to the Lake Loop, turning left at the T intersection. A bald cypress rises on the right. Watch for deer in the forest as the understory opens up underneath the spreading moss-draped live oaks. The trail veers to the right; go straight, walking under the open oaks at 2 miles. You reach a boardwalk out over Bonnet Lake, a pleasant resting spot and observation area where you can watch blue herons wading through the spatterdock and water lilies with broad white blooms drifting across the open water.

Turn around and return to the lakeshore, turning left to follow the white aster markers back to the main trail. Turn left again, walking through an open forest of pines. Scattered clumps of saw palmetto add a touch of green to the earth-toned landscape. Wind whistles through the needles of the longleaf pines. At 2.4 miles, you come to the Lake Loop sign and the Split Oak. Nearly 60 years ago, this centuries-old tree broke under the weight of its own branches, its main trunk falling in two to the ground. Over time, lateral branches grew up as tall and thick as tree trunks, creating an interesting tableau, the splayed trunks thick with resurrection fern and gold-foot fern. This is not an isolated phenomenon, but this tree is a grand one.

Take a left around the tree, where you'll

The Split Oak

KEVIN MIMS

pass a MOSS PARK sign. At marker 15, you reach a fork; keep left, passing the LAKE LOOP/SPLIT OAK sign. The trail meanders through a forest of young longleaf pine, crunchy underfoot due to dredged fill, the sand dense with fossil seashells. At 2.7 miles, you reach the trail junction for the Swamp Trail, which leads off to the left to Moss Park. Continue straight, as the pine flatwoods open up into scrubby flatwoods with sparser pines and more dense underbrush of gallberry, greenbrier, and saw palmettos. A wide firebreak comes in from the right; continue straight to reach the junction of the North Loop and South Loop, after 3.3 miles. This is your decision point. While it provides your best opportunity to see sandhill cranes, it takes another 3.1 miles to hike the perimeter of the South Loop, wandering through mostly open pine flatwoods. After a rain, the trail will flood up to your ankles in places. If you're happy with a shorter, tamer experience, turn right to follow the cross-trail 0.9 mile back to your car. Otherwise, continue straight as the trail veers to the left.

Wildlife is more prevalent along the South Loop, since fewer hikers bother to wander down into this part of the park. Watch for wild turkeys in the open prairies, gopher tortoises ambling down the trail, and the tall sandhill cranes. The trail is wide like a road, since it also serves as a firebreak between the open scrub and the more developed dense oak forest. After 3.6 miles, keep right. At the Y intersection at 3.9 miles, the trail turns right, away from the property line and into the pines. This section of the trail can be particularly wet, since a large bayhead swamp sits off to the right, draining across the trail as a tannic stream in several places. After 4.1 miles, take the right turn, and the trail veers through scrubby pine flatwoods with a dense palmetto understory. Young longleaf pines show off various shapes—some look like wiregrass,

others like bottlebrushes or saguaro cactus. Bracken fern grows densely under the pines. Watch for shards of clay turpentine pots, from the era when this forest served as a turpentine plantation. Signs indicate the last occurrence of a controlled burn, a critical part of managing pine flatwoods and scrub so they do not revert to oak hammocks. An oak toad hops across the trail, pursued by a rough green snake swimming across a puddle to chase its quarry. You pass a fence corner on the left. The trail swings to the right, paralleling a blackwater slough. You hear a sudden splash—alerted to your approach, an alligator slipped back into the water.

At 4.4 miles, you reach a boardwalk overlooking the sawgrass marsh, surrounded by pine flatwoods. Sit and take a break on the bench, watching for herons, ibises, and alligators. Returning to the trail, turn right. The trail leads back into the pine flatwoods. Stay right at the fork. The green markers assist in directing you around the loop. Take another right at 5.9 miles, but avoid the next one—continue straight as the trail enters a mixed forest of small live oaks, longleaf pines, and turkey oaks. Blueberries grow densely, intermingled with thousands of small oak trees clamoring for space, each showing off a bounty of oversized acorns.

The trail turns right again. You see another double-trunked longleaf pine, just outside a small grove of sand live oaks. Their gnarled branches form a low canopy over the trail. Stay left at the next fork. You'll pass a broken longleaf pine, its top destroyed by lightning. Called snags, these dead or dying longleaf pines provide excellent homes for several species of woodpeckers. Pink mushrooms poke up through a carpet of foamy deer moss. The trail enters an avenue of oaks, with interlocking branches overhead, then veers left toward an open prairie.

As you exit the oak hammock and enter

Lake Bonney

the prairie, walk softly, watching for sandhill cranes. Consider yourself fortunate to come across the a crane in the throes of its mating dance, as the males leap and prance with wings outspread, bowing and cackling to attract the attention of a mate. Sandhill cranes mate for life, returning to the same nesting site every year. After hatching in July, the chicks take two months to mature to where they can find their own food; in the meantime, both parents work to feed their brood of two. Tall grassy savannas, prairies on the edge of marshes, provide the perfect habitat for the sandhill crane, which feeds on insects, plants, amphibians, and fruit.

When you reach the fence line, continue straight across the prairie to the parking lot, off in the distance. Passing a kiosk on sandhill crane habitat and the purpose of this mitigation park, you'll return to the junction of the

North Loop and the South Loop. Bear left, away from the woods and back to the parking lot, completing a 6.4-mile hike.

SWAMP TRAIL

Camping out at Moss Park? If so, you can access the Split Oak Forest trail system directly from the campground. The Swamp Trail provides a 1.4-mile round-trip out to the perimeter trail around Split Oak Forest. Moss Park is a full-service county park with boating and canoe access, picnic pavilions, playgrounds, and a nice roomy campground in an oak hammock. From inside Moss Park, make the first right and follow the signs for Pavilions 5 & 6, at the far end of the park. Parking for the connector trail is on the right, across from Pavilion 6 and beyond the playground. Look for the arched entrance and kiosk.

The Swamp Trail is just that—a long causeway through a marsh, giving you an up-close look at cattails, duck potato, and pickerel-weed. Wax myrtles create a corridor for the old jeep trail, providing shelter for songbirds, ducks, and mergansers. After passing a jeep trail off to the left, the trail enters Split Oak Forest, changing to pine forest and oak hammock. Within a few hundred feet is a kiosk; stop here for a trail map. After 0.7 mile, the Swamp Trail ends at the North Loop trail. If you plan to hike only the northern loops of the park, turn right to visit the Split Oak (going in the opposite direction from the hike previously described); otherwise, turn left to head toward the South Loop. By starting and ending your hike at Moss Park, you complete an 7.8-mile loop.

DIRECTIONS

From the Orlando International Airport, follow SR 528 (Beeline Expressway) east to exit 13, Narcoossee. Take CR 15 (Narcoossee Road) south for 7 miles to Clapp-Simms-Duda Road, passing a turnoff for Moss Park and the SR 417 exchange en route. Turn left on Clapp-Simms-Duda Road and follow it 1.6 miles to the parking area and trailhead, on the right.

For Moss Park, take exit 13 on SR 528 (Beeline Expressway), just east of the Orlando International Airport. Turn south on CR 15 (Narcoossee Road). Drive 2.8 miles to Moss Park Road. Turn left, and follow Moss Park Road 4.5 miles until it ends at the park entrance.

LAND MANAGER

Florida Fish and Wildlife Conservation Commission
Farris Bryant Building
620 South Meridian Street
Tallahassee, FL 32399-1600
850-488-4676
www.myfwc.com

24

Hal Scott Regional Preserve

Total distance (circuit): 5 miles

Hiking time: 3 hours

Habitats: pine flatwoods, prairie, floodplain forest, oak hammock, seepage slope

Trailhead coordinates (lat-lon): 28.486333, -81.095833

Maps: USGS 7½' Narcoossee; St. Johns River Water Management District Recreation Guide to District Lands; Florida Trail Association Map Central 5

Admission: Free

Hours: Sunrise–sunset

Hal Scott Regional Preserve provides a buffer of public land along the Econlockhatchee ("Econ") River, protecting more than 8,000 acres of Central Florida's once-common pine flatwoods and prairies not far from the Orlando International Airport.

The parking lot is immense. Park near the kiosk. The trails here are multiuse, and especially popular with equestrians, so don't be surprised to see horse trailers in the lot. Most of this trail is in the open, so be sure to slather on the sunscreen and wear a hat.

Start at the entrance through the fence, walking along the narrow strip of grass between the fence line and the firebreak. Pine flatwoods stretch out into the distance on the right. On the far side of the parking lot is a small lake edged with cattails. An eastern kingbird warbles from its perch on a snag, its black- and-white tail feathers flashing in the sun.

After you round the corner at the horse gate, the trail heads straight south. It's easy to miss the turnoff for the north section of the loop, so watch carefully on the right for both a wide mown area *and* a post with white diamonds, which serve as blazes for the route. Follow the path into the pine flatwoods. Dew-drenched spiderwebs shimmer in the early morning light. Tall longleaf pines are sparsely interspersed in an unending sea of saw palmetto and wiregrass, a scene described by one Florida naturalist as the "palmetto prairie." Underfoot, the trail is a grassed-over jeep track with fine, delicate grasses, including the colorful blooms of yellow-star grass.

A small but deep ditch parallels the trail on

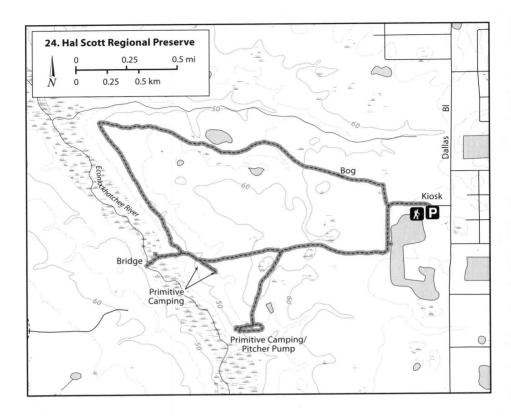

the left as you pass a tree banded in blue and white. Shiny lyonia grows over the ditch, shaking its blooms of tiny pink bells. This and other ditches throughout the preserve were likely built to drain the land for scrub cattle ranching, as pine flatwoods retain water for many days. After a rain, you'll find the next mile of the trail prone to scattered muddy puddles. At 0.6 mile, a ditch on the left drains a small wetland. Look closely along the ditch for the unmistakable curved form of the hooded pitcher plant, a carnivorous plant that is one of Florida's threatened species. In this region, its white-spotted trumpet-like leaves grow little more than a foot high, curving inward to create the "pitcher" that traps flying insects and ants that venture inside. Tiny

downward-pointing hairs force the insects into the trap, where glands at the bottom digest them. The pitcher plant blooms in spring, with thick, rubbery-looking flowers of red or yellow. There are several patches of these pitcher plants along this section of trail.

Just beyond the next firebreak, the distant cooling towers of the Orlando Utilities Commission coal-fired generating station appear briefly on the horizon. The elevation rises a little, and the trail underfoot becomes sandy. Residents of the scrubby flatwoods take root here, such as scrub live oak and sand live oak. The pink blooms of pale meadow beauty peek out from between the saw palmetto. The trail drops down to cross a very narrow drainage toward the Econ River, where the crossing may get your boots wet. Rising back up into the pine flatwoods, short saw palmetto seems to stretch to infinity off to your left. On the right, the blanket of palmettos comes to an abrupt halt at a wall of forest—loblolly bay and bald cypress, indicating the meander of a lazy tributary of the Econ River. Scattered purple asters bloom amid the wiregrass.

The trail reaches a T intersection at 0.8 miles. To the right, a trail blazed with red diamonds leads off to the tributary, where tall bald cypresses stand over the rush of dark water between their roots. To stay with the main loop, turn left, paralleling the river and its floodplain forest off in the distance. The white blossoms of narrow-leaved sabatia rise above the young saw palmettos.

The trail converges with the tree line, offering shade under sweetgum and live oaks.

Up near the top of a longleaf pine, a pileated woodpecker beats out a steady rhythm. A little ways farther, an indistinct path heads straight into the woods. Stay on the main trail, which swings slightly off to the left. You reach another T intersection at 2.7 miles, this time with the yellow-blazed trail.

Turn right for a walk down to the river. The trail drops down into the floodplain forest of the Econlockhatchee River, with its open understory beneath a canopy of sweetgum, live oaks, and bald cypress. The forest echoes with the screeches and chirps of birds—the blue-gray gnatcatcher, the tufted titmouse, and the wood thrush. Hairy wild pine and large pineapple-like bromeliads cling to the trees. Skirt the deep mud puddles, made messy by the frolic of feral hogs. The lazy meander of the river lies just beyond the cypress knees, dark waters cloaking their depth.

Campers at Hal Scott

KEVIN MIMS

Bromeliad near the Econ River

KEVIN MIMS

Orlando residents are familiar with busy Curry Ford Road, but probably not with the original Curry Ford, this narrow spot in the river near the Curry homestead. Travelers on horseback and stagecoaches crossed at this spot en route to Titusville until 1924, when the Cheney Highway opened through Bithlo. The old bridge has been rebuilt, enabling you to stand over the dark waters and watch them flow through the river swamp. Turn around and re-turn to the trail junction, heading straight along the yellow-blazed trail. A firebreak follows along on the right. The trail drops down through a churned-up streambed, where small fish dart in the shallows. Netted chain fern grows in the shadows of the eroded ravine, off to the right. Step over the water and climb up the sandy slope. The firebreak now parallels the trail on the left.

At 3.2 miles, you come to a post with a

white diamond and a blue marker indicating the campsite is down this trail. Turn right to follow this trail into the grassy prairie. Stretching off into the distance on both sides of the footpath, enveloping the small saw palmettos, the shortspike bluestem forms a wheat-colored haze beneath the scattered longleaf pines. Off to the right, the floodplain forest defines the edge of the prairie. After crossing several small ditches, the trail rises up into a hammock of live oak, where the gnarled branches are covered with a dense skin of resurrection fern and wild pine. The saw palmetto grows taller here, crowding in close to the trail on both sides. After 3.6 miles, a spur trail marked with blue diamonds leads off to the right past a portable toilet to the campsite. By the appearance of this man-made structure in the middle of the woods, it's easy to guess this campsite has become pretty popular, especially on weekends and with scouting groups, as there aren't a lot of primitive camping options for backpackers in the Orlando area. It's the perfect place to pitch a tent—a seamless canopy of live oak overhead, a picnic bench and several benches around a fire ring with a grill, and a pitcher pump nearby to provide water. Even if you're not planning an overnight stay, it's a great place to stop and take a break, listening to the sound of rushing water in the background as the canal drops down through a spillway. Lily pads float on the surface of the canal as a great blue heron picks its way along the bank. If you camp here, take the time to explore the levees on both sides of the canal.

Return back along the white-blazed trail through the prairie. A pine warbler explodes out of a saw palmetto, swooping past in a blur of yellow. Look carefully at the center of the trail for tiny but colorful wildflowers and dime-sized carnivorous sundew plants, glistening like drops of strawberry jam.

Back at the main loop after 4.1 miles, turn right. Tall wormwood grows along the disturbed ground between the trail and the firebreak. A drainage ditch leads off to the right. After you pass the ditch, the prairie yields to flatwoods again as thickets of saw palmetto choke out the grasses. Gallberry waves in the breeze, weighed down with a load of purplish-black berries. A pine woods snake moves quickly off the trail as you pass, disappearing into the wiregrass. Never growing more than a foot long, these snakes live under rotten logs and chase after lizards and toads, slathering them in toxic saliva.

At 4.6 miles, the trail comes to a sharp left turn. Ahead of you is the shimmer of a marshy lake, edged in cattails. Believe it or not, this portion of the preserve was once a large-scale phosphate mining operation. The preserve's name comes from a former president of the Florida Audubon Society who served as an environmental consultant to large mining companies such as IMC Agrico, who named this, their prize-winning reclamation project, after him. Turn left, following the lake. After walking past a pile of rock, you'll come to the beginning of the blue-blazed loop. Continue straight, jogging around the horse gate to follow the fence line back to where your car is parked at the kiosk, completing your 5-mile hike.

DIRECTIONS

From Orlando International Airport, drive east along SR 528 away from the airport, take Exit 24, Dallas Boulevard. Turn left. Drive 2.4 miles to the preserve entrance, on the left.

CONTACT

St. Johns Water Management District
Altamonte Springs Service Center
975 Keller Road
Altamonte Springs, FL 32714-1618
386-329-4404
www.sjrwmd.com

25

Tibet-Butler Preserve

Total distance (circuit and round-trip): 2.7 miles

Hiking time: 1.5 hours

Habitats: pine flatwoods, scrubby flat-woods, oak scrub, oak hammock, freshwa-ter marsh, bayheads, cypress domes

Trailhead coordinates (lat-lon): 28.442717, -81.541267

Maps: USGS 7½' Windermere; Preserve trail map available at nature center

Admission: Free

Hours: The park is open 8 AM–6 PM, Wed. through Sun., and is closed on Mon. and Tues.

It's been more than 25 years since Walt Disney World first opened its doors, and with the explosive growth of tourism in western Orange County, most of the land surrounding the theme park has been converted to housing developments, strip malls, hotels, and restaurants. Hiding just beyond the tourist amenities of Lake Buena Vista, Tibet-Butler Preserve protects a precious 440 acres of the region's original habitats along the shore of Lake Tibet. A network of well-maintained, family-friendly interpretive hiking trails wind through its forests. Combining various trails—if they are open, since certain trails may close due to flooding—you can hike up to a 3.5-mile loop.

The Vera Carter Environmental Center dominates the entrance to the preserve. Stop and take a look at the displays, which explain the various habitats in the park, and pick up an interpretive trail guide, which corresponds to numbers posted along the trails. Restrooms and picnic tables at the entrance invite you to linger.

Your hike starts behind the building. Be sure to sign in at the trail register, then turn right onto the Pine Circle trail. The trail is a low indentation into the pine flatwoods, meandering through tall slash pines, loblolly bay, and saw palmetto. Sphagnum moss creeps down along its edges. After passing the Screech Owl Trail, you skirt a damp area off to the left, alive with swamp lilies growing under dahoon holly and red bay. Deerberry jingles its dark black berries in the breeze. The trail rises and becomes sandy underfoot as you approach the intersection with the Pal-

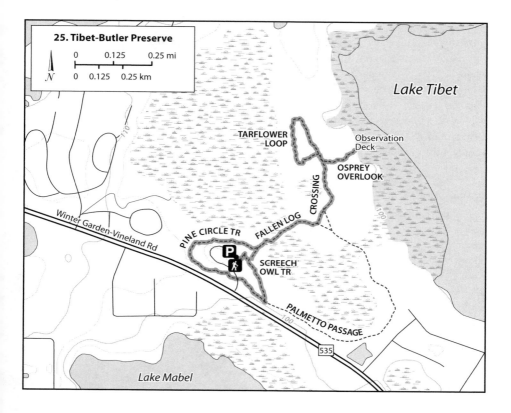

metto Passage Trail, at 0.2 mile. Turn right to stay on Pine Circle.

As the trail continues to rise, the habitat becomes scrubby flatwoods, where the pine canopy thins out. Gallberry, winged sumac, and grasses compete for the understory; deer moss grows on decomposing pine needles. Small stands of scrub live oak provide cover. You start to see the roof of the environmental center through the trees to the right as you wind down the sandy narrow passage. Cross the entry road on the crosswalk, making sure to check for cars. The trail now enters an oak hammock of large gnarled scrub live oaks draped in moss. Like Christmas tinsel, fallen pine needles decorate the branches of sand live oaks. As the trail circles

around, you pass an opening filled with royal ferns. The forest opens up as you enter the ecotone between the pine flatwoods and bayheads, where the slash pines are scattered amid an unbroken understory of saw palmetto. Watch for the palm warbler and the yellow-throated vireo as they flutter between the palmettos. Dense loblolly bay off to the left indicates the dampness of the area. A tall, thick clump of blueberry bushes—tempting you with their juicy fruits in April—sits off to the right. You see the roof of the environmental center again, this time off to the right.

At 0.8 mile, Pine Circle intersects with the Fallen Log Crossing. If you turn right, you'll end up back at the environmental center within a few moments. To enjoy the rest of the preserve, turn left, following the Fallen Log Crossing into a bayhead. This marshy forest was once a common sight in Central Florida, where water from the surrounding pine flatwoods drains down into a permanent depression, feeding the roots of damp-loving trees like bay magnolia, sweet bay, red bay, dahoon holly, and loblolly bay. As you walk along the boardwalk, look down and notice the tannic water collecting in the bottom of the bayhead. You'll pass the Screech Owl Trail again, a hummocky shady connector trail through the bayhead, which gets inundated with water after a heavy rain. Use it only if you want to return to the environmental center; otherwise, continue straight along the boardwalk, which ends back in the pine flatwoods. Wild iris grows in damp spots. Blueberries dominate the open, disturbed understory beneath the slash pines. A gopher tortoise strolls by, pausing briefly as you pass. Yellow buttons add a touch of color to the forest, as do the large white blooms of the bay magnolias. You reach another junction with the Palmetto Passage at 1.2 miles. Continue straight, passing a snag where a downy woodpecker is busy at work. Although it is Florida's most common woodpecker, this small black-and-white woodpecker goes almost unnoticed, thanks to its larger, showier cousins. The male is slightly larger than the female, and has a small red spot on the back of its head.

After passing a canopied bench, the trail rises into an oak scrub. At the OSPREY OVER-LOOK sign, turn right. This short spur trail follows the edge of the pine flatwoods along the oak scrub, entering a dense, shadowy forest of oaks and pines. As you walk up the boardwalk to the observation deck, notice the marsh ferns and small pond cypresses with their fern-like needle clusters. The covered deck provides a sweeping view of the marsh along the edge of Lake Tibet, a slim blue ribbon of water beyond the distant cy-

In the sand pine scrub

presses. Watch for purple gallinules picking their way through the duck potatoes, and osprey swooping down from the cypresses, heading out to the open waters of the lake in search of fish. If you are especially lucky, you may see a pair of river otters playing in the mud on their way to the lake. Growing up to 4 feet long, otters are the only aquatic mammals to have a lining of fur instead of blubber. They prefer living in marshes along wooded streams, rivers, and lakes, where they build their dens. Look for them on a morning hike, as they are most active from early evening through early morning.

Turn around and return to the trail junction, turning right. You are now on the Tarflower Loop, a walk through the preserve's small forest of oak scrub; head straight at the loop junction. The footpath becomes sugar-white sand, blindingly bright; the oaks hang heavy with ball moss and old man's beard, one of the more common lichens in Florida. Old man's beard is a crispy grayish-green fungal coating on the oak that can burst into any of several varieties—long, hair-like strands, wiry masses, or tangled fruiting clumps with small plates at the ends of the strands. As the Tarflower Loop ends at 2.1 miles, you'll retrace your steps back past the Osprey Overlook trail to the Palmetto Passage.

At the time of my visit, the Palmetto Passage was closed, and according to the folks at the environmental center, has been closed for years due to flooding. One glance at an aerial view of the park online will show you why. In the past decade, subdivisions have crept up to its boundaries, pouring their runoff into the pine flatwoods of the park. The low spot is the Palmetto Passage, which works its way through the bayhead next to the boardwalk. Chances are, the Palmetto Passage won't reopen. If it does, however, it's a lot of fun to hike—twisting and turning, ducking and scrambling, you make your way through the maze of trees to end up back at the Pine Circle. If you go this way, you'll complete a 3.5-mile hike by walking back behind the environmental center. If the Palmetto Passage is closed, continue back along the Fallen Log Crossing to complete a 2.7-mile hike.

DIRECTIONS

From Interstate 4, take exit 68 Lake Buena Vista. Drive north on SR 535. Pass the entrance to Walt Disney World at the first light, turning left at the second light to follow CR 535. The park entrance is 5.3 miles ahead on the right. The entrance road loops around to parking in front of the environmental center.

CONTACT

Tibet-Butler Preserve
8777 CR 535 (Winter Garden–Vineland Rd.)
Orlando, FL 32836
407-876-6696
www.orangecountyfl.net

26

Disney Wilderness Preserve

Total distance (circuit): 2.5 miles

Hiking time: 1.5 hours

Habitats: pine flatwoods, freshwater marsh, lake, oak scrub, scrubby flatwoods, floodplain forest, cypress domes, oak hammock

Maps: USGS 7½' Lake Tohopekaliga, park map

Trailhead coordinates (lat-lon): 28.129015, -81.430470

Admission: $2 per person suggested donation

In the early morning stillness, there are no sounds but the drone of cicadas, the cry of a red-shouldered hawk, the flapping wings of a flock of white ibis overhead. Preserved as mitigation (lands preserved in place of lands developed) for the construction of Walt Disney World on similar habitats, the 12,000 acres of forests and wetlands at the Disney Wilderness Preserve provide room for thousands of creatures to roam, and protect one of Florida's most rare treasures—a cypress-lined lake.

Take your time and watch for birds as you drive into the preserve. You might see a bald eagle perched regally on a snag, a little blue heron stalking the shallows of a flatwoods pond, or a belted kingfisher perched on a live oak branch. The hiking trails start at the Learning Center. Managed by The Nature Conservancy, the preserve is open from 9–5 daily. The Learning Center complex includes interpretive exhibits, a store, restrooms, and rocking chairs to sit and relax in, watching the sandhill cranes stride by. Pets are not permitted.

From the Learning Center, head through the breezeway past the restrooms, winding down a concrete path past the butterfly garden to get to the trailhead kiosk next to the pond. A small sign declares this the JOHN C. SAWHILL INTERPRETIVE TRAIL. A line of planted wax myrtle screens the back of the buildings from the trail, which offers a sweeping view of the pond. American lotuses float on the surface. Surrounded by smooth cordgrass, the viewing platform provides a place for early morning birding.

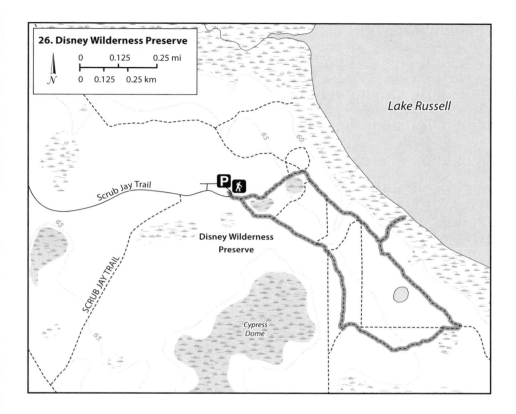

Entering the vast open longleaf pine flatwoods—which are indeed wet, as most in Central Florida are—the trail swings past the former entrance to the interpretive trail loop and turns right to start down a jeep track. Wild bachelor's button peeps up along the trail's edge, and winged sumac show off a tinge of fall color with leaves turning to crimson. The trail climbs a slight rise, and you see a red trail marker as a confirmation blaze. This property was formerly a cattle ranch, and few traces remain. Soon after, you reach an EXIT sign at 0.6 mile. Don't do it! Unless, of course, you don't mind missing the highlights of this trail system. Keep walking straight ahead through the vast open pine flatwoods.

The LAKE RUSSELL sign indicates the spur trail to the lake. Turn left and walk downhill through the floodplain forest of the lake, primarily pond cypress, to an open clearing with picnic tables and benches. Fed by Reedy Creek, Lake Russell is truly the jewel of this park. Once unspoiled by human construction along its shore, there are now the dim shapes of houses behind the far cypress shoreline. Still, the illusion is grand, and critical for wildlife. Watch for 10-foot-long alligators cruising the dark blue surface, their snouts and eyes barely protruding from the water; osprey, skimming low to grab a fish; flocks of white ibises crossing the vast expanse. Lake Russell drains south through marshlands to the Kissimmee River, feeding the Everglades with its northernmost trickle of water.

Cypress-lined Lake Russell

Returning along the spur trail to the main trail, turn left. The trail climbs up into scrubby flatwoods, stretching off to the right as far as the eye can see—longleaf pine, saw palmetto, and scattered lopsided indiangrass. The view is expansive around you, the saw palmetto short enough that you can see a mile or more in most directions. When naturalist William Bartram wandered through Florida in 1773, he reported vast grassy savannas with scattered trees. The dense thickets of saw palmetto we see today in the pine flatwoods are *not* the natural understory, but the result of more than a hundred years of fire suppression in Florida, allowing the palmettos to take over.

Cypress domes and strands look like mountains in the distance. For the remainder of the hike, there are only minor variations on this theme—longleaf pine savanna surrounds you, with puddles gathering in the trail in the deep tire tracks left by the swamp buggy, which is sometimes offered as an alternate way of exploring the preserve.

At 1.3 miles, you reach a sign that reads TRAIL CONTINUES. The trail used to go straight ahead, but is now closed. An unfortunate side effect of the preserve being boxed in by residential developments over the past decade is that the flow of water across the landscape has been altered, placing the farther reaches of the preserve perpetually underwater. Turn right. The footpath narrows to an actual trail with tall grass all around and a cypress-lined pond to the left. You head down a straightaway and then the trail makes a sharp left at a bench, working its way around the pond.

The landscape is a little elevated here, as there are no wet spots in the trail and the saw palmetto have an orange tinge, indicating distress in a time of drought. Winding through the saw palmetto, the trail comes to a confusing junction with a bench. Look for the next trail marker. You pop out onto the original outer loop next to another AUTHORIZED PERSONNEL ONLY sign. Turn right to continue on the loop. You've walked 1.8 miles. Notice the star-shaped yellow flowers on small rosemary like-bushes scattered between the saw palmetto. This is St. John's Wort, *Hypericum angustifolium,* one of the few colorful shrubs in the pine flatwoods, blooming in summer and fall. Originally used in Europe to fend off evil spirits—its generic Latin name, *Hypericum,* comes from the Greek for "above an icon"—its essential oils are now used to produce a popular herbal antidepressant. Don't munch on the plant or its flowers to lift your spirits, however, as they have a distinctly bitter aroma and taste.

This next segment of the trail tends to be wet. It's lower than the surrounding landscape, so water gathers in sheets across the footpath. On a dry day, it's not a problem, but on a wet day, you'll have to wade. Watch the leopard frogs bounce out of your way, and keep alert for water snakes. The savanna opens up even more around you, and you catch a glimpse of the Learning Center off in the distance. Meeting up with the junction with the shorter loop, the trail jogs left and goes through a drainage area, where it's likely you'll find standing water. The trail then rises up and makes a beeline across the savanna toward the pond at the education center. Heading around the pond, it meets up with the sidewalk at the trail kiosk marking the start of the interpretive trail. Turn left to exit, completing a 2.5-mile walk as you reach the parking lot.

The palmetto prairie

DIRECTIONS

The Disney Wilderness Preserve is well off the beaten track in Osceola County. Take I-4 west from Orlando to exit 27, Lake Buena Vista, heading south on SR 535. After 2.9 miles, turn right on Poinciana Boulevard. Heading south, this road crosses both US 192 and US 17/92 en route to Poinciana. It's 15 miles from the SR 535 intersection with Poinciana Boulevard to your next turn. If you are coming from the west on I-4, use exit 24 and head south toward Kissimmee; turn left on US 17/92, then right on Poinciana Boulevard. You'll pass the Osceola District Schools Environmental Study Center on the way.

Make a right at the traffic light at Pleasant Hill Road, immediately getting into the left lane. Make the first left onto Old Pleasant Hill Road, using the left turn lane 0.5 mile down the road. Follow this road for 0.6 mile, turning left onto Scrub Jay Trail, which immediately passes under a large sign for the preserve. It's a slow 1.6-mile drive through the property back to the Learning Center, where the trail starts.

LAND MANAGER

The Nature Conservancy
2700 Scrub Jay Trail
Kissimmee, FL 34759
407-935-0002
www.nature.org

IV. Lake Wales Ridge

Cordgrass and scrub

27

Crooked River Preserve

Total distance (circuit): 1.7 miles

Hiking time: 1 hour

Habitats: hardwood hammock, floodplain forest, lakeshore, oak scrub, river bluff, sandhill, sand pine scrub, sinkhole

Trailhead coordinates (lat-lon): 28.507938, -81.750393

Maps: USGS 7½' Clermont East; Preserve map at kiosk

Admission: Free

Hours: Sunrise–sunset

At the northernmost end of the Lake Wales Ridge, a significant landform that stretches from Minneola down toward Lake Okeechobee, creating the "spine" of the Florida peninsula, Crooked River Preserve showcases a wide variety of habitats in a short hike. The high, well-drained sandy soils of the Lake Wales Ridge were prized by citrus growers, who found them ideal for their groves. At one time, US 27—which follows the ridge, and still gives you a good taste of the hills that make up the middle of Florida's peninsula—was known as the Orange Blossom Highway. It was guaranteed, at least when I was growing up, that a drive down the highway with your windows down meant breathing in the sweet scent of citrus blossoms during their blooming season all winter and into the spring.

Situated just a few miles off US 27 south of Clermont, this is a small preserve, only 64 acres. The orange groves gave way to massive residential and commercial developments over the past decade, so the preserve is tightly hemmed in by the press of development that has otherwise smothered the natural habitats of the northern end of the Lake Wales Ridge. However, Crooked River Preserve not only showcases the scrub but also takes you on a walk down to an untrammeled corner of Lake Louisa by following part of the Palatlakaha River.

Sign in at the kiosk at the trailhead and pick up a map to start down the orange-blazed Cypress Trail. Starting out under a canopy of laurel oaks in a second- or third-growth forest, the trail is edged by giant

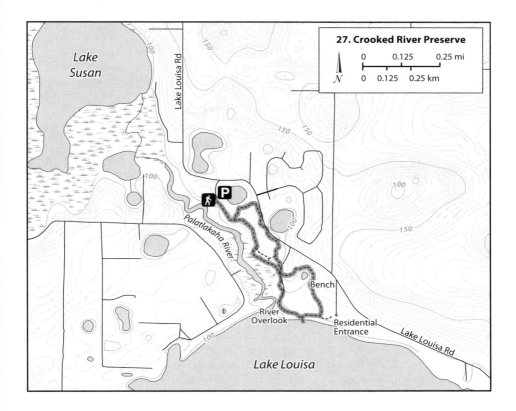

mounds of grapevines. The footpath is sand, but relatively compact. A line of cypress behind the oaks defines the floodplain of the river. Interpretive markers point out specific plants and trees, like the red bay, which likes to have its roots in the wet rim of the floodplain. A tiger swallowtail settles on a patch of fleabane, slowly pumping its wings. In an open area with tall longleaf pines and blueberry bushes, prickly pear cactus and grapevines intermingle as scrub and oak hammock meet.

At an intersection with a yellow-tipped post, turn right. This trail swings closer to the river, affording a shady canopy overhead. It's a crispy, crunchy tunnel of sand live oaks paralleled by a line of cypress. Through an open-

ing between the cypress, you can see Palatlakaha River Park on the opposite shore, another public land (with hiking trails) protecting the watershed of the this little-known river. Rising from the Green Swamp, the Palatlakaha River connects a chain of 11 lakes flowing north from Lake Louisa into Lake Minnehaha, Lake Minneola, and Lake Cherry.

Reaching an intersection with the Cypress Trail and the blue-blazed Sink Trail, keep right. You quickly come upon another junction of the two trails. Keep right again to stay close to the river forest. Turn right at the next yellow-blazed trail. You feel the presence of the river before you see it. A massive oak has an equally massive root ball where it's split into five separate trunks, creating an octopus of

Lake Louisa's north shore

a split oak tree. As you catch a glimpse of the far riverbank, the sparkle of water finally breaks through the understory as the trail gets within sight of houses on the far side of the sinuous stream. The Palatlakaha River is tannic but clear and sand-bottomed, with ripples across the bottom that make the stream almost seem tidal. It's hard to tell from this vantage point on the small bluff, but the river flows north. At a half mile, a picnic bench offers a place to watch for birds and savor the view as Lake Louisa gently pours through a gateway of cypresses into the river.

After watching a great blue heron spear a bluegill in the depths of a river curve, continue straight past the picnic bench to join the blue-blazed Sink Trail, a straightaway beneath tall oaks well-draped in Spanish moss and resurrection fern. Bracken fern crowds the understory. You emerge along the cypresses on the shore of Lake Louisa. Surprisingly, the far shore is pristine, unlike the near shores with their tightly packed lakefront homes. The lake is large enough to sport whitecaps when the wind picks up and is a favorite of local anglers. The far shore is protected by Lake

Louisa State Park, a former ranch and orange groves still undergoing restoration to longleaf pine forest. Along this sandy shoreline, watch for alligators as you marvel at the oddly shaped, almost bonsai-like bald cypress, each a short, stout sentinel proclaiming the age and wildness of this place, with trunks that are mostly hollow. An osprey cries as it banks through the air, scouting the lake for the strike of a fish at the surface. The imprint of a bobcat's paws is deeply embedded in a spit of sand that snakes out into the lake.

Return to the trail and turn right to continue along the blue blazes. Southern woods fern rises tall in the shaded understory. It's a fern that prefers dampness, and the humidity from the big lake suits it just fine. At the next trail junction, the trail straight ahead exits into a neighborhood. Turn left to follow the Sink Trail into a sandhill habitat, with longleaf pines and turkey oaks. Passing ground rooted up by an armadillo, look up and see the twisty branches of longleaf pines. Soon after, the sinkhole, rather significant in size, comes into view. A pond fills the bottom. Sinkholes commonly form in high, well-drained soils like the sand of the Lake Wales Ridge, especially where there are many oak trees. The word "karst," which describes the underlying bedrock full of holes like a sponge, is derived from the Czech word for "oak tree." The tannic acid that leaches from oak leaves accelerates erosion in karst. When a cavity beneath the surface erodes to the point it weakens, a sinkhole forms as the cavity collapses in on itself.

Leaving the sinkhole, turn left at the base of a tall longleaf pine tree—it has its own interpretive marker. The trail sweeps down to follow the rim of the sinkhole. Young longleaf pines shade the path as the trail continues to provide more vantage points across the sinkhole. At the trail junction, turn right at 1.1 miles. You pass another junction on the right a few moments later. Keep to the right, and

The Palatlakaha River

you're back on the orange blazes, following the perimeter of the preserve into its other highlight, the ancient scrub. The scrub of the Lake Wales Ridge is characterized by bright, almost powder-white sand that hosts a variety of woody shrubs and lichens. It is some of the oldest land in the Florida peninsula, teeming with biodiversity and species found nowhere else on earth—which is why this little patch means so much amid the sprawl that now surrounds it. In one spot, the open scrub is covered with sandspike moss, looking like slender fingers rising from the sand. Notice the "scrub olive" marker, indicating a native olive species that only grows in this well-drained sand. It sports small but fragrant flowers, and its fruits are larger than those of the wild olive found commonly throughout Florida.

The hill trends down toward Lake Louisa Road, as does the trail, drawing close to the fence line. The sand gets softer and the walking more difficult. You can see the line of cypress in the distance after the trail leaves the fence line and makes a sharp left into the scrub. Open patches of scrub with diminutive plants are all around you, including more patches of sandspike moss. Reaching the final trail junction at 1.6 miles, turn right to exit down the grapevine-lined corridor. Don't forget to sign out at the trail register!

DIRECTIONS

From US 27 in Clermont, drive south from its intersection of SR 50 for 1 mile. Turn right on Lake Louisa Road and follow it for 2.7miles to the trailhead on the left.

CONTACT

Lake County Water Authority
107 North Lake Avenue
Tavares, FL 32778
352-343-3777
www.lcwa.org

Crooked River Preserve

28

Catfish Creek Preserve State Park

Total distance: 3.5 miles

Hiking time: 2 hours

Habitats: scrub, wet prairie, dry prairie, sandhills

Trailhead coordinates (lat-lon): 27.983800, -81.496800

Maps: USGS 7½' Lake Hatchineha; Trail system map available on the trail

Admission: Free

Hours: 8 AM–sunset

Allan David Broussard Catfish Creek Preserve State Park isn't just "a perfect example of Lake Wales Ridge Scrub," it's a landscape unlike any other you'll find in Florida. The Lake Wales Ridge is a long, slender ridge of ancient sand that stretches from Clermont most of the way toward Lake Okeechobee.

Protecting more than 8,000 acres of untouched wilderness in a very off-the-beaten-path location between Lake Hatchineha, Lake Rosalie, and Lake Pierce (and not far as the crow flies from Lake Kissimmee State Park, Hike 29), Catfish Creek Preserve State Park contains a series of tall, steep ridges of sand that sparkles like fresh snow, featuring ascents and descents so steep you'd think you were traversing ski slopes along the trail system.

You have to love the scrub or a physical challenge to enjoy this trail. Scrub is Florida's desert, and you're in the very heart of it here. The forests are diminutive. Some are a bit on the crispy side, given fire is necessary to replenish the habitat, which makes them downright ugly. The trails are deep in soft sand and broad like roads. There is hardly any shade. But the incredible sweeping views, the extraordinary contrasts between "desert" and lakes, the bountiful wildlife, strange plants, and the physical challenge make this one of my new top picks for an amazing Florida hike. It will get your heart pumping! Given the complexity of the trail system, this is only one of many trail routes you can take on a visit to Catfish Creek Preserve.

Even a short walk through this preserve should not be taken lightly. This is a very

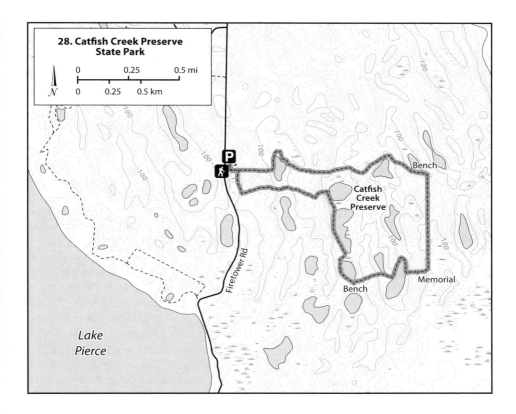

open, exposed hike with strenuous climbs. Get out quickly if you see a thunderstorm approaching. Shade is at a premium. Hiking poles are recommended due to the extremely steep slopes. Sunscreen, sunglasses, and a hat are a must to protect you from the elements. Equestrian trails share portions of the hiking trails, making those sections a much tougher hike due to churned-up sand.

Starting at the trailhead kiosk, follow the white-tipped blaze posts to begin your hike. The trail is a broad jeep road in deep soft sand, as this portion is shared with horses. Anywhere you see the posts tipped in red or red and white together, equestrians are allowed, and the sand tends to be churned up. A red mailbox catches your eye: "trail maps."

Stop and get one. This is a trail system where carrying a map, plus a compass or GPS, is a smart idea. Markers throughout the preserve are keyed to the map, but there are also so many cross-trails between major trails that you can lose yourself in this maze.

Turn right at the trail map box at Marker 2 to start walking the outer loop counterclockwise. The first of many ephemeral ponds is off to the right. The trail makes a moderate incline, paralleling Firetower Road, before it reaches a RESTRICTED AREA sign. Turn left. A Florida scrub-jay lands atop a tall dead tree, seen in silhouette against the blue sky. It's probably the sentinel of a scrub-jay family, watching out for danger from a high post to warn the others.

Passing Marker 4 and 5 in quick succession at 0.5 mile, where equestrian trails go off to the left and right, you climb up to a vantage point at Marker 6—with difficulty, since the sand is so soft—and can see a broad panorama of prairie and open water, and a distant gash of sand indicating a trail climbing the ridge on the far side of the next valley. You descend down a very steep slope into this lush prairie. A strong breeze makes the lack of shade more tolerable on a hot day.

At the base of the hill, you come to a T intersection with a blue-tipped post, which indicates a connector trail, at Marker 8. Turn right to follow this trail along a broad prairie studded with interconnecting lakes, depending on rainfall to provide depth. The trail follows its well-defined shoreline, with sand less-trammeled and more like a well-packed beach. Lily pads float on the surface. It's a Florida landscape on a grandiose, "Big Sky" scale. At an intersection with a white-blazed trail at a T junction, turn left. The shoreline swoops around to a trail junction at a shady spot with a bench at 1.2 miles. Fishing is permitted here, as evidenced by the monofilament disposal tube next to the bench, so these lakes are not ephemeral. A pair of sandhill cranes slowly work their way through the

Rolling ridges

grass along the lakeshore, seeking their afternoon meal.

Pass Marker 24 and head straight past the bench to continue your hike. At Marker 23, the white blazes go off to the right and left, and the blue blazes lead straight ahead. Continue straight to ascend to a very pretty overlook over a very long and slender prairie with a shimmering pond, with the crests of the ridges beyond. The trail makes a sharp left. At Marker 22, the blue blazed trail leads off to the left. Continue around the prairie, where you begin to see some of the more interesting and unusual plants of the Lake Wales Ridge. The quality of the sand changes—it's extremely white, and was one of the few parts of Florida that protruded from the sea when the state was once underwater. As a result, there's a Noah's Ark of ancient plant species here found nowhere else in the world, including 21 species that are considered endangered due to their rarity, including scrub plum (*Prunus geniculata*), scrub morning glory (*Bonamia grandiflora*), and pygmy fringe tree (*Chionanthus pygmaeus*).

A extremely steep ascent faces you, one of the steepest in Florida. Consider making your own switchbacks as you make the climb to this lofty spot, which lets you survey all of the hiking you've done so far. At 1.7 miles, it's here you find the memorial to Allan David Broussard, for whom the preserve was dedicated. The family left quotes on the engraved memorial, and a scrub-jay perches on Allan's shoulder on the bust atop the granite, looking out over this incredible panorama. A rare cluster of beargrass grows near the foot of the memorial.

What goes up must come down, and facing this next slope back down off the high ridge, you'll want a toboggan. Keep left at the fork as the descent slides down to the next prairie's edge. Reaching Marker 19 at a T intersection, make a left and walk along the

Beargrass

prairie. After a few footfalls you come to the junction of the white and blue blazed trails, reaching the outer combination hiking/equestrian trail at Marker 18. Continue straight. Many interesting lichens and mosses, including patches of spike moss and odd-looking fungi, grow beneath small woody shrubs. You start a long ascent up the ridge, an ascent where you can see the trail kiss the sky a good quarter mile up ahead. Colorful sprays of Ashe's calamint, cloaked in pink blooms, attract bumblebees and butterflies. A deer pauses at the top of the slope before vanishing into a forest only a few feet taller than you. At the crest, don't follow the curvature, which drops down into a deep valley. Go straight ahead and meet the outer loop at Marker 16. Turn left and walk down to the prairie. At the fork at Marker 15, the horse trail diverges to the right, and the hiking trail continues to the left. Enough shade is cast by a hammock of older sand live oaks on the south side of the trail to encourage you to stop and rest on a bench overlooking this prairie. You've hiked 2.3 miles.

After ascending up and over the ridge, the trail provides you a panorama of a broad prairie rimmed in saw palmetto. Tall stalks of wheat-colored pinewood dropseed wave in the afternoon breeze. Past Marker 17, off to the left is a prairie showcasing the textures of at least seven types of grasses in succes-

sion from sprays of sand cordgrass to tall stands of shortspike bluestem. This is the northern end of the long chain of lakes and prairies. When you reach Marker 13, continue straight to start walking along the red-tipped posts of the equestrian trail. The sand is more churned up, but this route is worth it. As you climb the hill, look back at the view behind you, across the prairie, framed inside a small oak hammock, the sweep of a liquid landscape.

The outer equestrian trail joins in from the right at Marker 43, where several scrub plums with weirdly jointed branches flourish. Marker 42 is next to another pretty prairie pond. An unmarked trail leads off to the right, but the main trail skirts around the prairie, where the live oaks arch out to provide a spot of shade. The trail turns and follows the prairie rim, its grasses waving in the wind, and then makes a steep uphill to the right past Marker 41. This is the final climb out of the preserve, so take it easy. You complete the loop at the map box at Marker 2 after 3.4 miles. Continue straight, with the oak hammock to your right, to exit the preserve at the trailhead at 3.5 miles.

DIRECTIONS

From US 27 in Dundee, follow CR 542 east to Hatchineha Road. Turn right and continue 8 miles to Firetower Road. Turn right. Continue 3 miles. The park trailhead is on the left before the FFA Leadership Camp entrance. If you reach their gate, turn around and come back—Firetower Road dead-ends at the camp.

CONTACT

Catfish Creek State Park
c/o Lake Kissimmee State Park
14248 Camp Mack Road
Lake Wales, FL 33898
863-696-1112
www.floridastateparks.org/catfishcreek

29

Lake Kissimmee State Park

Total distance (three circuits): 15.4 miles

Hiking time: 8 hours or 2 days

Habitats: prairie, oak scrub, pine flat-woods, scrubby flatwoods, oak hammock, freshwater marsh

Trailhead coordinates (lat-lon): 27.943847, -81.354761

Maps: USGS 7½' Lake Weohyakapka Northeast; Florida Trail Association Map South 1; Florida State Park map

Admission: $2 pedestrians/bicyclist, $4 single motorist, $5 carload

Hours: 8 AM–sunset

Situated on the western shore of Florida's third largest lake, Lake Kissimmee State Park provides a weekend's worth of hiking and more wildlife sightings than you can imagine. Herds of white-tailed deer browse uncon-cernedly along the entrance road. Sandhill cranes stride through the tall prairie grasses. Alligators bask in the sunshine along a canal filled with colorful purple pickerelweed blooms.

The vast prairies and scrub along Lake Kissimmee provided free-range grazing ground for a scruffy breed of wild cattle known as the scrub cow, descendents of cat-tle brought to Florida in 1539 by explorer Her-nando de Soto. Cattle ranching became popular because cattle could be shipped to the Caribbean in exchange for gold, and the only effort expended was to round them up. By 1860, south-central Florida had 13 times more cattle than people! After the fall of Vicks-burg, Florida beef became a crucial commod-ity to the Confederacy during the Civil War, inspiring Union Army raids on cattle drives.

The park road twists and winds through the oak hammocks that dominate the North Loop. Continue along it until you reach the parking area next to the marina. All of the park's trails radiate from this point. For a quick starter hike—an easy one for the kids—take a stroll over to the Charlie Gafford Flatwoods Pond Trail. It begins on the other side of the road. This 0.4-mile interpretive trail takes about 15 minutes to complete. It meanders around a marshy pond in the pine flatwoods, showing you the succession of habitat from pine flatwoods to oak hammock.

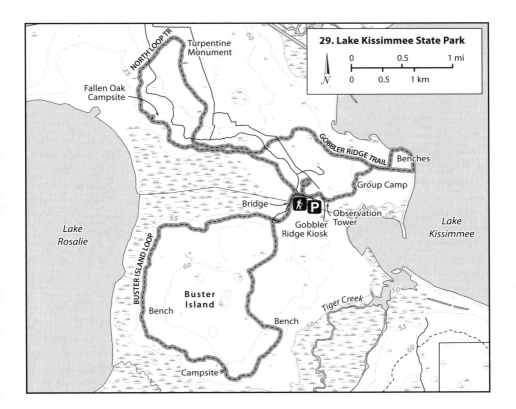

The other trails require some planning be-fore you start hiking. The popular Buster Is-land Trail is a 6.9-mile loop trail that takes about 3.5 hours to hike. The North Loop Trail and the Gobbler Ridge Trail are stacked loops that take you through a wide variety of habitats past a primitive campsite in the oak hammock and out along the shores of Lake Kissimmee. Hiking the outer perimeter of these two loops takes about 4 hours to cover 8.5 miles.

To enjoy all of the major hikes in this park, hike Buster Island first, stay overnight in the full-service campground, and rise early the second day to tackle the northern trails. If you enjoy backpacking, you may prefer to split the two hikes into two weekend trips, taking ad-

vantage of the primitive campsites provided along the trails. Prefer the comforts of home? There's the Liar's Lodge Motel nearby down at Camp Mack Fish Camp at the end of the road outside the park. No matter which option you choose, Lake Kissimmee State Park re-quires at least two days for you to enjoy all it has to offer.

DAY ONE

Buster Island Loop
(6.9 miles)

Starting at the marina parking lot, sign in at the hiker kiosk. Follow the blue blazes through an oak hammock and out to a road you passed on the way in—the "1876 Cow Camp." Turn left at the trail junction and follow the road over the bridge. At the fork in the road, the right side leads to the trail; the left side leads to the cow camp.

When it came time to bring cattle to market, Florida cowmen, called "Crackers" for the sound of their bullwhip over the herd, rounded up the cows and drove them toward a port. Frederick Remington described the Crackers as "wild looking individuals, whose hanging hair and drooping hats and generally bedraggled appearance would remind you of Spanish moss." At the park's 1876 Cow Camp, open on weekends, you can visit an encampment of these cowmen (never call them cowboys!), and learn what it took to live and work in the rough conditions of frontier Florida, in the days before mosquito control and paved roads. A herd of more than 200 scrub cattle roam in the park, a tribute to Florida's frontier history.

The blue blazes end as the Cow Camp Road ends, so follow the white blazes to continue along the Buster Island Loop. After a half mile, you reach the actual start of the loop trail. Turn right into the pine flatwoods to walk it counterclockwise. Thin-needled sprays of wild pine decorate the gnarled branches of live oaks.

Comprised of wet prairies, pine flatwoods, oak hammocks, and scrub, Buster Island is indeed an island, surrounded by three lakes and their associated waterways; you just can't tell from the trail. Right away, you notice you're on a corridor of high ground. Just beyond the cool shade of the live oaks and slash pines is the prairie, stretching off to the distance to your right and left. Like the short interpretive trail, the Buster Island Trail provides a close-up look at succession of the pine flatwoods to Florida's climax forest, the live oak hammock. Fire is an integral part of the natural pine flatwoods ecosystem, burning off the thick mat of pine needles from the forest floor, preventing it from becoming dark

rich soil. When fire is absent, oaks easily take root in the new topsoil, quickly choking out the growth of small pines. Over time, the oaks become the dominant tree, hosting a vast array of epiphytes—air plants—and ferns on their branches. The size and shape of many of the live oaks in this forest indicate a century or more of growth.

Watch for signs of the turpentine industry of the 1900s. Although all of the original pine forest was logged more than a century ago, some of the tall stumps and snags of long-dead pines have the v-shaped marks that indicate the pine was tapped for resin. One such snag along the trail has the metal strips still embedded in the wood. To catch the resin, a clay cup was dangled below the "v" created by the two metal strips.

Where the ground gets moist, ferns appear, particularly the cinnamon fern and the woods fern, both lovers of the acidic soil provided by pine needles. Thickets of saw palmetto grow tall under the oaks, straining skyward for sunlight on enormous thick trunks. A white-tailed deer pauses between two trees. Several more lie in the tall grasses at the edge of the hammock.

As you cross a jeep trail at 1.1 miles, there is an old section of fencing off to the left. This land was once farmland owned by the Zipprer family, who sold it to the state in 1969. After walking through a low area of tall grass and ferns, you return to the familiar hammock and pines. Deer trails crisscross the main trail—always keep to the white blazes, as it's easy to wander off on the well-established footpath of a deer trail without realizing you've gone the wrong way. For a while, the corridor widens, the prairie disappearing beyond the trees. Fallen over like a log, an old oak tree sprouts branches as thick as trunks. It's a great perch to sit and take a break. Look up, and notice the large bromeliads clinging to the slash pines in front of you—an odd perch

KEVIN MIMS

Along the Lake Kissimmee lakeshore at Gobbler Ridge

for them, with not much of a foothold. In many places, bromeliads lie scattered on the ground, victims of strong winds and weak attachments to their hosts.

After 2.2 miles of hiking, you see open scrub off to the left. It may have been burned recently to remove the dense undergrowth. As the trail enters the scrubby flatwoods, it becomes a distinct pine-needle footpath edged by grass. Gallberry takes over the understory. You cross another jeep trail into an area where the grass creates a chestnut haze beneath the slash pines. At 3.4 miles, the trail turns left at a double blaze, briefly following a jeep road before turning left again, back to an oak hammock. Butterfly orchids dangle overhead, catching your eye with their long, grass-like leaves and tall yellow-green flowers with white lips striped purple. The butterfly orchid is Florida's most common wild orchid, blooming from late spring to

early fall. Yet it also a protected species, thanks to the thousands of orchid lovers who have removed far too many specimens from the wild.

Turning left into pine flatwoods, you hear a distant, constant buzz—airboats on Lake Rosalie. Invented in the 1920s, the airboat's original purpose was to carry people into the depths of the Everglades. Like a kayak, it needs only a couple of inches of water to be able to skim the surface and propel forward. Unlike a kayak, the airboat is made up of a airplane engine and propeller contained in a wire cage and strapped to a flat-bottomed craft. Like airport maintenance workers, airboat operators wear heavy headphones to block out the constant drone, which carries for miles and miles, especially across these open prairies in the Kissimmee River basin. But the importance of their traditional uses— aiding ranchers and anglers to get into the

Lake Kissimmee State Park

shallows of the meandering waterways and lake edges—outweigh the noise factor.

Half-hidden by tall cinnamon ferns, blueberry bushes rise from the needle-carpeted forest floor. The brilliant pink petals of a pale meadow beauty catch your eye. A chorus of frogs sings as the trail skirts around a large flatwoods pond, coming up on the sign for the primitive campsite. Nestled under live oaks, the campsite has two picnic tables and several fire rings. It's a great place to stop and take a lunch break after 3.8 miles of hiking. If you want to backpack in to the campsite, be sure to first register at the ranger station. There is no water at this site, so you'll need to bring adequate supplies for drinking and cooking.

Returning to the trail, turn right. The footpath becomes a narrow corridor between dense saw palmettos. Spanish moss drapes over the live oak limbs overhead. You begin to be able to see the prairie on the right, a savanna of tall grass just beyond the tree line. As you walk through a gap between two trunks of a divided oak, look for the butterfly orchids overhead. A near-seamless canopy of live oak branches shades the trail. At 4.4 miles, the trail passes through a massive divided oak, where each trunk is at least 10 feet around. The grasslands become more visible as you cross a horse trail. As the hammock narrows, the trail jumps on and off a jeep trail several times over the next half mile before it makes a sharp left into the scrub.

Short scrub live oak and myrtle oak trees characterize this scrub habitat, with only scattered lonely slash pines. Florida rosemary grows in small clearings between the saw palmettos. A grassy marsh pond sits off to the right. At 5.2 miles, the trail turns right onto a jeep road, continuing into pine flatwoods. Watch for the double blaze where the trail turns away from the jeep trail, making a right into the pine flatwoods. As you pass another

marshy pond on the right, the forest floor gleams green with the gentle needles of thousands of small slash pines taking root. Dark earth gives way to white sand as the elevation increases slightly, bringing you into a sand pine scrub. After 6.1 miles, the trail enters the vast prairie at the heart of Buster Island, and you cross over a jeep track. A red-tailed hawk circles over the grassland. Looking off to the left, you can see the sweep of tree line in the distance, your route through the oak hammock and pine flatwoods. You reach the beginning of the white trail loop at 6.5 miles. Turn right, retracing your steps back to the parking area along the blue-blazed trail.

Vary the end of your return trip by turning right just before the bridge over the Zipprer Canal, which drains Lake Rosalie into Lake Kissimmee. Walking along a grassy strip, cross the canal on a pedestrian bridge, and follow the canal down to the marina for the opportunity to watch for wading birds. Otters sometimes play in the water. A bridge leads out to an island in the canal, a great spot to see alligators sunning on the steep banks. The marina store has camping and fishing supplies, and there is a soft drink machine next to the restrooms. The trailhead and parking lot is just behind the marina.

DAY TWO

North and Gobbler Ridge Loop Trails (8.5 miles)

To start your next day's sojourn, return to the marina parking lot. Begin at the kiosk, making sure to sign in. Follow the blue blazes through the oak hammock to Cow Camp Road. This time, continue straight across the road. The blue blazes lead you under a large live oak. The trail skirts the edge of the prairie on its way toward the pine flatwoods. A large sign confirms your choice of route; continue straight until you reach the yellow-blazed loop trail, at 0.4 mile. Turn left, wandering through open cabbage palms and dense gallberry. A flock of wild turkey vanishes quickly into the underbrush. The trail shows signs of sporadic wetness, and is dug up in many places by armadillos. Entering a tall stand of pines, the trail makes its way to where you see prairie between the trees off to the left. A mirror image of the Buster Island Loop, this trail parallels the south edge of the same open prairie. A white-tailed deer looks up, startled. In search of mushrooms, a Florida box turtle wanders across the footpath.

You walk through a stand of young cabbage palms decked out in their full mass of fronds at ground level, growing out before they grow tall. The trail swings to the right, away from the prairie and then jogs back to the left. Scattered live oaks and saw palmetto clumps break up the pine forest. A broad ditch, perhaps a seasonal stream, drains into a flatwoods pond. The forest yields to an oak hammock, where a damp fur of resurrection fern covers the sprawling limbs of live oaks. Butterfly orchids grow here, too, with several large clusters on trees off to the right. Saw palmettos with trunks up to 20 feet long sprout out from the protection of the base of one large live oak. Photographs from the early 1900s commonly show saw palmettos of this size and girth; most of today's specimens are tiny by comparison, revegetating habitats that have been plowed under, drained, and used for cattle grazing.

After you cross a jeep trail, the soil under-

Scrubby flatwoods

foot becomes an unusual deep cinnamon color, the result of deep layers of decomposing pine needles. Passing another flatwoods pond, the trail reaches the sign for the primitive campsite at 1.9 miles. Turn right to check out the campsite, 0.1 mile down a blue-blazed trail. The nearest water (which must be filtered) is in that flatwoods pond you last passed; the campsite is high and dry under the live oaks, with picnic tables and two fire rings.

Continuing on the white loop, the trail veers to the right into the pine flatwoods. To the left, glimpses of open sky show that the prairie isn't far away. But you soon run out of park. The trail makes a hard right within sight of the fence line, passing through a hammock of sand live oak before it enters the open scrubby flatwoods. Another hard right leads you straight down a long corridor of saw palmetto and across the park entrance road. This stark but compelling landscape of dense, low saw palmetto and scattered longleaf pines goes on for the next half mile, broken only by small circular wet prairies and one tiny oak hammock. A small rise in elevation creates an oak scrub, dense with miniature versions of sand live oak, Chapman oak, and myrtle oak competing for space. At 3.2 miles, you reach a pen containing an unusual occupant—an old snag catfaced for turpentine, hung with the traditional clay.

Wiregrass invades the trail as the scrubby flatwoods take back over, choking out the last few Chapman oaks. Long strands of Spanish moss dangle like beards from the tall longleaf pines. After 4 miles of hiking, the forest becomes denser, turning to pine flatwoods that offer well-appreciated shade. Crossing the park road again, you enter a hammock of pines and oaks. Soft pine needles obscure the footpath; watch carefully for the blazes as the trail swings quickly to the left after the road crossing. A fox squirrel perches in the high branches of an oak, nibbling on a shelf mushroom. Its tawny bronze and black coat gives away its hiding place.

Squeezed between the park road and the prairie, this narrow strip of hammock contains both the trail you're on and the trail you've been on, not more than a hundred feet apart in places. Be very cautious about stepping off the footpath, as you might end up stepping back on to the wrong yellow-blazed trail segment! Skirting a prairie on the left, the trail passes through a burned area and gets very narrow through a densely wooded area, becoming damp underfoot in places. Walking across the park road, you enter another stretch of pine flatwoods, crossing a jeep trail under a power line. Watch for the first blaze on the right, painted on a catfaced snag, where you can run your fingers across the deep notches created by the turpentine crews.

At 5.6 miles, you reach the trail junction for the Gobbler Ridge Trail. Continue straight, following the orange blazes on this loop out to Lake Kissimmee and the perimeter of the prairie. A cabin hides off in the woods to the left. After crossing a jeep trail, the trail veers to the right, paralleling the jeep trail by weaving in and out of small oak hammocks along the Gobbler Ridge. The "ridge" is only a few inches high, but high enough to keep the sweeping prairie off to the left at bay. In the distance, cattle browse in the tall grass. A brown anole races up an oak trunk. Where the trail becomes open, the ground is almost desert-like. Clusters of seafoam-colored deer moss sprawl across the blinding white sugar sand. A herd of six white-tailed deer explode from where they were sitting, a large buck flashing his 12-point rack.

Where the trail seems to end at a T with a jeep track, turn left, following the jeep track through the tall grass. Head straight another hundred feet onto the "beach" of Lake

Kissimmee, relict sand dunes with clumps of saw palmetto. The marshy shores of the lake lap at the sand; you can see clear water not far off in the distance, beyond the airboat trail through the reeds. Because of its extensive marshes, Lake Kissimmee remains the domain of boaters; this may be the only place in Central Florida where you can actually walk up to the shore of the lake.

Turn right at the post along the lakeshore and start following the trail around the lake. It offers expansive views of the lake and its surrounding prairie. As the waters fade into the distance, you enter the shade of the oak hammock, passing a campground for youth groups. The old observation tower stands sentinel above the prairie. A victim of old age and battering by storms, it's no longer accessible for its scenic view. The Gobbler Ridge Trail ends at the observation tower parking area. Continue along the edge of the pavement and picnic area back around to the marina, completing your hike at the marina parking lot after 8.5 miles.

DIRECTIONS

From the interchange of US 27 and SR 60 in Lake Wales, head east on SR 60 for 9.7 miles, driving through the village of Hesperides before you reach Boy Scout Camp Road. There should be a prominent sign pointing out the turn. Turn left and drive 3.5 miles to Camp Mack Road. Turn right, following this road 5.4 miles to the park entrance on the right.

CONTACT

Lake Kissimmee State Park
14248 Camp Mack Road
Lake Wales, FL 33853
863-696-1112
www.floridastateparks.org/lakekissimmee

30

Crooked Lake Prairie

Total distance (circuit): 2 miles

Hiking time: 1.5 hours

Habitats: freshwater marsh, oak scrub, sand pine scrub, scrubby flatwoods

Trailhead coordinates (lat-lon): 27.806483, -81.559483

Maps: USGS 7½' Babson Park; Preserve map at kiosk

Admission: Free

Hours: Sunrise–sunset

At Crooked Lake Prairie near Frostproof, the dunes of the Lake Wales Ridge meet showy prairie grasslands along the eastern shore of Crooked Lake. This hike is a refreshing excursion into habitats found on the high hills of the Lake Wales Ridge, a counterpoint to the spreading residential development that is replacing the scrub forests and orange groves on these high hills with tightly packed housing. Crooked Lake Prairie is notable for its interface of wetland and scrub habitats, where a birding excursion means you're as likely to spot a Louisiana heron as you are to encounter a family of Florida scrub-jays.

The network of interlinking loop trails includes four trails. This route follows the perimeter of the trail system on the orange-blazed Scrub Trail, the blue-blazed Piney Woods Trail, and the yellow-blazed Prairie Path, showcasing the best of the habitats found here. Stop at the kiosk and pick up a trail map. The trails are well marked, and the habitat is extremely open—desert-like, as to be expected of the Lake Wales Ridge—so sunscreen, sunglasses, and a hat are a smart idea.

Walk through the baffle and into the preserve. Stop at the kiosk for a map. A sign points you down the Scrub Trail, so follow it on a narrow orange-blazed path into an oak hammock. As you reach a picnic table tucked under the shade of an oak tree, views open up to your right of the open scrub. Continuing along a corridor fringed by saw palmetto and young sand live oaks, the trail continues through oak scrub, jogging right at an orange-tipped post with an arrow. From the shade of

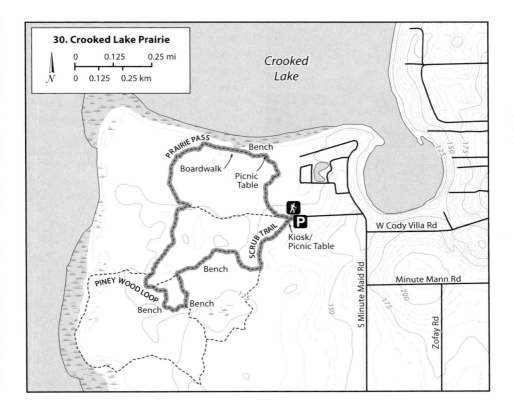

the oak hammock, you emerge into the blinding white sand of the Lake Wales Ridge. Soft and powdery, it's not easy to walk through, especially as the trail joins a jeep road along the perimeter of the hammock, a restoration area where the habitat is being restored to the diminutive forest that the Florida scrub-jay prefers. The next arrow points you back into a short stretch of shade before the trail makes a sharp right out into the open scrub.

Crossing a jeep road, you return to another stretch of oak hammock with scenic views of the open scrub. This area, too, is undergoing restoration, so it may not be open when you visit. A gopher tortoise burrow is half-hidden by dense grasses. Joining another jeep road in soft sand, the trail jogs off it

briefly to reach a bench at the half mile mark. It's not exactly a pleasant place to tarry, given the lack of shade, but if you hear the "shreep" of a scrub-jay, hang in there. This preserve is actively managed for the benefit of the Florida scrub-jay families that reside here. These large, colorful members of the jay family are only found in Florida, their population in decline and severely limited by lack of habitat. Preferring young scrub forests—which regenerate naturally when fire sweeps through the scrub, something that has been actively suppressed along much of the Lake Wales Ridge due to development—they don't migrate far. Living in family groups, where the prior season's youngsters stick around to assist with the next brood, they are large and colorful and

Boardwalk along Crooked Lake

unmistakable when one swoops down to land on a snag in front of you.

The trail turns off the jeep road and becomes a footpath again, winding through an oak scrub where tiny myrtle oaks and Chapman oaks grow in front of the larger sand live oaks. Two benches provide more comfortable birding spots. Puffs of deer moss and spiky red-tipped reindeer lichen emerge from the leaf litter on the forest floor as you pass a large old oak tree. The footpath returns to the open. Keep alert to the orange blaze posts as you zigzag along and across several jeep trails. Longleaf pines become a dominant feature above the classic sea of saw palmetto that defines Central Florida's palmetto prairies. Grand sentinels, they are picturesque reminders of the grander forests that once swept across this part of the peninsula.

At 1.3 miles, you reach the junction with the Piney Woods Trail coming in from the right. Turn left to remain on the perimeter of the trail system. Meandering beneath the tall pines, you catch sweeping views of the cordgrass prairie in the distance to the right. Pass-

ing under a stand of cabbage palms, the trail emerges along the prairie's edge as it tacks from oak hammock to oak hammock across the ancient sands of the Lake Wales Ridge. Swaying clumps of sand cordgrass rise around you as you reach the berm along Crooked Lake. A mowed path offers excellent views of the lake as you reach the boardwalk. You'll want to tarry here. Herons and egrets poke around the shallows, and the view back across the cordgrass prairie is spectacular, with showy sprays of slender grass waving in unison in the breeze.

Leaving the boardwalk, you reach a picnic table sitting beneath long streamers of swaying Spanish moss amid an oak hammock at 1.7 miles. This is a lovely spot to sit and enjoy the lake before you turn to leave. Exiting the moss-draped oak hammock, the trail leads you back along the ecotone where sand pine scrub and open prairie meet. Prickly pear cactus rise from the grasses as you come up to the intersection with the Piney Woods Trail. Turn left to exit, passing a portable toilet as you come up to the baffle leading out to the parking lot, completing the 2- mile hike.

DIRECTIONS

From the junction of SR 17 and CR 630 in Frostproof, drive north 3.8 miles to Cody Villa Road; turn left at sign for Crooked Prairie Preserve. Follow road to where it makes a sharp right; turn right and make an immediate left into the preserve. The entrance road leads through a citrus grove to the trailhead parking area.

CONTACT

Polk County Environmental Lands Program
4177 Ben Durrance Road
Bartow, FL 33830
863-534-7377
www.polk-county.net

31

Tiger Creek Preserve

Total distance (circuit): 8.4 miles (two trails)

Hiking time: 5 hours

Habitats: oak scrub, sand pine scrub, pine flatwoods, scrubby flatwoods, bayheads, floodplain forest, hydric hammock, sand-hills, seepage slopes, prairie

Trailhead coordinates (lat-lon): 27.807983, -81.492050

Maps: USGS 7½' Lake Weohyakapka; Florida Trail Association Map South 1

Admission: Free

Hours: Sunrise–sunset

Few Florida habitats are talked about with such reverence as the scrub of the Lake Wales Ridge, thought to be the oldest land in the state. When the rest of Florida was under a few feet of water, all the way back to Miocene times, these long, thin dune-capped islands stood well above the waves. As a result, strange and unusual plant species evolved on the Lake Wales Ridge, making this one of North America's most diverse biological communities, with the highest concentration of rare and endangered plants in the continental United States. These are also the "mountains" of peninsular Florida, rising up to 300 feet.

Managed by The Nature Conservancy, Tiger Creek Preserve protects nearly 4,900 acres of this sensitive habitat, leaving it open only to those who enjoy walking the trails. Two of the preserve's three trails—the George Cooley Trail and the Highlands Trail—start from Pfundstein Road, south of Babson Park. The third, the Jenkins Trail, is presently under restoration. Pets are not permitted in these fragile habitats.

GEORGE COOLEY TRAIL

There is no obvious trailhead for the George Cooley Trailhead, which starts at the first power pole on the left. Look for the NATURE CONSERVANCY sign. Two or three cars can fit along the road. The short (0.8 mile) but diverse George Cooley Trail is a great introduction to the habitats of the Lake Wales Ridge and is a fun outing for families. Follow the footpath away from the road, passing through a series of spaced poles that prevent

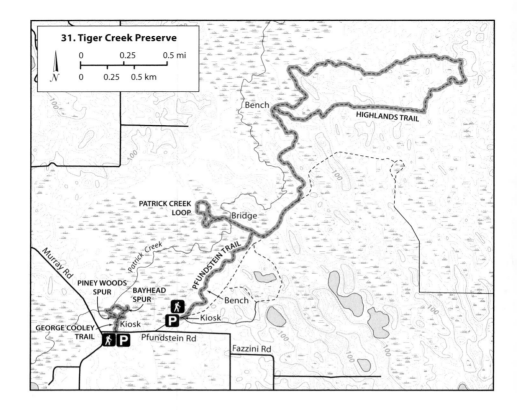

31. Tiger Creek Preserve

0   0.25   0.5 mi

0   0.25   0.5 km

N

Bench

HIGHLANDS TRAIL

PATRICK CREEK LOOP

Bridge

Patrick Creek

PFUNDSTEIN TRAIL

Murray Rd

PINEY WOODS SPUR

BAYHEAD SPUR

Bench

Kiosk

GEORGE COOLEY TRAIL

Kiosk

Pfundstein Rd

Fazzini Rd

vehicles from entering the area. Notice the fine creamy turquoise lichens tipped in bright red, clustered on the tops of the poles. Called British soldiers, *Cladonia leporina* thrives on the rough ends of dead wood. These slow-growing lichens are a symbiotic relationship between a specific fungus and an alga, neither of which can live on its own. A close relative to this lichen is the perforate reindeer lichen, with similar red tips. Along with 19 other species of plants and six species of animals found on the Lake Wales Ridge, it is on the federal endangered species list.

Several benches are clustered around the "official" trailhead, tucked away under myrtle oaks. Metal NATURE CONSERVANCY diamond-shaped markers serve as blazes. At the COO-

LEY NATURE TRAIL sign, turn right. A side trail takes off to the right; follow it over a scrubby ridge, where crispy gray-green lichen coats the limbs of dead oaks, and old man's beard dangles in long wisps from the trees. The trail weaves to a dead end on a hilltop overlooking a bayhead. Retrace your steps back to the main trail and turn right. At the next trail junction, turn right to walk down into the cool, damp bayhead, with cinnamon ferns growing up to shoulder height. At the END OF TRAIL sign, turn around and return to the main trail. Turn right, following the trail as it rises through an oak scrub to a cutthroat seep, a grassy wetland in the scrub. Veer right at the next trail junction to walk down to Patrick Creek. Peer into the clear water to watch the current tug at strands of eelgrass. Walk back to the trail junction, taking the right fork. Turn right to walk through a short stretch of pine flatwoods, where blue flag iris blooms in and around the trail. The footpath peters out in wet ground under a stand of dahoon holly. Retrace your steps, heading straight to follow the Circle Trail. You'll soon return to the original CIRCLE TRAIL sign, having walked 0.7 mile through seven different habitats. Turn right to return to where your car is parked along the road.

HIGHLANDS TRAIL

If you're now ready for a more rugged immersion into the Lake Wales Ridge, drive up the road another 0.2 mile to the Highlands Trail trailhead, turning in to the entrance road on the left with the NATURE CONSERVANCY sign. Across from the parking area, a FLORIDA TRAIL sign indicates the start of the trail, through the gate just beyond the kiosk. Most of this trail is very dry, open, and desert-like. Take plenty of water along, and wear a hat and sunglasses to keep the glare of the sugar-white sands to a minimum.

The orange-blazed trail immediately makes a left into the grassy scrub, passing a cutthroat grass restoration area. Found nowhere else in the world but Florida, cutthroat grass grows only along seepage slopes in the scrub, where moisture seeping from the sand feeds its minimal water requirements. These endangered tufts of grass are protected along the Lake Wales Ridge. Underfoot, the glistening white sand path is made up of

Prairie on the Highlands Trail

ancient particles of quartzite. It winds through the oak scrub, a forest in miniature. As you walk down the trail, notice how few of the oaks tower above your head. Myrtle oak, Chapman oak, and scrub live oak thrive here, as do stunted wax myrtle and the pygmy fringe tree. Although the bright white sand reminds you of a desert, this area receives up to 50 inches of rain each year. The well-drained sand soaks up the rain so rapidly that scrub plants barely have an opportunity to use the water. Instead, the oaks and shrubs rely on deep taproots and waxy coatings to maximize their survival.

Minutes into this hike, you notice its most spectacular quality—the absence of human touch. The tracks of deer, raccoon, coyotes, and bobcats define the footpath, crisscrossing with their own well-defined trails; the hiking trail is almost an afterthought, lightly used. Yours may be the first footprints in weeks. No candy wrappers or cigarette butts defile the pristine scrub. You reflect that you are but a visitor, an incidental movement across this ancient landscape, and you slacken your pace, wandering through the scrub in wide-eyed wonder.

Where the orange blazes lead into the pine flatwoods, wiregrass creates a hazy forest floor under the tall longleaf pines. As the trail continues over gently rolling hills, it meanders back and forth between scrub and flatwoods until it comes to a junction with a jeep trail. To the left lies the Patrick Creek Loop; to the right is the bulk of the main trail, starting at the HIGHLANDS LOOP sign. Turn left. Blazed in blue, the jeep trail drops down quickly to beautiful Patrick Creek, here a broader and swifter creek than your previous encounter with it, and stained a dark black from tannic acids leaching out of oaks and cypresses along the waterway. Large epiphytes cluster in the creekside trees; royal and cinnamon ferns grow along its edge. Cross the

long bridge, its end marking the beginning of the 0.5-mile loop. Turn left, where the trail quickly rises, changing from a mucky marsh to a hardwood hammock of pignut hickory, water oaks, and large live oaks. Watch for the double blazes that escort you around the loop as it descends back into the hydric hammock, closely crowded by tall cinnamon ferns. Returning to the bridge, turn left to cross Patrick Creek and return to the trail junction.

Take a right past the HIGHLANDS LOOP sign to begin your trek into the rolling terrain of the Lake Wales Ridge highlands. At the first T intersection, make a left, walking down a jeep road into a bayhead swamp sweet with the scent of magnolia blossoms. Tannic water flows across the road; do your best to skirt around it. Rising out of the bayhead, the trail comes to a fork; keep to the left, dropping through a stand of longleaf pine and through a second bayhead with its thick earthy aroma, jumping over sheets of water flowing across the road. Rising up into the scrub, the trail makes a sharp left off the jeep road—don't miss it! Scattered hickory trees and turkey oaks creep into the scrub, indicating a transition to sandhill. After dropping down into damp pine flatwoods, the trail rises up to another HIGHLANDS LOOP sign at 2.8 miles. This is the beginning of the long loop out into the scrub and sandhill.

Head past the HIGHLANDS LOOP sign to follow the trail down off the sandhill into scrubby flatwoods, dense with saw palmetto and gallberry. The many short scrubby plants with yellow star-shaped flowers are varieties of St. John's Wort, some endemic to this preserve. Rustling the palm fronds, an armadillo grazes, out of sight. The trail is crowded by scrub vegetation in many places, so carefully watch for the orange blazes—if you don't see an orange blaze after five minutes of walking, retrace your steps. There are many false leads on game trails throughout the loop, so be es-

One of many dead ends on the Cooley Trail

pecially attentive for double blazes. Keep watching for signs of wildlife—bobcat and deer tracks in the soft sugar sand, and a blur of yellow and brown as a pair of brown thrashers scoot across the trail. Slightly larger than a robin, the male thrasher has the broadest vocal repertoire of any North American songbird, with more than 1,100 different songs.

After you walk down a corridor of 5-foot-tall oaks, the trail turns left onto a jeep road, left onto another jeep road, then right to head back out into the open scrub. Several cabbage palms are growing in a low grassy area off to the left—an indicator of a seepage slope. Longleaf pines edge an open prairie. Turning left on another jeep road, the trail rises through the scrub, the footpath blinding white sand. Keep alert for a sharp right as the jeep road rises farther up into the sandhill, where the trail leaves the jeep road

to climb up through the turkey oaks. Don't be surprised to flush a turkey or a covey of quail as you kick through crunchy fallen turkey oak leaves. When you reach the scrub-jay sign, you've hiked 3.1 miles.

Over the next mile, be especially alert, as the trail makes many sudden twists and turns on and off jeep roads. As you walk along a broad, sandy arc between clumps of saw palmetto, notice how the sand is covered with crispy silver lichen, *Cladonia prostrata*. If you pour a little water on it, it will unfold and become light green. Look closely for winding tracks through the sand, the telltale trail of the Florida sand skink. The only sand-swimming lizard in North America, the sand skink actually swims just under the surface of the sand. Atrophied limbs and a transparent lid over its eyes help it to move freely. An endangered species that prefers rosemary scrub, the skink is found only in Central Florida, from the

Tiger Creek Preserve

Lake Wales Ridge north to the Ocala National Forest. Don't be surprised to see a sand skink or two in motion as you hike—but they do notice your footfalls, and they will burrow quickly for cover.

After 6 miles, you return to the HIGHLANDS LOOP sign. Turn left to retrace your path back to the trailhead. Be especially careful to not miss the sharp right turn after you walk through the second bayhead, since the trail immediately turns off the jeep road and into the woods. By 7.1 miles, you've returned to the original HIGHLANDS LOOP sign at the trail junction with the Highlands Trail and the Patrick Creek Loop. Turn left, following the orange blazes back through the pine flatwoods and scrub to the parking lot, for a total hike of 7.9 miles.

DIRECTIONS

Follow US 27 south from Lake Wales to CR 640 east. CR 640 turns into SR 17, passing through Babson Park. Two miles south, turn left on North Lake Moody Road, then left again on Murray Road. The road plunges downhill through orange groves and comes to a DEAD END sign at Pfundstein Road. Turn left.

CONTACT

The Nature Conservancy
222 South Westmonte Drive
Suite 300
Altamonte Springs, FL 32714
863-635-7506
www.nature.org/florida

CCC-era swinging bridge over the Hillsborough River

32

James E. Grey Preserve

Total distance (circuit): 1.3 miles

Hiking time: 1 hour

Habitats: river bluff, scrub, palm hammock

Trailhead coordinates (lat-lon):
28.236561, -82.700258

Maps: USGS 7½' Elfers; Park map at kiosk

Admission: Free

Hours: Sunrise–sunset

In an urban corridor surrounded by modern-day subdivisions, a tiny patch of rural Florida exists down a bumpy one-lane limerock road. A handful of homes along a palm-lined waterway hearken back to a gentler time in New Port Richey, before the march of residential construction smothered farms and ranches. Hidden amid it all is James E. Grey Preserve, a quiet rural breather along the Pithlachascotee River, known locally as the Cotee. An extensive boardwalk follows the sinuous path of the Cotee, creating the well-shaded Palmetto Loop, which has beautiful overlooks along the river and a large cove on the opposite side. A secondary loop provides a walk through an upland scrub habitat, where roserush and tarflower bloom in abundance.

Start your hike at the first parking area on the left, a circle at the canoe launch. A large kiosk showcases the park map and points you in the right direction, headed down a broad jeep road through the scrub forest to start the first of two loops in the park, the Palmetto Loop. In summer, fragrant tarflower blooms add a splash of color to the otherwise crispy forest, which runs right up to the edge of the floodplain forest along the Pithlachascotee (also called "Cotee" in these parts) River. You quickly reach a YOU ARE HERE sign with map and a picnic shelter just beyond it. The boardwalk starts here; turn left to follow it. It's a sturdy structure, built to withstand heavy flooding, and it quickly swings out through the floodplain forest to follow the river channel, providing a view of a sluggish waterway and a cove framed by oak branches.

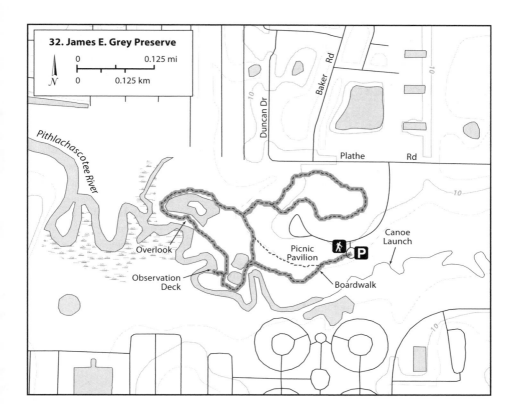

The boardwalk leaves the cove and continues meandering through a dense palm hammock, where songbirds fill the air with their calls. You can still see the river through a screen of trees to your left, with a few residences in view on the far shore. There is a break in the boardwalk at 0.1 mile, on the left, with a trail taking off into the forest. Stay on the boardwalk, and you'll come up to a lake on the right, with the Cotee remaining in your left. When you cross the bridge, it's obvious that the two connect—the lake is a cove off the river, and a rather large one, lined by lush palm hammocks. The boardwalk continues to wind along the waterway, well-shaded by cabbage palms, with glimpses of water from both sides. With all of the water surrounding

you, there's always a nice breeze, making this a cooler-than-average walk for a summer day.

After 0.3 mile, a side boardwalk leads to an observation deck—don't miss it! The setting is spectacular, with a panorama of the wild river shorelines. It's hard to believe you're in the middle of New Port Richey. Returning to the main boardwalk, turn left. The boardwalk ends, depositing you on a berm surrounded by a forest with ferns thickly carpeting its floor. You're leaving the river now, as the trail keeps close to the shore of the cove on the right. An opening on the right with a bench provides a quiet place to sit and watch herons picking their way through the shallows.

Still in deep shade, the trail narrows, and

Helpful kiosk along the trail system

the footpath becomes gravel. Glimpses of the cove are less frequent, but you can still see it through openings in the forest. Might that shimmer in the water be a manatee? The footpath broadens again, back to the width of a jeep trail, as you approach the sign for the Upper Trail at 0.6 mile. Turn left to explore this loop, which focuses on the upland scrub forest near the river and offers two benches for resting. Pale pink roserush blooms in summer amid the grasses. Bear left at the loop junction and follow the wide bark chip path as it leads you into the shade of mature sand live oaks. The trail follows what looks like an old road, veering right as it leaves the bark chips to loop around. A Florida box turtle makes its way across the trail, its pattern of radiating gold stripes on a black shell shimmering in the sun. A subspecies of the Eastern box turtle, the Florida box turtle is found only in Florida. Besides its distinctive shell pattern, it differs from other Eastern box turtles in that each turtle only has three toes on its hind feet. Just like the gopher tortoise, the Florida box turtle is a threatened species due to habitat destruction.

Transitioning to sandhills, the footpath re-joins the bark chips as you're surrounded by turkey oaks that offer little shade, and the trail winds its way through this open, sunny habitat where you'll notice gopher tortoise burrows along the way. By 0.9 mile, you reach the end of the loop. Continue straight to rejoin the main trail—the Palmetto Loop—and take a left. You're back on a jeep road with very little shade, and this leads straight back to the trailhead, if you prefer to be direct. Why not savor the river on your way out? An unmarked side trail at 1.1 miles tempts. Dive into the cool shade of the palm hammock, and you're back along the edge of the cove again, approaching the opening in the boardwalk. Step up and return to the boardwalk. Turn left to retrace your approach through the floodplain forest back to the boardwalk's end at the picnic pavilion. Turn right to exit, completing a 1.3-mile hike.

DIRECTIONS

Take SR 54 east from US 19 in New Port Richey for 2.7 miles to Rowan Road. Turn left and drive north 1.6 miles, past the light at Trouble Creek Road, to the turnoff for Plathe Road on the left. Plathe Road quickly turns into a one-lane limerock road through a residential area. Never fear, you're in the right place! The turnoff for the park is rather obvious, and it's on your left after 0.3 mile on the left. Drive in and park in the first parking area on the left to start your hike.

CONTACT

James E. Grey Preserve
City of New Port Richey
6938 Plathe Road
New Port Richey, FL 34653
727-841-4560
www.cityofnewportrichey.org

33

Hillsborough River State Park

Total distance (three circuits, one round-trip): 8.4 miles

Hiking time: 4 hours

Habitats: bluff forest, floodplain forest, freshwater wetlands, hardwood hammock, pine flatwoods

Trailhead coordinates (lat-lon): 28.149129, -82.227341

Maps: USGS 7½' Thontonassa; Hillsborough River State Park map; Florida Trail Association Map Central 3

Admission: $2 pedestrian/bicyclist, $4 single motorist, $6 carload

Hours: 8 AM–sunset

One of Florida's oldest state parks, Hillsborough River State Park offers something you just don't run across every day in Florida—rapids. Limestone boulders create a mild stretch of scenic whitewater along the Hillsborough River, which flows out of Green Swamp on its lazy way to Tampa Bay. The soothing sound of burbling water is enough for any hiker to make the trek out to Thonotosassa, northeast of Tampa, to enjoy this state park.

If you are interested in backpacking out to a quiet primitive campsite along this hike, register at the entrance station before hitting the trail with your pack. The park's two full-service campgrounds—Rivers Edge and Hammock Circle—cater to tent and trailer campers.

Turn right onto the one-way loop road that circles the park. After passing the interpretive center, stop at the next parking lot (parking lot #2) with the sign NATURE TRAIL. Start your hike here, passing the PRAYER OF THE WOODS sign, and enter the forest under a canopy of tall live oaks, pignut hickory, laurel oak, and cabbage palms. Oaks are the dominant tree along the river, with surprisingly large and ancient live oaks along some of the trails. The Native Americans who called these woods home dubbed the area *Locksa Apoka*, the place for eating acorns.

This hike links together three riverside trails—the River Rapids Nature Trail, the Baynard Trail, and the Florida Trail—to create a loop out and back along the river and its surrounding habitats. You can vary the length of the loop according to your interest and time.

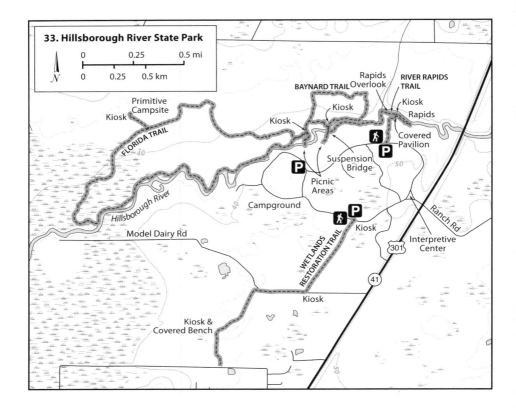

33. Hillsborough River State Park

0   0.25   0.5 mi

0   0.25   0.5 km

Primitive Campsite

Kiosk

FLORIDA TRAIL

40

Hillsborough River

Model Dairy Rd

Kiosk & Covered Bench

Baynard Trail

Rapids Overlook

Kiosk

Suspension Bridge

Picnic Areas

Campground

WETLANDS RESTORATION TRAIL

Kiosk

RIVER RAPIDS TRAIL

Kiosk

Rapids

Covered Pavilion

50

Kiosk

Ranch Rd

Interpretive Center

301

41

Kiosk

A fourth trail, the Wetlands Restoration Trail, is accessed from a separate trailhead.

RIVER RAPIDS NATURE TRAIL

Start by following the River Rapids Nature Trail, a broad and well-maintained interpretive trail ideal for all members of the family. At the first trail junction, a trail comes in from the left. Continue straight, crossing a small bridge over one of the river's side channels, lined with saw palmettos. The sound of rushing water fills your ears. When you reach the log Civilian Conservation Corps shelter at 0.2 mile, walk over to the rapids overlook. The dark, tannic water tumbles over dark red and black boulders, outcrops of Suwannee limestone, creating a small series of rapids. A

striking bald cypress rises from its roots in a rocky island, its trunk and branches furry with air plants, primarily wild pine. As water rushes over the rocks, frothy bubbles float downstream. Swimming is not permitted in the river—the park boasts a half-acre swimming pool near the concession area—but you'll see canoes and kayaks headed downstream and families fishing along lazy bends in the river.

Turn left and follow the trail downstream, past larger islands with bald cypress and royal ferns. A large Florida cooter suns on the exposed trunk of a drowned cabbage palm. Since the Rapids Trail is the oldest trail in the park, it swings back and forth out onto observation decks along the river, bypassing spots where decks once stood, but now only pilings remain. Meandering under bay magnolias, pignut hickory, and swamp tupelo, the trail passes under an arching live oak thick with wild pine and resurrection fern. At 0.3 mile, you'll cross a high boardwalk over one of the Hillsborough River's many floodplain cypress swamps. This one is tucked into a bend in the river. During periods of high water, these elevated floodplain swamps act as side channels for the river; the receding floodwaters leave behind enough water in each depression to support a small forest of bald cypresses. Stop at the next observation platform to take a look at the now-quiet surface of the river. A blue heron skims above the water, its massive wingspan nearly half the width of the river. After you pass a live oak with a trunk full of holes—an ideal hideout for raccoons—numerous unofficial trails beat their way through the forest above the river. Follow the most distinct path past some wooden benches that look like they date back to the park's opening in 1936. After 0.6 mile, turn right and cross the lofty suspension bridge that spans the river. The bridge bounces underfoot as you walk.

BAYNARD TRAIL

On the north side of the river, a marker indicates the start of the Baynard Trail, named for Oscar E. Baynard, the first superintendent of the park. Turn right, passing a floodplain cypress forest on the left. Curving to the right, the trail follows the river upstream. Hickory trees drop their pignuts on the ground. A long black racer slithers across the path into a saw palmetto thicket. At 0.8 mile, the trail turns away from the river, heading into a tall canopy of cabbage palms and hickory trees, past small groups of wild oranges. There are many side trails created by bicycles. Stay with the distinct path. Roots appear in the sand underfoot as you take a sharp left. A few cypress knees poke out of the footpath. After a

mile, the trail rises slightly, paralleling a fence on the right. Wild coffee grows under tall water oaks. Past 1.3 miles, the trail takes a sharp left and becomes grassy underfoot, with a sparse canopy of hickory and sweetgum overhead.

FLORIDA TRAIL

Start your walk on the Florida Trail at 1.5 miles, turning right at the FT sign. This is your bailout point—if you need to cut your hike short, follow the picnic area sign over to the bridge. The Florida Trail starts with blue blazes past a swampy hollow full of cypress trees. Yaupon holly grows to the right. Reaching the loop trail sign, turn right. For the next 3.3 miles, you'll be following the orange blazes. Passing a low swampy area on the left, the trail continues through sweetgum and hickory forest before edging around the massive base of a pond cypress. Watch carefully for a gopher tortoise burrow with a roof—it hides under a moss-covered hollow log on the right. Overgrown in places, the trail is rough underfoot. Hickory and cypress form the sparse canopy for a while, and then are replaced by ancient live oaks. The dead limb of one tree arches over the trail, green with resurrection fern. In this damp, nutrient-rich environment, many of the ferns grow unusually large.

After crossing a small bridge at 1.9 miles, the trail wanders through tall cabbage palms, their trunks aglow with green and yellow sphagnum moss. A slight elevation drop changes the character of the forest. Sweetgum and elm take over, and the ground underfoot becomes very damp, rich dark soil busy with pennywort. Crossing another bridge at 2.3 miles, the trail turns sharply left to follow the creek through a palm hammock. Notice the thin blades of shoelace fern cascading down the trunk of a cabbage palm at the end of the bridge. Dark but clear, the

The Hillsborough Rapids

KEVIN MIMS

tannic creek moves placidly toward the Hillsborough River. Roots and muck make walking rough as you approach the sign for the primitive campsite. To access the campsite, follow the blue blazed trail off to the right for 0.1 mile. Continuing on the main trail, the elevation rises, resulting in white sand underfoot as you walk through a mixed oak and palm hammock. Blanketed in ferns, one solitary live oak on the left rises more than 100 feet high. Dropping back into the dark soil of the palm hammock, notice the bright orange polypores on rotting logs. Crossing a bridge at 2.9 miles, the trail continues under low cabbage palms arching overhead. Sunlight glints off the glossy leaves of a southern magnolia. Watch for armadillo holes hidden around fallen logs. As the trail turns back toward the river, you'll come across one of the largest live oaks you've ever seen, a tree that is easily several centuries old. The base is a mass of moss-covered knobs, and the center has a hollow more than 20 feet tall. Climb up the knobs and peer inside. Veering around another grand live oak, the trail emerges on a sand bluff above the river at 3.4 miles.

The remainder of the Florida Trail loop follows the Hillsborough River upstream. The constant proximity to the river makes this a delightful hike as the trail winds through forests of live oak and cabbage palm, hickory and sweetgum, water oak and holly. The limbs of many old live oaks arch down to the water, nearly 20 feet below. The trail dips in and out of small hollows created as tributaries drain into the river, winding through a grove of sugarberry trees with shiny dark leaves. .

After veering away from the river to skirt a floodplain cypress swamp, the trail heads back through a corridor of saw palmetto to a bridge over a tributary, at 3.9 miles. The footpath turns to bright white sand as you round the river bend. Dry floodplain channels parallel the river to your left; the trail walks a narrow high path between the two. Crossing another small bridge, you'll clamber up tree roots to the next sand bluff. The canopy opens up overhead as the forest turns to young hickory and water oak. At the end of the next bridge, sword ferns edge along the left side of the trail. Dropping down a hill at 4.3 miles, the trail crosses a bridge into another sugarberry grove. Watch the details along the trail—tiny seafoam-colored star-shaped lichens growing on the trunks of cabbage palms, and fungus as orange as the trail's blazes. When you start to hear the shouts of children playing in the distant swimming pool, you'll soon see the picnic area on the other side of the river.

Coming to the end of the loop at 4.8 miles, pass the sign and head straight down the blue-blazed trail to the junction with the Baynard Trail. Turn right and follow the trail past the floodplain cypress swamp to the river's edge. The bridge in front of you leads to the picnic area, restrooms, and swimming pool—take a side trip if you need it. Your return loop to your car continues on this side of the river. Turn left on the Bayard Trail, following the river upstream. The trail runs close to the bluff's edge, where you can see small rapids sending tiny bubbles downstream. As you climb down and across a small stream channel, you'll hear the sound of running water. The trail pops out at the suspension bridge; you've walked 5.1 miles so far. Turn right and cross the bridge.

You have two choices to return to the parking area—take a different route through the floodplain cypress swamp by heading straight into the clearing and turning onto the trail on the left, or return the way you came in, along the River Rapids Nature Trail. Unless you're simply looking for variety, stick to the river. It's a prettier trail, and you'll have one last chance to savor the river's unique rapids.

Reaching the rapids overlook, take a quick out-and-back hike (0.2 mile) upriver on an older trail that leads up a stretch of rapids where water pours through a small chute—one of Florida's few natural waterfalls. Turn around at the old stone retention wall, built by the CCC. Beyond this point, the trail becomes dangerously overgrown and indistinct.

Back at the rapids overlook, turn around and hike past the CCC shelter to follow the trail back to the parking area. Two white-tailed deer cross your path as the sun drops beneath the canopy of oaks. Reaching the parking lot, you've hiked 6 miles.

WETLANDS RESTORATION TRAIL

With a separate trailhead from the rest of the trail system, the Wetlands Restoration Trail is an out-and-back trek through low-lying habitats starting more than 3/4 of the way around the one-way drive through the park. Pull off at the trailhead and start your hike. This is a multiuse trail that simply goes out on an old road to the park boundary and back, so the main reason to walk along it is for birding. Unlike the other trails in the park, this one is mostly in the sun, so be sure to have your sunscreen and hat at hand. The trail is a broad jeep road with benches along the route. Start at the kiosk and walk through the wet flatwoods. Cabbage palms rise tall overhead.

At a large intersection, turn right, passing a kiosk at 0.4 mile. The trail continues along the park's fence line under a power line. The sand gets deep underfoot. At the next fork, keep left. An arrow points to the left, along with a fort symbol. Dog fennel grows tall in open prairies dotted with Florida myrtle. The trail passes cypress domes on the right and left before reaching a covered bench with a kiosk beneath a large oak after a mile. The kiosk goes into detail about how the surrounding landscape was reclaimed from the former Modal Dairy Farm. The Wetlands Restoration Trail ends after 1.2 miles at the park boundary at a LEAVING HILLSBOROUGH RIVER STATE PARK sign, but the trail continues, connecting to other mountain biking trails throughout adjoining Flatwoods Park. Turn around and walk back to the trailhead for a 2.4-mile round-trip.

DIRECTIONS

From I-75, take exit 265, Temple Terrace (Fowler Avenue/SR 582), heading east to the intersection with US 301. Follow US 301 north 10.5 miles to the park entrance on the left.

CONTACT

Hillsborough River State Park
15402 US 301 North
Thonotosassa, FL 33592
813-987-6771
www.floridastateparks.org/hillsboroughriver

34

Lettuce Lake Park

Total distance (circuit): 1.8 miles

Hiking time: 1 hour

Habitats: floodplain forest, oak hammock, pine flatwoods, scrubby flatwoods, freshwater marsh, cypress domes

Trailhead coordinates (lat-lon): 28.074253, -82.374654

Maps: USGS 7½' Sulphur Springs; Park map

Admission: $2 per vehicle

Hours: 8 AM–7:30 PM, spring and summer; 8 AM–5:30 PM, fall and winter.

Black as midnight, sluggish as molasses, the Hillsborough River laps at the bases of bald cypresses, trapped between the trees in ponds clogged with water lettuce. Creaky weathered boardwalks span this backwater, where in times of high water the river cuts itself off at a bend, forming a vast treed swamp–Lettuce Lake. Along the network of boardwalks through the swamp, canopied and open benches enable you to sit and watch the wildlife. Limpkins plumb the shallows for apple snails, while turtles sun themselves on fallen logs. Canoeists ply the tangle of passageways through the swamp forest.

Located at the north end of Tampa, Lettuce Lake Park protects 240 acres along the Hillsborough River, providing urban residents a quiet spot to hike, bike, and picnic along the river. An open grassy space in the center of the park is ideal for Frisbee or volleyball and has a playground for the kids. Before you hike, stop at the Audubon Resource Center, accessed by the trail on the opposite side of the parking lot. Browse through their resource library, examine the natural history exhibits, and take a look in the nature store. Pick up a copy of *Lettuce Lake Park: A Companion Field Guide,* containing the park map and information about wildlife you'll see along your walk.

Start your hike by following the weathered boardwalk down past the picnic tables and into the blackwater cypress swamp. Scattered red maples show off crimson and gold leaves in the fall. The tall purple blooms of water hyacinths catch your attention. A white heron intently watches the water for the

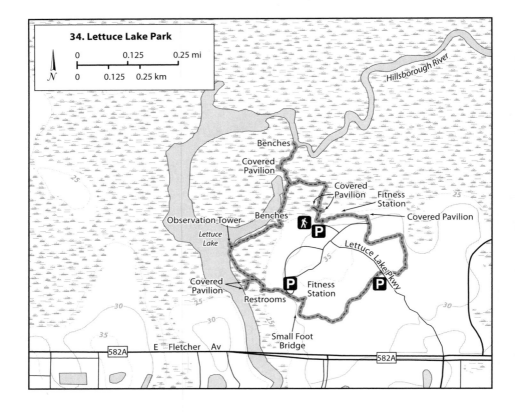

telltale shimmer of fish. Water bugs glide across the surface. At the T intersection, turn right. The boardwalk slips past massive bald cypresses, where duckweed forms a thick blanket over the swamp. You pass a side trail, a boardwalk leading to a canopied bench with a clear view of open waters of Lettuce Lake. Pause to take in the scene, watching a great blue heron soar overhead. A cottonmouth moccasin swims past, iridescent black scales rippling against the dark water.

Back on the main trail, notice how cinnamon and marsh ferns take advantage of rotting logs to gain a foothold in the slower waters of the swamp. The boardwalk ends at a platform overlooking the narrows of the Hillsborough River, a fast-flowing channel

through the cypresses. As a canoe slips silently by, a flock of white ibises pick through the high ground between cypress knees, searching for insects. Turn around and return to the T intersection, heading straight. The boardwalk swings out along Lettuce Lake, providing a breezy walk along the open water, then ducks back under the cypresses. Look closely for swamp lilies in the shallows, with their broad grassy leaves and showy strap-shaped white blooms. White-tailed deer seek out the tasty blooms, just like they munch on flower beds in suburban gardens.

When you reach a junction where a cypress is encircled by the boardwalk, turn right to follow the river. At 0.8 mile, you reach the observation tower, climbing five stories high for a scenic view of the floodplain forest and the Hillsborough River, looking down the entire length of Lettuce Lake. An osprey swoops past, bass clutched tightly in its talons. The boardwalk continues past the junction of Lettuce Lake and the river, sweeping away from the water and into the dense stand of bald cypress. Where the boardwalk ends, two short boardwalks take off to the right, both leading to picnic tables along the river. Follow the sand path through a live oak hammock up to its junction with the paved 1.5-mile loop trail (popular with joggers, in-line skaters, and bikers), in front of the restrooms and water fountain. You've walked a mile. Turn right on the paved trail, following it into the oak hammock, past an American beautyberry flaunting its brilliant clusters of purple berries.

Turn right at the NATURE TRAIL sign at the split-rail fence, entering the pine flatwoods. Since the trail wanders along the edge of the park, traffic sounds from Fletcher Avenue carry into the woods. Slash pines tower overhead, dropping a deep carpet of pine needles onto the footpath. Stay to the main trail as you pass a side trail on the left, walking into a shady oak hammock with a dense understory of saw palmetto. Palm warblers scurry between breaks in the saw palmetto, wagging their tails and displaying their yellow breast feathers.

The trail emerges into scrubby flatwoods, open and sunny. Winged sumacs display deep red leaves in the fall. At 1.3 miles, you rejoin the paved trail. Turn right, crossing the park entrance road. Soon after, the nature trail ducks off to the left, into a dense forest of pines and saw palmetto, dropping down into a low area where young cypresses are

Oak Hammock

KEVIN MIMS

Lettuce Lake

forming a new cypress dome. The trail climbs back up under spreading live oaks and slash pines. Passing a loop trail off to the left, continue straight, making a right at the next fork. You emerge into a parking lot. Cross the parking lot and road to rejoin the paved trail. Make a left, walking along the edge of the cypress swamp to return to where your car is parked, for a total hike of 1.8 miles.

DIRECTIONS

From I-75, take exit 266, Temple Terrace, and follow Fletcher Avenue 0.8 mile west to the park's entrance on the right, Lettuce Lake Park Road. Follow the entry road to a T intersection, making a right, then the first left into the parking area. The hiking trail starts here, a wheelchair-accessible boardwalk between the picnic tables.

CONTACT

Lettuce Lake Park
6920 East Fletcher Avenue
Tampa FL 33637
813-987-6204
www.hillsboroughcounty.org/parks

35

John Chesnut Sr. Park

Total distance (circuit): 2.7 miles

Hiking time: 1.5 hours

Habitats: bayhead, floodplain forest, freshwater marsh, hardwood hammock, pine flatwoods

Trailhead coordinates (lat-lon)
South Loop: 28.085158, -82.702635
North Loop: 28.096832, -82.709669

Maps: USGS 7½' Oldsmar; Pinellas County Parks map

Admission: Free

Hours: 7 AM–sunset

With its extensive boardwalks along the shores of Lake Tarpon, John Chesnut Sr. Park provides Pinellas County residents with a popular place to picnic, fish, watch birds, or just amble along the trails and enjoy the cool breeze off the lake. With most of Lake Tarpon's shores heavily developed and inaccessible to the general public, this is one of the few waterfronts along the lake that remains in its natural state—a crowded floodplain forest of tall cypresses. Although it only encompasses 255 acres, the park manages to provide an excellent urban hiking experience. If you bring a picnic lunch, you have your choice of enjoying it in a secluded cypress forest or along the lakeshore.

John Chesnut Sr. Park sits on the southeast shore of Lake Tarpon and offers public boat ramp access as well as several large picnic pavilions that groups can reserve in advance. Dogs are welcome. Except for the observation tower, the boardwalk trails and the Peggy Park Trail are wheelchair-accessible.

SOUTH LOOP/PEGGY PARK NATURE TRAIL

Named after a local wildlife officer who was killed in the line of duty, the interpretive Peggy Park Nature Trail introduces you to the floodplain forest along Lake Tarpon and the banks of Brooker Creek. Pick up an interpretive guide at the trailhead. Starting off in a lush pine flatwoods, the trail winds through stands of stately slash pine with abundant cinnamon ferns at their bases. One of the easier ferns to identify, the cinnamon fern sprouts a prominent frilly cinnamon-colored frond above its

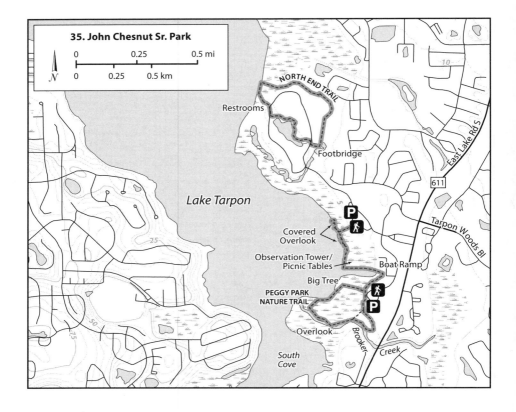

35. John Chesnut Sr. Park

0   0.25   0.5 mi

0   0.25   0.5 km

NORTH END TRAIL

Restrooms

Footbridge

Lake Tarpon

East Lake Rd S

611

Tarpon Woods Bl

Covered Overlook

Observation Tower/ Picnic Tables

Boat Ramp

Big Tree

PEGGY PARK NATURE TRAIL

Overlook

Brooker Creek

South Cove

---

greenery. This showy fertile frond contains its active spores, ready for germination—unlike most species of ferns, which bear their spores on the undersides of their fronds.

The trail rises up onto a boardwalk through the floodplain forest of cypresses. One stately bald cypress towers well above the rest. Estimated to be 230 years old, it still doesn't match the size and breadth of cypresses described by naturalist William Bartram during his travels through Florida in 1774. Older cypresses like this one have noticeably deep buttresses at their bases, helping to hold the tree straight and tall in marshy ground. Of the trees that still existed in Bartram's time, before cypress logging decimated Florida's grand giants, Bartram wrote that the but-

tresses, "in full grown trees, project out on every side to such a distance that several men might easily hide themselves in the hollows between."

Tannic water, stained to the color of tea by the leaves of oaks, red maples, swamp bay and sweetgum, flows sluggishly underneath the boardwalk, feeding clusters of giant leather fern, some exceeding 8 feet in height. You feel as if you are walking through a prehistoric forest. Elephant ears and royal ferns cluster between the bases of the cypresses. The boardwalk swings left as it reaches the edge of Lake Tarpon, providing your first glimpse of the dark, undulating surface of the lake. Reeds protect the curving shoreline. Soft splashes fill the air as the lake gently laps

---

against the cypress trees. A deep hollow trunk provides a good home for a family of raccoons. Watch out for mooching gray squirrels along this section of the boardwalk; they've been habituated to human presence, and will follow you along the railing, begging for a handout.

Veering left away from the lake, the boardwalk curves through the darkness of the floodplain forest. Both pond cypresses and bald cypresses grow in this part of the swamp. Notice the difference between their needles. Those of the pond cypress sweep upward from the stem, creating a wispy effect. The needles of the bald cypress spread flat like a hawk's feather.

The boardwalk meets Brooker Creek near its discharge into Lake Tarpon. When the boardwalk ends, a trail continues along the placid creek, with many opportunities to you to sit on benches along its shore and watch

for fish and turtles. Daisy fleabane spills over grapevines on the far shore. A tufted titmouse flutters in and out of a clump of saw palmetto. Crushed white shells create a crunchy footpath under the cabbage palms, slash pines, and live oaks—look for giant bromeliads overhead. A johnboat putters by; the creek provides access to Lake Tarpon for private boaters putting in farther upstream.

At 0.5 mile, you reach a trail junction with a sign that reads SHORT WAY PARKING AREA pointing to the left. Turn right to continue following Brooker Creek through the cypresses, slash pines, and gnarled oaks. As the road noise increases, the trail turns left, away from the creek, then left again to loop back toward the trailhead, entering a forest with a tall canopy of laurel oaks and slash pines. Joining up with the shortcut trail at 0.7 mile, turn right along the crunchy shell path, passing several picnic tables as you stroll

Observation decks along Lake Tarpon

through the narrow band of oak hammock. At 0.8 mile, you reach the trailhead. Return your interpretive guide to the box.

Continue your hike by walking to the Lookout Tower Trail. Walk clockwise away from the Peggy Park trailhead along the edge of the parking lot until you come to a break in the woods, an unmarked trail. Follow this path through the oak hammock past pavilion 1 to join up with a pebbly path of Chattahoochee stone, curving over toward the boat ramp. Make a left and walk across the top of the boat ramp to reach the other side; turn left onto the stone path. At 1 mile, the boardwalk starts. Go straight at the trail junction, following along the edge of the channel. Parents, mind your children—there is no railing! Benches enable you to sit and ponder the channel, and several short boardwalks lead off into the cypresses on the right to elevated picnic tables, where you can enjoy a private lunch in the middle of a swamp.

As you reach where the channel meets the lake, look down. Although the tannic water of Lake Tarpon looks jet black from a distance, when you see it lapping up on the sand in the shallows, the water is clear, cast with a yellow hue. The boardwalk turns left to follow the lake, first coming to the 40-foot-tall observation tower, with five levels of decks. Clamber up to take in the view and the refreshing stiff breeze. Continuing along the lakeshore, the boardwalk sticks to the edge of the floodplain forest. Crimson leaves from red maples flutter down into the water. Short boardwalks lead off to the left to elevated lakeside picnic tables, a great place to sit and watch for wildlife. The third turnoff is perhaps the best, as it overlooks a small bay protected from the main portion of the lake by cattails and reeds. A moorhen emits a raspy screech and flutters its wings as a alligator approaches. Overhead, an osprey lets out a piercing cry.

At the next trail junction, continue straight. The boardwalk leads to more picnic tables, more platforms along the lake, coming to a dead-end after 1.2 miles. Turn around and return to the trail junction; turn left. The boardwalk heads into the cypress swamp, coming to a T intersection. Turn right; the trail to the left leads to the north parking lot. The boardwalk ends, and the trail becomes a footpath of crushed seashells, winding through the cool shade of the cypress swamp. Cinnamon ferns and cypress knees crowd close. As the trail swings to the right, zigzagging back toward the boat ramp, the understory of the cypress swamp becomes a sea of waving ferns. At the T intersection, turn left, retracing your steps back around the boat ramp and pavilion 1 to return to the south parking lot, completing your 1.8-mile hike.

NORTH LOOP

The northern trail in John Chesnut Sr. County Park has no specific name, but it starts within sight of Lake Tarpon at a spot that was once the park's beach. From the marina, follow the park road north 0.7 mile past the dog park and playground. After you cross the bridge, keep left at the fork. The parking area adjoins restrooms and a short boardwalk along the lake at Pavilion 10. The trail starts immediately to the left of the restrooms at a kiosk with interpretive information about exotic species. Follow the crushed-shell footpath, which is immediately behind the floodplain forest and a screen of tall cattails along Lake Tarpon. Soon after you reach the beginning of the boardwalk, there's a short observation deck amid the cattails with a couple of benches, an ideal place for birding, a blind of sorts hidden by natural vegetation. An osprey cries out overhead to its mate.

Returning to the boardwalk, turn left and follow it as it makes a sharp right. The cypress swamp here was likely logged out

Boardwalk along the North Loop

more than 50 years ago, since the cypresses and their knees are rather small in comparison to the ones seen near Brooker Creek. Highly prized because of their resistance to rot, old-growth cypresses were felled and dragged out of forests along lakes and in swamps throughout Florida to be transported to the nearest sawmill. Carved into boards, the giant cypresses became packing crates for the shipment of citrus fruit, supporting the region's primary industry through the 1970s.

Well-shaded by the forest canopy, the boardwalk is long and narrow; it shows its age. Since the southern boardwalks were being replaced as I revisited this park, don't be surprised to find this one widened as well. Cabbage palms and cinnamon ferns grow throughout the understory. The boardwalk ends, becoming a crushed-shell path again. You can see a park road off to the right.

The trail continues along the ecotone, with cypress swamp on the left and pine flatwoods on the right. At 0.2 mile, the next segment of boardwalk begins. It, too, is narrow, wiggling through an intermingled mix of pines and cypress fighting for control of the forest. A bench overlooks a willow marsh with deeper water, where you might see a young alligator drifting across the open water. Frogs kick up a noticeable chorus until a red-shouldered hawk glides in and lands on a low branch.

An overfed squirrel sits on the railing where the boardwalk ends. Avoid temptation and don't feed the wildlife here—and you might have to stomp your feet to chase habituated squirrels away. The trail is once again a crunchy crushed-shell path as you pass a STAY ON TRAIL sign within sight of a neighborhood behind the trees, where a trail comes in from the left. On the right is a marsh that looks like an intentionally created aquatic garden/retention area, now becoming more of a wild wetland. The next boardwalk begins soon after, leading through palms to a bayhead, where more frogs kick up a fuss. The blooms of buttonbush look like miniature fireworks. A yellow-crowned night heron succeeds at stalking a frog in the shallows. Older cypress knees rise from the shallows, including one that looks very much like a planter covered in colorful bromeliads.

After a half mile, the boardwalk ends within sight of a long, linear man-made waterway. Cross the path and take the bridge over the small canal. This is one of the many "islands" providing picnic spots in this part of the park. Turn right to walk along the canal. Turn right again and cross the canal on the wooden park road bridge. Turn left near the PAVILION 13 sign and start following the waterway along the pine duff on the edge of the shoreline, beneath a stand of extremely tall longleaf pines. Note the BEWARE OF ALLIGATORS sign and watch your step! A bench swing provides a perch and a resting point. Continue around this man-made pond, fol-lowing the shoreline, until an obvious path veers to the right past a picnic spot and you reach the park road at Pavilion 10. Cross the road, and you're back at the parking area by the restrooms, after a 0.9-mile walk.

DIRECTIONS

From the junction of SR 60 (Gulf to Bay) and McMullen Booth Road (CR 611) in Clearwater, drive north on McMullen Booth Road. Four miles north of Safety Harbor, it crosses CR 752 (Tampa Road) in Oldsmar on an overpass. Continue north on CR 611, which now changes its name to East Lake Road. Continue another 2 miles. The park entrance is on the left just after you cross Brooker Creek. Once you're inside the park, follow the road to the South Parking Loop to find the trailhead for the Peggy Park Nature Trail.

CONTACT

John Chesnut Sr. Park
2200 East Lake Road
Palm Harbor, FL 34685
727-669-1951
www.pinellascounty.org/park

36

Honeymoon Island State Park

Total distance (circuit): 2.5 miles

Hiking time: 1.25 hours

Habitats: pine flatwoods, salt marsh, mangrove swamp, coastal hammock

Trailhead coordinates (lat-lon): 28.071667, -82.832267

Maps: USGS 7½' Dunedin; Park map

Admission: $2 pedestrian/bicyclist, $4 individual motorist, $8 carload

Hours: 8 AM–sunset

West of Tampa, the Gulf Coast town of Dunedin evokes a seaside Scottish village, with its narrow streets, colonial-style townhouses, vibrant shade trees, and eclectic art galleries and eateries. It's only when the flocks of green monk parakeets flutter overhead that you remember you're virtually in the tropics. Escapees from birdcages, the monk parakeets fill the void of North America's only native parakeet, the Carolina Parakeet, which was driven to extinction in the 1920s.

Since Dunedin sits along a bay, its beaches are several miles to the north of town on the former Hog Island, the site of a hog farm in the late 1800s. The island's image took a turn for the better in the 1940s, when a contest in *Life* magazine offered a week in paradise on "Honeymoon Island," where visitors enjoyed the languid seaside life from the doorsteps of their tropical thatched bungalows. The island changed hands several times, but thankfully remained pristine, accessible only by boat until the 1960s. When Dunedin donated its beaches to the state in 1982, the northern tip of the former Hog Island became Honeymoon Island State Park. Beachgoers can enjoy 22 acres of oceanfront or hop the ferryboat to adjoining Caladesi Island State Park (Hike 37) for sparser crowds.

Protected by its own barrier island, a sand spit called Pelican Point, the northern tip of Honeymoon Island guards 80 precious acres of virgin slash pine, a rare commodity in Central Florida. Because of the age and the size of the pines, an osprey rookery—another rare commodity—is going strong in this forest. The

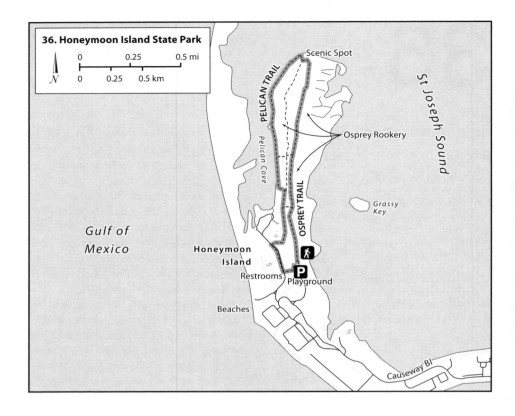

osprey is a large black-and-white raptor, up to 2 feet tall and with a 6-foot wingspan. Although ospreys are found worldwide, the effects of pesticides—particularly DDT—almost wiped out these grand birds in the United States, where they are still considered a threatened species. As runoff from pesticides entered waterways and became concentrated in fish, the osprey's almost purely fish diet resulted in an extremely high concentration of the chemical in the bird. Besides causing the bird to become ill, the DDT caused the osprey's eggshells to be too thin, killing off subsequent generations. After DDT was banned in 1972, the osprey population slowly recovered. Now, you'll see osprey around most waterways in Florida, particu-larly during the cooler months. Some of Florida's ospreys are not permanent residents, but "snowbirds" that migrate south for the winter.

Your hike starts at the OSPREY TRAIL sign. After looking at the map, take the right fork. This is a broad, grassy trail, an easy walking route. Sea grapes cluster under the massive pines, many of which have strange twists and turns to their trunks. Daisies and yarrow nudge up to the trail's edge. As you hike, take the time to look for osprey nests in the tall bare pine snags. Constructed of loose sticks, the nests look like inverted wigs, and can be up to 5 feet in diameter and several feet thick. Although ospreys will build nests in live pines, they prefer the dead trees because of the ease of landing without dropping a fish. After fishing, the osprey returns to its nest to eat.

This is an interpretive trail, with benches, signs, and small kiosks along the way. Stay to the right past the kiosk. A necklace pod tree catches your attention with its bright yellow blossoms and seed cases that look like strings of beads. A salt-tolerant species, the blooms of the necklace pod tree provide the fuel for flocks of Florida's ruby-throated hummingbirds, as they fill up on nectar before migrating for the winter across the Gulf of Mexico to the Yucatan peninsula.

At the half mile marker, keep to the right. A cluster of saw palmettos lifts their strong trunks skyward. An osprey glides overhead. If you want to see osprey tending their young, the best time to enjoy this hike is between December and April. Ospreys mate for life, returning to the same nest every season. The eggs take five weeks to hatch. Although the female sits on the eggs the majority of the time, the male will take over occasionally to give her a break to go fishing. After the chicks hatch, the male cares for the family's needs for the next six weeks. Once the chicks are large enough to be left alone, both parents participate in feeding them until they are old enough to be taught to fly—and fish.

After a mile, you reach a kiosk that explains the osprey's fishing behavior. It's amazing to watch an osprey fishing. They circle 50 feet or more above the water, scanning for prey, and often hover in place as they watch. When an osprey sees its target, it drops from the sky like a rock, hitting the water feetfirst. Specially adapted toes allow it to grasp a squirming fish and hold it firmly as it lifts off.

The junction with the Pelican Trail is just after the kiosk. To enjoy a walk along breezy Pelican Cove, keep to the right. The narrow trail drops down into the mangroves, crossing a jeep trail before it emerges on a picturesque windswept beach. Take a moment to

Osprey nest

sit on the bench and contemplate the serene scene. Turning left, the trail continues through the sea oats along the sparkling blue shallows of the cove. Looking to the left, you see more osprey nests in the trees. You would think the leaping mullet in Pelican Cove would be a great target for the osprey, but not necessarily so. According to John James Audubon's observations in *Birds of America,* the osprey "never attempts to secure its prey in the air," preferring to pluck leaping fish out of the water after they had vanished beneath the surface.

All along the waterfront are benches set as memorials, providing plenty of places to perch and watch birds along the shoreline. Within the next half-mile, black and red mangroves take over the waterfront, forcing the trail several feet back away from the cove, creating damp spots underfoot. Once you've hiked 1.6 miles, you reach two side trails that allow you to retreat to the Osprey Trail in the drier pine flatwoods, if you so choose—a good way out if the trail ahead is badly flooded.

Longleaf pines along the Osprey Trail

Continuing forward on the Pelican Trail, watch for the tiny sand fiddler crabs that scuttle out of harm's way as they sense your footfalls. They're responsible for the thousands of tiny holes on and around the trail. Grasses and flowers adapted to salty environments thrive here, like the red-tipped glasswort, bristly bulrushes, and thick-leaved sea purslane.

At 1.9 miles, the trail climbs uphill, away from the salt marsh, rejoining the western side of the Osprey Trail. Turn right, following the wide jeep trail, as it becomes a soft, sandy track through the pinewoods. Watch for catfaces on several of the larger slash pines. At the next trail junction, there is a PIC-NIC AREA sign. Keep to the left; the trail to the right wanders a short ways out to Pelican Cove. Your trail emerges at the rear of the picnic area, conveniently behind the restrooms. Turn left to cross the boardwalk back to the parking area, completing a loop of 2.5 miles.

DIRECTIONS

To get to Honeymoon Island, drive north from Dunedin along US 19A. Turn left onto Causeway Boulevard (SR 589), and follow it 2.8 miles to the park entrance. After paying your entrance fee, follow the park road to its very end, beyond North Beach. Turn right into the picnic area. Follow the NATURE TRAIL signs to park at the extreme northern end of the picnic area, just after you drive past the trailhead.

CONTACT

Honeymoon Island State Park
#1 Causeway Boulevard
Dunedin, FL 34698
727-469-5942
www.floridastateparks.org/honeymoonisland

37

Caladesi Island State Park

Total distance (circuit): 3 miles

Hiking time: 1.5 hours

Habitats: coastal scrub, palm hammock, pine flatwoods, coastal hammock, salt marsh, mangrove swamp, coastal dunes

Trailhead coordinates (lat-lon): 28.031762, -82.819508

Maps: USGS 7½' Dunedin; Park map

Admission: If arriving directly: $2 per person or $6 per boat. If arriving via ferryboat from Honeymoon Island: $2 pedestrian /bicyclist, $4 single motorist, $6 per carload, plus ferryboat fee of $12 per adult, $6 ages 6–12, under 6 free.

Hours: 8 AM–sunset. However, if you take the ferryboat to the island, you are subject to their return schedule. Pay attention to it so you don't get stranded!

A windswept sentinel off the coast of Dunedin, Caladesi Island enthralls visitors with its remoteness, its quiet beaches, its extensive forests and mangrove swamps. Shifting sands continually redefine the barrier islands in the Gulf of Mexico. In 1921, an unnamed hurricane sliced Hog Island in two, the sands reforming to create Honeymoon Island (Hike 36) to the north, and Caladesi Island to the south. When Hurricane Elena swept through in 1985, the shoreline reshaped again, as Dunedin Pass filled in with sand, joining Caladesi to the greater bulk of Clearwater Beach Island.

To reach the trails of Caladesi Island, you can park in a public lot on Clearwater Beach and walk north on the beachfront nearly 5 miles, crossing the sand-filled pass. However, this makes for a long, tiring day—beach walks may be beautiful, but they're tough on the feet—so most folks visit Caladesi Island by boat. You can kayak the placid waters of St. Joseph Sound from the Dunedin causeway, floating through Hurricane Pass to land on the shore, or ease your private boat up the mangrove-lined channels and into the 99-slip marina. Or do as the majority of visitors do—take the Caladesi Island Connection, a 20-minute ferryboat ride ($12 round-trip) from Honeymoon Island State Park, watching dolphins chase the boat's wake.

Pay your Florida State Parks entrance fee at the Honeymoon Island entrance station—if you walk or boat privately to Caladesi Island, you'll have to pay the fee there—and follow the signs for the ferryboat dock, turning left into the parking area next to the dog

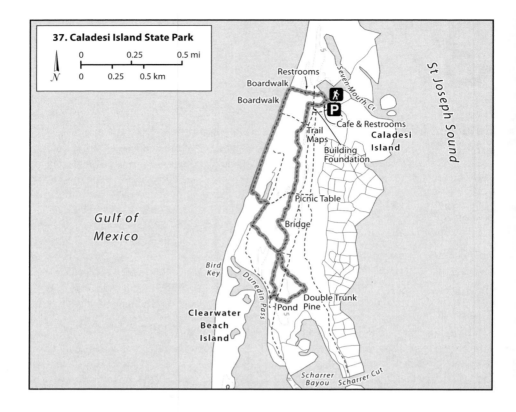

beach. Ferryboats run hourly, but are subject to the whims of nature—check with the park as to the current schedule, and arrive early so you have plenty of time to hike *and* enjoy the beach. Dogs are not permitted on the ferryboat.

On the ferryboat ride, enjoy the sweeping view of Dunedin and the mangrove maze that the boat must navigate to reach the Caladesi Island marina. Belted kingfishers skim the water as your ferryboat pulls into the dock. Don't forget to bring swimming gear! Taking a leisurely hour and a half to explore the trails, you have a couple of hours to laze on the beach or grab a snack at the concession stand before catching the ferryboat back to your car. Although they run through a variety of habitats, the trails are mild enough for sports sandals.

Your hike starts at the kiosk at the dock. Walk up the boardwalk and around the back of the concession stand, following the boardwalk into the beach scrub with its scattered cabbage palms. Southern red cedar, a frequent inhabitant of barrier islands, grows along the trail. Colorful lantana shows off its pink, orange, and yellow blossoms, vying with the bright purple of the American beautyberry bush for attention. Just before you reach a T intersection of boardwalks, look for the ISLAND TRAIL sign. Turn left, passing a concrete building foundation (now full of palms) and an old picnic area with restrooms. The trail meanders into the coastal scrub. Look for a trail guide box on the left. Grab an interpretive guide, which contains a map of the island's three trails. The Island Trail connects you to the Hammock Loop, which encircles the old-growth forests of Caladesi Island, and the Beach Trail, which leads through the salt marshes and mangrove swamps down to the beach.

At 0.4 mile, there is a SHAPED BY FIRE sign on the left. If you visit after a recent burn, you'll see how the scrub forest regenerates itself. It's an especially arid and open environment. Watch for the tracks of lizards and gopher tortoises in the sugar-white sand underfoot, and the tiny, delicate wildflowers of the coastal scrub—blue-eyed grass, white heliotrope, and dayflower. The larger bushes along the trail are groundsel bush, or sea myrtle, *Baccharis halimifolia.* Like red mangroves, these woody-stemmed shrubs have

special glands in their leaves that can remove salt, allowing them to survive in a saline environment. Along this shoreline, salt spray shapes the habitat, since only certain plants can tolerate the occasional coating of salt. The gnarled, windswept oaks farther along this trail are sand live oaks—virtually the only oak found on barrier islands, as their waxy, curved leaves minimize the toxic effects of deposited salt.

When you reach the trail intersection with the Beach Trail at 0.6 mile, in front of a BIRDS OF PREY sign, continue straight across through the palm hammock into the shady pine flatwoods, where cabbage palms and sand live oaks are interspersed among a high canopy of slash pines. The trail veers to the right into a tangled forest where muscadine grapes and greenbrier smothers the understory. With their fronds spilling out of the

Docking the ferryboat

KEVIN MIMS

top of a cabbage palm, a cluster of goldfoot ferns evokes the thought of tropical huts on the beach. As you cross a bridge, the forest closes in. Ascending a small ridge, you reach a spot with a bench overlooking a small man-made pond, dug for mosquito control and stocked with mosquitofish. If you sit long enough, you may catch a fat raccoon wad-dling down to the pond on a fishing expedi-tion.

The trail continues to climb, and tall slash pines dominate the forest. Several pines on the right show the catface scars where visit-ing sailors tapped them for emergency naval stores of turpentine and pine tar. After a mile of hiking, you reach a post with an arrow. Bear right and then turn left to follow the Hammock Loop. The trail follows the edge of the island's high ground. Walk softly along this cathedral of pines, one of Central Florida's last remaining strands of virgin slash pine. Veering down to the left, you catch sight of the glimmering waters of Dunedin Pass. The tang of salt lays heavy in the air. There is a short side trail off to the right at 1.2 miles that leads to a bench overlooking the water. You can see dunes and the sea beyond, where the channel closed shut in 1985.

Returning to the main trail, it crosses a sand road under a power line. An arrow indi-cates where the trail vanishes into the woods, transitioning from pine flatwoods to coastal hammock. Because of the beauty of coastal hammocks—such as the grand old sand live oak along the trail, with its thick branches spreading in all directions—few of them re-main today; most were developed into resi-dential beachfront property. At 1.4 miles, you come to a tannic pond—a natural freshwater spring, the largest source of water on the is-land. When you reach a kiosk in a clearing a little farther on, take a look at the unusual twin pine in the middle of the clearing, a pine with a rare double trunk. The adjoining kiosk ex-

KEVIN MIMS

Interpretive kiosk at the old homestead

plains the story of the island's first European settler, Henry Scharrer, who arrived in 1883 from Switzerland and homesteaded Hog Is-land for 50 years. The discovery of shell im-plements and a burial mound give evidence of earlier human activity, but it is unknown which of Florida's early coastal tribes lived here.

The trail rises through the coastal ham-mock back up into the pine flatwoods, cross-ing the sand road and power line again at 1.6 miles. The footpath narrows, passing through a seasonally wet area, before it completes the Hammock Loop. Turn right at the NATURE TRAIL sign, then make an immediate left onto the Beach Trail. The trail is low and flooded in places, making for a sticky walk through the mucky spots. Black-eyed Susans grow amid the cordgrass. Where the trail veers left, a sprawling prickly pear cactus shows off its bulbous red fruits. Necklace pod trees show off their bright yellow blossoms and strange, bead-like seed cases.

A sign at the 2-mile mark indicates the marina is off to the left, back along the Shortcut Trail. Turn left, crossing over a bridge along a mangrove-lined canal and lagoon. This is a great bird-watching spot. Examine the edges of the lagoon and the mangrove trees closely for Louisiana heron, reddish egret, snowy egrets, and the rare and beautiful roseate spoonbill.

Continue down the trail, and a few minutes later, you're at the beach, walking between the windswept sea oats atop tall sand dunes. Turn right. Clusters of white beach morning glories unfurl their blossoms against the sand. Walk along the water's edge, and you're bound to spy a stingray skimming past, or a horseshoe crab walking along the bottom. Watch the dolphins frolic in the waves, just a hundred feet offshore. If you're not pressed for time, settle down and enjoy the sun, the sand, and the surf, with no high-rise buildings or houses to spoil your view. *This is why people come to Caladesi Island.*

You'll wander a half-mile north along the beach before coming to the first boardwalk inland, across the dunes. It was closed at the time of this hike, so continue on to the second crossover at 2.8 miles. To finish your hiking loop, head up this boardwalk and around the bathhouse, coming to an intersection of boardwalks. Turn right, passing the start of the Island Trail. Retrace your steps back to the concession stand and around it to the ferryboat dock, for a 3-mile hike.

DIRECTIONS

Drive north from Dunedin (several miles north of Clearwater Beach) along US 19A. Turn left onto Causeway Boulevard (SR 589), and follow it 2.8 miles to where it ends by entering Honeymoon Island State Park. Once inside the park, make the first left to the ferryboat parking area for the Caladesi Connection Ferry.

CONTACT

Caladesi Island State Park
#1 Causeway Boulevard
Dunedin, FL 34698
727-469-5918
www.floridastateparks.org/caladesiisland

38

Eagle Lake Park

Total distance (circuit): 3 miles

Hiking time: 1.5 hours

Habitats: freshwater marsh, lakeshore, oak hammock, pine flatwoods

Trailhead coordinates (lat-lon): 27.930247, -82.763418

Maps: USGS 7½' St. Petersburg; Park map at trailhead kiosk

Admission: Free

Hours: 7:30 AM–sunset

In the mid-1800s, settlers came to this pine-forested peninsula west of Tampa Bay and staked out homesteads for ranching and citrus groves. Pinellas County became known for its citrus industry, which faded out after the post–World War II land rush, when servicemen stationed in the region poured in to purchase affordable housing in this tropical setting, housing that was built atop the agricultural base that had sustained the county for so long.

Largo's original nickname was "Citrus City," and it was in large part due to the Taylor family. Born in March 1871, John Stansel Taylor is known as the "father of Pinellas County." He was a substantial landowner and citrus grower, the president of the Florida Citrus Exchange, and the first state senator to serve from this county. The Taylor groves and packing plant sustained the local economy for many decades, particularly through the Great Depression. For years, I'd see these remaining orange groves as I drove from Belleair to US 19 and marvel that there was still a hint of the past remaining in the midst of this urban area.

Eagle Lake Park, the first new Pinellas County Park to open in the past decade, celebrates the legacy of the Taylor family's groves, with an 18-acre remnant of the citrus grove to walk through, picnic pavilions that look like pole barns, and an adorable playground with a citrus grove theme. Not all of the 163 acres was given over to citrus, so there are natural habitats as well, including oak hammocks, natural lakes, and restored marshes. Old-growth longleaf pine

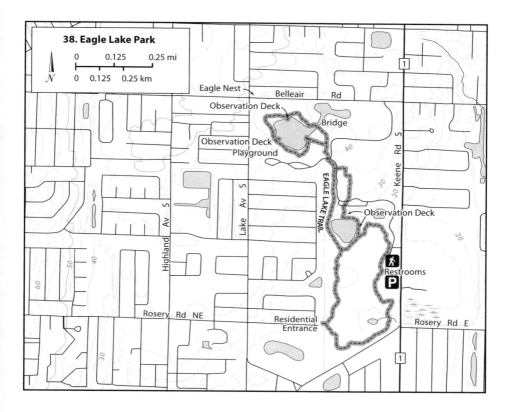

38. Eagle Lake Park

towers over many of the trails.

Most of the trail system is paved. While I generally don't include paved trails in the "50 Hikes" series, Eagle Lake Park is impressive and diverse enough to rate an exception. This is truly an urban forest, so if it makes urban folks more comfortable to walk through the woods on pavement, I'm glad they're getting outdoors. The entire trail system can be bicycled as well as hiked, which makes it great for families with small children and people with limited mobility. This hike describes one of dozens of possible routes you can take through the park's extensive trail system, so it's possible to tailor the length of the hike to your needs.

Starting from the parking area near the dog park, follow the paved path to the right of the restrooms and through the oak hammock. After you pass the main entrance of the park on the right, turn left on the first side trail, which leads to a boardwalk around a marshy slough. Turn left again to cross another slough flowing between the marshes. A green heron picks its way across the green surface of the water within sight of a snowy egret. Tall longleaf pines—the reason Pinellas County has its name—rise well above from patches of forest.

This trail emerges on the outer loop, facing a forest of young longleaf pines. Turn right. In the early morning hours, spiderwebs sparkle with dew as they stretch between the pine needles. Following the perimeter of the

Ducklings in the marsh

property, the trail works its way along a pond on the right. A natural surface path comes in from the left. Elderberry shows off its white blossoms.

A fork in the path at 0.5 mile is at the edge of another parking area. Continue straight, passing the parking area and its picnic pavilions, with the remains of the old orange grove off in the distance. The trail jogs to the left, slipping around a half-fallen tree and remnant of old farm fence line. Passing a crosswalk off to the right, where buildings from the Taylor farm sit at the edge of the orange grove, the path continues up to a crosswalk and comes to a T. This marks the start of the loop around Eagle Lake. Turn right. Make the first left into the oak hammock at the PICNIC PAVILION 4 sign. This path leads to Pier 3, the first of several overlooks on Eagle Lake. Ironically, the signs say NO FISHING, despite this being designated a pier. Only certain piers throughout

the park may be used to cast a line. Check the park map for details.

Leaving Pier 3, turn right and follow the path around the lake. Spiderwort grows in colorful clusters in a shady spot along the edge of the trail. From the comfortable shade of an oak hammock past Picnic Pavilion 5, you see the playground off to the left, a fanciful fantasy of a citrus grove complete with barn. The trail continues around the lake. Keep to the right, avoiding the trails that branch off to the left, including one that leads to a gate into the local neighborhood. As you emerge from the shade of the laurel oaks past Pier 2, the path crosses a small bridge over the outflow of Eagle Lake, where young cypresses have been planted along its banks. The bald eagle nest comes into view in a tall pine just outside the park boundary, to the right-hand side of the corner of the park on your left. Bald eagles build nests of incredible

Eagle Lake

size, which require trees such as the old-growth longleaf pines for support. There is no mistaking a bald eagle nest for that of any other bird, since the nest stands 10 to 20 feet tall, a deep pocket of branches filling the crook of a large tree. In springtime, you'll see the nest busy with activity.

Rounding the corner, Pier 4 comes into view. Stop for a moment at this spot, where fishing is permitted. The lily pads of American lotus fill the shallows. A coot fusses as it scurries through the grasses. Back on the paved path, you cross a steel bridge that is so sturdy and well built you could probably drive a semi over it, perhaps built atop a frame from when tractors had to cross into this part of the grove. The bridge crosses a stream flowing into Eagle Lake, a stream so clear you can see coontail waving in the current at the bottom, with fish darting in and out of the aquatic garden below.

At 1.6 miles, you complete the loop around Eagle Lake. Cross the crosswalk again, and up ahead, make a left at the stop sign. Ramble along the edge of the big parking area to where you can see the farmstead, including the historic home and barns. The county plans to renovate these structures, but for now, turn right when you see them. Turn left at the fifth orange tree (or sixth, or seventh) and wander a little ways into the citrus grove to follow an old gravel path between the trees. In spring, some of the trees are laden with oranges, while others are full of fragrant blossoms. This stand of citrus is a remnant of the once-mighty industry that Pinellas County relied on as an economic base up through the 1980s, when the combination of a bitter freeze in 1983 and hyperinflated tax values on agricultural land forced most growers to sell out to developers. Thankfully, the Taylor family kept their homestead and groves, selling to the county to preserve this urban forest and showcase of their citrus legacy.

Cross the park road to walk past Picnic Shelter 3 and Restrooms 2, and work your way down to Pier 2. This overlook is great for birding, as there's always activity going on, from red-winged blackbirds fussing and squawking from the trees to blue-winged teals cruising the open water. Follow the boardwalk around to the right between the series of ponds. Past the next pier, make a right, and you're back at the first wetland area you encountered. Now the green heron is hiding in the branches of a wax myrtle. Popping out at the paved perimeter path, take a left this time. A thicket of terrible thistle tempts you over with its big brilliant purple blooms. Just avoid brushing the spiny leaves and stems!

At 2.2 miles under the tall longleaf pines, you reach a T intersection. Turn right. A boardwalk crosses reconstructed marshlands, where ducklings scurry to follow their mother into the tall reeds. Several coots climb up on the shore and make a fuss. The longleaf pines are quite old at this end of the park, with oaks making up the understory. This paved trail ends at an exit at Rosary Road into a local neighborhood. Turn left on a shellrock path and follow it into the pine flatwoods. Take the right fork at the Y intersection. The draping blooms of pawpaw catch your eye as the trail nears the southern boundary of the park—there are many pawpaw here, resplendent in spring.

The trail swings to the left to follow the park boundary, where the sound of traffic becomes noticeable. Although Eagle Lake Park is surrounded by busy roads, there is so much birdsong in the air and so many views to delight the senses that you don't really notice the traffic until you hit this corner of the park, where you finally see the urban interface—cars rushing by to an intersection with Keene Road. Curving left again, the trail comes up to a short boardwalk over a wetland area. Take a peek at the aquatic plants as you continue across a bridge flanked by willows. Lizard-tail grows in the shallows of this natural waterway.

At the next major pedestrian entrance to the park, the Keene Road entrance, at 2.8 miles, turn left. Beyond a bench, another paved path heads over a bridge to the left. Continue straight, since you're now within sight of the parking lot where you started your walk. Passing the dog park on the right, you come up to Picnic Pavilion 1 and its adjoining restrooms, completing a 3-mile walk.

DIRECTIONS

Eagle Lake Park sits between US 19A and US 19 immediately south of Clearwater off Bellaire Boulevard. From the junction of US 19 and SR 60 (Gulf to Bay Boulevard) in Clearwater, drive west 2 miles to Keene Road. Turn left. Continue south 2.1 miles, crossing Belleair Boulevard, to the park entrance on the right. Inside the park, turn left and park in the parking area near the dog park and restrooms.

CONTACT

Eagle Lake Park
1800 Keene Road
Largo, FL 33771
727-518-3186
www.pinellascounty.org/park

39

Sawgrass Lake Park

Total distance (circuit): 1.9 miles

Hiking time: 1.5 hours

Habitats: freshwater marsh, floodplain forest, lake, hardwood hammock

Trailhead coordinates (lat-lon): 27.838964, -82.667900

Maps: USGS 7½' St. Petersburg; Southwest Florida Water Management District map; Park map

Admission: Free

Hours: 7 AM–sunset

Tucked away at the end of a suburban street in Pinellas Park, Sawgrass Lake Park provides the city dweller with a quiet place to commune with nature. Weathered boardwalks cross a red maple swamp, where alligators cruise silently through the dark waters. Trails wind through a tangle jungle of vines and saw palmetto, along rolling hills covered in turf and punctuated by ponds, looking like a golf course for hikers. As you enter the park, past the open canal where extremely large alligators can be caught sunning on the banks, the John Anderson Environmental Education Center and trailhead parking is on the left, just before the road ends.

Take the time to look through the environmental center before you hit the trail. An aquarium brims with local fish, such as Florida gar, greater siren, and the common mosquito fish. Other tanks hold turtles and snakes. There are many exhibits in the center, including ones on wildflowers, seashells, birds of prey, and the history of the Tocobaga tribes who once inhabited this region, displaying arrowheads and tools collected from middens in the area.

As you walk out of the back of the environmental center, past the restrooms, the trail starts. Follow the sidewalk down to the canal, then turn left and cross the bridge onto the boardwalk. When you come to the fork in the boardwalk, turn left, down the Sawgrass Trail. All around you are massive ferns—royal ferns, cinnamon ferns, marsh ferns, maiden ferns, and the tall and stately forms of giant leather ferns—jogging your memories of *Jurassic Park*, thoughts of velociraptors lurking nearby.

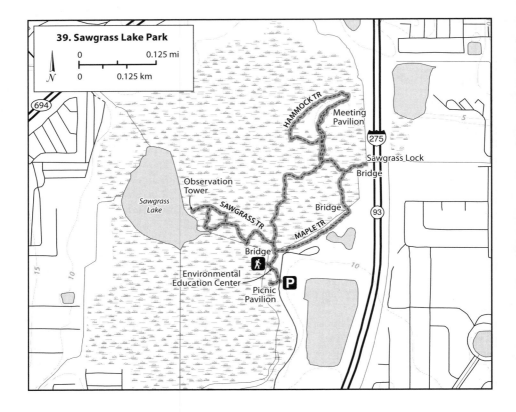

You are walking through a floodplain forest, the floodplain of Sawgrass Lake, where water-loving trees like red maple, dahoon holly, Virginia willow, and red bay dominate. The park encompasses 400 acres, most of it the largest remaining red maple swamp in the Tampa Bay area. Elderberry grows up to 6 feet tall, forming a thicket in the swamp.

Pause at the canopied overlook along the canal, where silent creatures are watching and waiting. As you wander out on the observation platform, an alligator senses your presence and propels itself smoothly across the canal to rest within feeding distance. A Florida gar drifts past, more than 2 feet long. Softshell turtles, up to 19 inches long, float with their snouts sticking out of the clear but dark water, a respectful distance from the alligator. The Florida softshell turtle has an unusual appearance, with alligator-like protruding eyes, a tubular head, and a pointed snout. The most amazing part of the softshell turtle is its blood-vessel-packed leathery skin covering an almost pancake-flat shell. The skin is an adaptation that allows them to remain submerged much longer than other turtle species, since they are able to take in oxygen and expel carbon dioxide through the skin. Because of their special skin, they dry out quickly, so softshell turtles don't bask in the sun as much as other turtles. Softshell turtles compete with alligators when hunting fish, frogs, and small waterfowl.

As you exit the platform, turn left, passing

by tall shiny-leafed wild coffee bushes. At 0.3 mile, you reach another fork in the boardwalk, with a sign marked OVERLOOK TOWER. Turn left, paralleling the canal. Pineapple-sized bromeliads grow in the trees, as do butterfly orchids. Near a clump of giant leather fern, look closely at the water for two types of aquatic ferns, ferns that float on still waters—water spangles and mosquito fern. Water spangles have small, round leaves that radiate from a base; mosquito fern grows in strands.

When you reach the next trail junction, turn left. As the habitat transitions from red maple swamp to the open waters of Sawgrass Lake, you reach the two-story covered observation tower. Climb up to the top to sit and observe alligators floating across the still surface of the lake. All around you, anhingas cope with their daily routine, diving into the water to chase fish. Surfacing, their long-necked heads look like snakes at attention, which is why the anhinga is also called the snakebird, or water turkey. After dining their fill, they retreat to the limbs of maples along the lakes, stretching out their wings to dry.

Leaving the observation tower, keep left at the next two trail junctions. You'll retrace your steps briefly, passing by the canopied overlook on the canal and back to the first trail junction on the boardwalk, with signs for the MAPLE TRAIL and HAMMOCK TRAIL. Turn left, walking through a forest of 75-foot-tall red maples. In late fall and early winter, the maples shed their leaves, dropping crimson reminders of seasonal change onto the boardwalk. Dense royal ferns and leather ferns crowd at their bases, some with fronds 5 feet long. You pass a covered bench amid the maple swamp. Notice how small hummocks of land create islands in the swamps, where ferns cluster more closely to the trees. You start to see cabbage palms interspersed throughout the forest. After another covered

Observation tower above Sawgrass Lake

bench, the boardwalk passes an uprooted oak; with the ball of roots dangling in the air, the cavity it left behind has filled in as a small pond. At 1 mile, you come to another junction in the boardwalk, with a covered bench and a HAMMOCK TRAIL sign. Turn left.

The boardwalk soon ends at a covered bench, spilling you onto the blinding white sands of an oak hammock. Look closely for fox tracks—despite the small size and the urban surroundings of this park, gray foxes have been sighted here. Numerous short trails wind through the hammock, leading back to this point. Feel free to explore. A new educational and meeting pavilion is here to host school groups.

The main trail seems to wander off to the left, then veers right past a bench. At the T intersection, turn left, climbing up onto a short boardwalk, where vines drape like curtains from the live oak canopy. The trail curves around, meeting back up with the starting point. Turn right to return to the main boardwalk. When you reach the next junction, at 1.4 miles, turn left.

Ferns galore at Sawgrass Lake Park

KEVIN MIMS

Walk along the edge of the hardwood hammock on the other branch of the Hammock Trail, where swamp tupelo, laurel oaks, and dahoon holly compete for space. Highway noise increases as you reach the next trail junction. Turn left, walking out of the forest and over a bridge on the Sawgrass Canal, at the Sawgrass Lock. To ensure the health and availability of water resources in the St. Petersburg area, these wetlands and waterways are managed by the Southwest Florida Water Management District and Pinellas County Parks. Here at the lock, you can see traffic whizzing by on Interstate 275 just a few hundred feet away. But it doesn't seem to ruffle the feathers of the great blue heron or the little blue heron on the edge of the canal, looking for fish. Peer into the water, and you'll see turtles and alligators going about their business, as though the city and the highway didn't exist.

Turn around and cross the bridge, retracing your steps back to the trail junction. Turn left, passing another covered bench, walking through the swamp forest of red maples and cabbage palms. Emerging back out to the canal, cross the bridge and turn right to walk along a concrete path along the canal's edge—a great place to wander slowly, watching for alligators. When you pass the next bridge, turn left to return to the environmental center, completing your 1.9-mile walk.

DIRECTIONS

Although Sawgrass Lake Park fronts Interstate 275 just north of St. Petersburg, access is a bit convoluted. Take exit 14B, heading west on 54th Avenue North. Turn right onto North 31st Street, then right onto 62nd Avenue North, which leads you back toward the interstate. Turn left at the traffic light just before the interstate overpass, onto North 25th Street. Follow the road a half-mile into the neighborhood and through the gate for the park.

CONTACT

Sawgrass Lake Park
7400 25th Street North
St. Petersburg, FL 33702
727-217-7256
www.pinellascounty.org/park

40

Fort De Soto Park

Total distance (4 circuits): 4.9 miles

Hiking time: 3.5 hours

Habitats: coastal dunes, coastal hammock, palm hammock, pine flatwoods, mangrove forest, mudflats, saltwater marsh

Trailhead coordinates (lat-lon)
Barrier-Free Nature Trail:
27.622782, -82.714243;
Soldier's Hole Trail:
27.617618, -82.728671;
Arrowhead Nature Trail:
27.642037, -82.734662;
Fort De Soto Historical Trail:
27.617064, -82.735437

Maps: USGS 7½' Pass-a-Grille Beach; Park map

Admission: Free

Hours: 7 AM–sunset

Dangling out into Tampa Bay like a giant anchor, the islands (call them "keys" in Florida) that make up Fort De Soto Park have plenty to offer. Canoeing the saltwater inlets of Soldier's Hole. Casting for snook off the Bay Pier. Relaxing on North Beach. Biking down the paved trail. Climbing the masonry fort, first built to protect Tampa Bay during the Spanish-American War. Hiking the historical route, or any of three hiking trails through coastal terrain. Dog lovers: bring your furry friends! Pets are permitted on the hiking trails, and there is a dedicated dog park with dog showers and water fountains in one corner of this 1,136-acre preserve. You'll find out quickly that a day just isn't enough to enjoy all this Pinellas County Park has to offer, which is why the campground is so popular.

Mullet Key, the largest of the islands in the group, first showed up on the map in February 1849 when a group of United States Army Engineers surveyed Florida's coastline. Colonel Robert E. Lee recommended that both Mullet Key and nearby Egmont Key be preserved for military use, placing the land off-limits to civilians. During the Civil War, the Union Blockading Squadron ran ships between the two keys, along the mouth of Tampa Bay, attempting to prevent Confederate blockade runners from reaching port. Egmont Key became a refugee camp for Confederate defectors, guarded by and eventually evacuated by the Union Navy.

In 1898, the Spanish-American War broke out, leading Tampa's citizens to demand protection. Tampa tycoon Henry Plant succeeded in convincing the Secretary of

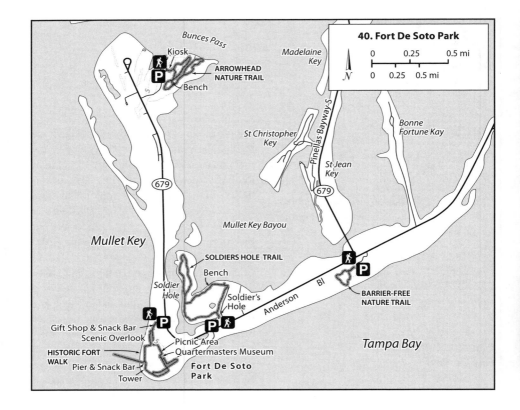

The map shows Fort De Soto Park with labels: 40. Fort De Soto Park, scale bars (0, 0.25, 0.5 mi), Bunces Pass, Kiosk, ARROWHEAD NATURE TRAIL, Bench, Madelaine Key, St Christopher Key, Bonne Fortune Kay, St Jean Key, Pinellas Bayway-S, 679, Mullet Key, Mullet Key Bayou, SOLDIERS HOLE TRAIL, Bench, Soldier Hole, Soldier's Hole, Anderson Bl, BARRIER-FREE NATURE TRAIL, Gift Shop & Snack Bar, Scenic Overlook, HISTORIC FORT WALK, Pier & Snack Bar, Tower, Picnic Area, Quartermasters Museum, Fort De Soto Park, Tampa Bay

War to build fortifications on both keys. By 1900, the forts were complete—Fort De Soto on Mullet Key, and Fort Dade on Egmont Key. It took another six years to build and outfit the adjoining army post for Fort De Soto, which included barracks, the mess hall, and 27 other buildings. By the time the men were stationed, the war was over. During World War I, the heavy mortars installed to protect Tampa were dismounted and shipped to San Diego. Twenty-four men remained on duty, never needing to fire a shot. In 1922, the Army decided that the forts were no longer needed for Florida's coastal defense. The island lay fallow and wave-battered for many years, used as a quarantine station and then a bombing range before the Army sold the land back to Pinellas County. The park opened to the public in 1963.

Fort De Soto Park encompasses all of Mullet Key, and the trails are dispersed, so you'll have to drive to each trailhead. The campground entrance is ahead on the left. If you enjoy camping, take note—this is one of the prettiest campgrounds in Central Florida. Virtually every space in the campground has a commanding view of the water. After you pass the campground entrance, you'll notice a ribbon of pavement paralleling the road—the park's biking and jogging trail, a 7-mile loop. When you get to the T intersection, turn left. Make a right into the parking lot for the park headquarters, driving down to the far end of the building to find the first trailhead.

Beach along the Barrier-Free Nature Trail

BARRIER-FREE NATURE TRAIL

Built as a Boy Scout project, the short Barrier-free Nature Trail provides all visitors a chance to experience the natural communities of Mullet Key, featuring a graded path wide enough for two wheelchairs to pass, and six touch-activated speaker boxes covering each of the interpretive stations. A concrete strip just before each station alerts the visually impaired as to the location of the speaker box. Rest areas with benches and water fountains allow the elderly to enjoy the trail at their own pace. Pick up an interpretive guide at the trailhead. Starting off in a palm hammock, the trail meanders through a tall stand of cabbage palms. A strangler fig envelops one unfortunate tree. When the seeds of a strangler fig are dropped into the top of a cabbage palm, they germinate as an epiphyte, sending dozens of tendril-like roots plummeting toward the ground. The roots grab hold of the host tree, and as both the tree and the fig grow, the dense net of fig roots can strangle the host tree's growth. If it doesn't, the host tree will eventually die under the leafy shade of the strangler fig, as it grows into a full-sized tree up to 60 feet tall.

When you come to the fork in the trail, keep to the right. The ditch on your right is one of many mosquito-control projects on Mullet Key, built to attempt to break the breeding cycle of the mosquito. Mosquitofish in the ditch eat the mosquito larvae. Although it's a freshwater fish, the mosquitofish quickly adapted to brackish pools like these. Black mangroves grow along the edge of the ditch. Watch for the belted kingfisher, a showy blue-and-white bird with a prominent crest and beak, as it loves diving for the tiny fish.

As the trail rounds a bend to the left, it emerges from the cabbage palms into the coastal dunes. Sea grapes clamber over the sandy hills. You catch a glimpse of the Sunshine Skyway Bridge off in the distance, an important link between St. Petersburg and the mainland. Sea oats rustle in the breeze. The trail turns left back into the palm hammock, when bracken ferns and hay-scented ferns carpet the forest floor. Returning to the trail junction, turn right to return to the trailhead, completing a 0.4-mile walk.

Stop in the ranger station to pick up a map of the park. If you're interested in the self-guided tour of the fort, pick up a free copy of *The History of Fort De Soto Park*, which contains the interpretive map and guide.

The next trailhead starts at Soldier's Hole, a popular canoe trail route. Leaving the ranger station, turn left. Pass CR 679 and continue up to the BAY PIER sign. A dirt track leads off to the right, where a canoe concessionaire may be parked. Follow the dirt track down past a gate on the right, and find a place to park on the left. The trail starts at the gate.

SOLDIER'S HOLE NATURE TRAIL

Check the box on the gate for an interpretive brochure before starting your hike on the Soldier's Hole Nature Trail. This is an open trail through mangrove swamps, so sunscreen and insect repellent are a must. At the entrance is a tidal pond—Soldier's Hole, named for its use as a surreptitious departure point for deserters from Fort De Soto. Small boats can quickly slip into the mangrove channels and vanish. Three varieties of mangroves grow here: black mangrove, white mangrove, and red mangrove. How do you quickly tell them apart? Compare their shapes. Red mangroves have a distinct network of prop roots, roots that look like arches holding up the tree. Black mangroves are broader, and are surrounded by a network of short breathing roots protruding from the soil under the plant, looking like miniature cypress knees. White mangroves look the most tree-like, with oval light green leaves—the other mangroves have dark green, elliptical leaves.

Veering off to the right, the trail follows a grassy jeep road. Beware of poison ivy along the footpath. After passing several jeep roads coming in from the right, the trail comes up to a fork near interpretive station 6. Turn left past the sea oats, walking along the mangroves on the edge of the tidal lagoon. Notice the thousands of tiny balls and holes in the trail, created by the burrowing fiddler crabs. Take a moment to walk down to Mullet Key Bayou at station 7. Dolphins and manatees both venture into these shallow waters, so keep alert! Mild waves wash horseshoe crabs up on the shore.

At station 12, the trail turns left. If you want to double the length of your hike, turn right and walk the loop out to the end of the Soldier's Hole peninsula, through the forests of mangroves, returning to this point. You cross over a mosquito-control ditch, where wild poinsettia grows near the base of sea grapes. At station 14, you come to an open area filled with glasswort, a thick salt-tolerant grass with red and yellow tips. When you reach the T intersection, turn right, walking back past the tidal pond to the gate, completing your mile-long walk.

Leaving Soldier's Hole, turn right on the park road and follow it down past the fort to the North Beach Swim Area. Watch for the small ARROWHEAD PICNIC AREA sign on the right; it comes up quickly. Turn into the picnic area and follow the one-way road around until you see the trail kiosk on the right. Park nearby and start your hike by picking up an interpretive guide at the kiosk.

ARROWHEAD NATURE TRAIL

Winding through coastal hammocks and mangrove swamp, the Arrowhead Nature Trail is a 1.5-mile series of loops best done by following the trail stations in sequence. There are lots of places where you can skip or redo certain loops, so it's easy to get mixed up unless you follow the numbers in the proper order. Winding under the slash pines, cabbage palms, and sand live oaks, the trail meanders off to the right. Watch for the sign for numbers 4, 5, and 6; turn right, performing a loop up a small hill, in sight of a tall tower. After you complete the loop, turn right on the Spur Trail, a grassy jeep track leading out along a mangrove-lined canal. The aroma of salt fills the air as you near the bay. At the fork, turn right, passing by tall saw palmettos and southern red cedar. Glasswort clusters along the edge of the trail. As the trail veers left along the coast of the bay, you catch a glimmer of water through the mangroves. A

Tampa Bay through the mangroves of Solider's Hole

short side trail winds beneath tall black and red mangroves to the water's edge. A green heron makes its way through the shallows as horseshoe crabs scurry along the bottom.

Returning to the trail, turn right and follow it back around to the fork to complete the loop. Stay straight until you reach the T intersection and then turn right to pass station 7. You're back on the main trail. Turn right at the sign for TRAIL STATIONS 8–13 at 0.9 mile. The trail follows the other side of the mangrove-lined canal with a vista of an open coastal savanna, where scattered cabbage palms tower above of a sea of tall marsh grasses. Pause at station 10 to check out an unusual coastal vine called coin vine or fish poison vine. These vines create an impenetrable tangle in mangrove forests, and used to be used to catch fish. When immersed, the vines let off a chemical that blocks the uptake of oxygen to fish gills, causing death. It's now illegal to stun or kill fish using the coin vine.

At station 11, the trail swings out along the edge of Bunce's Pass. Sandpipers scurry along the mudflats, bathed in a reddish-pink hue from the sun's reflection against the mud. Smooth cordgrass grows out of the mud, dotted with the tiny shells of periwinkles. Returning to the trail, turn right and follow it back through the savanna. After you pass station 13, turn right at the T intersection, into the pine flatwoods. Turn right again to return to the trail kiosk and parking lot. You've walked 1.5 miles.

If you haven't stopped for a picnic yet, there are some benches with beautiful bay views along the road, beyond the trailhead. Continue driving around the one-way loop to exit the Arrowhead Picnic Area. Turn left to continue down to North Beach and the fort.

FORT DE SOTO HISTORICAL TRAIL

Although this isn't technically a hiking trail, a self-guided tour of Fort De Soto lets you explore the fort and the ruins of the Army post on a 2-mile circuit. Start your walk from the gift shop/snack bar area to walk up and around to the remains of Fort De Soto—two key batteries that protected Tampa Bay. Stairs enable you to climb atop Battery Laidley for a sweeping view of the bay. The brick road along the battery is the original road on Mullet Key, built in 1898. Skirting around the edge of the parking area nearest the road, the historical trail continues down toward the bay, passing various storehouses and living quarters on its way to the bay. Reaching the old quartermaster's wharf, the trail turns right to follow the waterfront around to the Gulf Pier, passing the officer's quarters, a tall observation tower, and the Army barracks. Loop back around along the edge of the parking lot to return past Battery Laidley to your starting point. Guided tours of the fort—ideal for groups—are also available by appointment; call ahead to 727-582-2267 for details.

DIRECTIONS

Take Interstate 275 south from St. Petersburg to exit 17, Pass-a-Grille Beach. Head west on 54th Avenue South (Pinellas Boulevard), which is a toll road. Drive 2.5 miles to CR 679 south. Turn left, following CR 679 for 5.5 miles to the park entrance, where there is another toll on a drawbridge.

CONTACT

Fort De Soto Park
3500 Pinellas Bayway South
Tierra Verde, FL 33715
727-893-9185
www.pinellascounty.org/park

41

Little Manatee River State Park

Total distance (circuit): 6.5 miles

Hiking time: 4 hours

Habitats: pine flatwoods, scrub, sandhill, oak hammock, palm hammock, floodplain forest

Trailhead coordinates (lat-lon): 27.674285, -82.351256

Maps: USGS 7½' Wimauma; Florida Trail Association; Park map

Admission: $2 pedestrians/bicyclists, $4 single motorist, $5 carload

Hours: 8 AM–sunset (for registered backpackers, 24 hours)

In southern Hillsborough County, the Little Manatee River flows a lazy 38 miles from its swampy backwater sources into the broad sweep of Tampa Bay. Tucked between US 301 and Interstate 75, the Little Manatee River State Park provides access to a preserved sliver of wilderness along the river, encompassing a variety of habitats, numerous waterways, and one of the most beautiful creeks in the state. A primitive backcountry campsite awaits hikers who want to spend a peaceful night under the stars. Or use the full-service campground in the main part of the park, and you'll be able to spend a full weekend hiking and canoeing along this outstanding Florida waterway.

After checking in at the ranger station at the south end of the park, drive back north along US 301 to the opposite side of the Little Manatee River to find the hidden entrance to the trailhead, per their instructions. Use the lock combination they gave you to enter the trailhead parking area. Turn the lock on the gate to match the combination on the map. Lift the end of the gate up, and it will swing inwards. After you drive in, secure the gate behind you. This park is multiuse, but the hiking trail is strictly for hikers—the gate and fencing along the road help ensure that the trails stay untrammeled except by feet. Swing around to the parking area, where the trailhead is clearly marked. A blue-blazed connector trail leads from the trailhead to the main orange loop trail, winding through a hardwood hammock lushly carpeted in ferns. Stop and look closely at the many species, including giant sword ferns, marsh ferns, netted chain, and cinna-

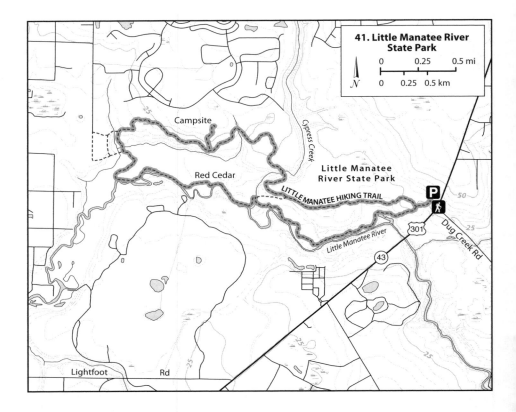

mon ferns. Enjoying the damp environment, ferns crowd close on both sides of the slightly mushy footpath.

After 0.1 mile, you reach the beginning of the orange loop. Turn right into a dense slash pine forest, where water oak, Yaupon holly, and bay magnolia share the sunlight. Emerging into a meadow, you pass under a power line before the trail curves to the left, back into a pine and oak forest, dominated by laurel oaks. After you cross a bridge over a small creek, the trail enters a tunnel through a grove of wax myrtle, then parts a dense thicket of blackberries. The easy access to the blackberry bushes makes this stretch a berry picker's delight in April, when blackberries grow ripe and full. Signifying seasonal marshy

conditions, red maples poke up through the sea of berry bushes. At 0.5 mile, the trail enters an oak hammock with a bridge over a small winding creek with short sand bluffs. Cinnamon ferns cluster close to the water. Watch for poison ivy! For the next 5 miles you'll see a good bit of it in the deep dark hammocks. It grows close to the trail in places, and rises on stems up to 2 feet high.

The trail enters a pine flatwoods, where the sparseness of the slash pines and the many snags—dead standing trees—along the trail show the long-lasting effect of wildfire. As the footpath becomes sand, the habitat transitions to sand pine scrub, with a dense understory of scrub palmetto stretching off in every direction. An armadillo rustles under the dried fronds, rooting for grubs. Young sand pines huddle along the edge of the trail like a row of tiny Christmas trees. Thickets of dense oak scrub break up the desert-like habitat, where the trees rarely grow more than 10 feet tall. Chapman's oak, scrub live oak, and myrtle oak make up these islands of oak. Scrub relies on wildfire to replenish the habitat. When fire happens infrequently, the oaks cluster together tightly, and sand pines grow to the immense heights you see along this section of trail.

At 1.1 miles, you reach a junction with a blue-blazed cross-trail. If you want a much shorter hike, turn here to head down to Cypress Creek, for a total circuit hike of 2.9

Bromeliads grow thickly near the Little Manatee River

KEVIN MIMS

miles. You'll miss some of the prettiest terrain, however, so continue straight ahead into the sand pine forest, following the sign toward the campground. The trail soon curves to the right along the edge of a depression filled with saw palmetto—the floodplain for Cypress Creek. As the trail turns abruptly left at 1.4 miles, you descend steeply down the bluff into the floodplain, crossing a bridge over a side channel. After you scramble up the next rise, Cypress Creek comes into view. Enjoy a few minutes of solitude on the broad bridge over the creek. This is by far one of the most beautiful and serene creeks in Central Florida, where the clear tea-colored water flows gently over rippled sand. Small fish dart through the shallows.

Leaving Cypress Creek behind, the trail ascends up over the bluff through a switchback to return to the sand pine forest. After you cross a small bridge, the forest opens up, and you're back in open scrub, out in the bright sunshine, among a broad open sea of scrub palmetto. A pileated woodpecker beats a rhythm against a distant snag as you pass through alternating open scrub and islands of oaks. Taller sand post oaks, laurel oaks, and bracken fern indicate the habitat's shift to sandhill, where oaks dominate and moister conditions make it possible for the bracken to flourish.

After 2.3 miles, you reach the blue-blazed 0.2-mile side trail to the primitive campground. Even if you're not spending the night, it's worth a stroll down the trail for a relaxing break at the picnic tables. If you are camping, be sure to get a permit from the park office before you start hiking. There is no water at the campsite, so you must carry in your water for drinking and cooking, or filter water at Cypress Creek to lug back to the campground. The campground is surrounded by oak hammock, with young longleaf pines growing in the sunny open spaces.

Continuing past the trail to the campground, turn back and look at the sign. A sand pine fell square on it, hammering the signpost like a nail into the ground. The trail continues past a red cedar densely draped with orchids into an oak scrub with more fallen pines, passing briefly under a stand of spreading live oaks. As a radio tower looms in the distance, the trail starts curving to the left, beginning its route toward the river. The habitat changes to a moister pine flatwoods, where damp indentations fill with swamp lilies. After the trail follows a fence line within sight of a golf course development for a short distance, it swings farther to the left, passing a couple of side trails. Stick with the main orange-blazed trail as it returns to a scrub habitat along the western boundary of the park.

At 3.2 miles, you cross a long boardwalk over a slow-flowing tannic creek. You've finished your trek through the scrub and pine flatwoods, and are entering the hardwood forests along the Little Manatee River, where cabbage palms and laurel oaks dominate. Not far beyond the bridge, the trail makes an abrupt hard left turn—watch for the blazes! It's easy to miss this one, as it seems like the trail continues straight ahead. As you walk through the forest, the trail crosses bridges over small channels that feed down into the river. You'll walk along the edges of small marshy ponds, some thick with swamp lilies, others coated with a slimy-looking surface of duckweed. As you approach a tall orange-blazed slash pine in the trail, look for an odd oak tree off on the right. The trunk fell over at

Young sand pine forest

KEVIN MIMS

some point early in the tree's development, leaving the branches to grow straight up—looking like mature trees sprouting out of a long log.

Emerging on a sand bluff, you get a sweeping view of a horseshoe bend in the Little Manatee River. Reaching this point at 3.6 miles, the trail swings left and follows the river upstream for most of the remainder of the hike. Although it jogs around numerous floodplain side channels of the river, the trail always returns to the sandy bluffs along the river's edge.

Two canoes drift by. Another has landed on one of the many sandy beaches on the river bends, where the family is enjoying a fishing expedition. It's a gentle paddle, a three-hour trip from the landing just off US 301 on the south side of the river. Largemouth bass rocket through the depths, headed downstream. A great white heron stands guard over the shallows. In a side channel off to the left, notice the Japanese climbing fern, filling the channel, climbing up a cabbage palm, and almost smothering a small saw palmetto. Each cluster has several different types of leaves. Although beautiful, this fern is an exotic species actively being eradicated from southern Florida, where it grows like a weed, smothering everything in its path. You'll see many more instances of this fern along this next stretch of trail.

The trail turns sharply left away from the river for a while to skirt a deep floodplain inlet, the trail broadening as it rises from a marshy area into a forest of sweetgum, water oaks, and laurel oaks. Watch for pineapple-sized bromeliads in the trees, particularly when you come up to the only red cedar thus far on the trail, at 4.2 miles. It's unusual to see a red cedar hosting any sort of air plants, but this cedar is more than 40 feet tall, its branches thick with air plants and large bromeliads. Soon after, you return to the river's edge, crossing a series of bridges spanning a floodplain channel next to the river. Lilies grow densely in the thick mud. Several fallen trees lie with their tops in the river, creating some minor obstacles along the footpath. The trail follows a narrow strip between the river and its floodplain forest, eventually coming to an area where cabbage palms dominate the landscape.

Climbing up a steep bluff, the trail turns left to follow Cypress Creek. Look off to the right to see where the creek enters the Little Manatee River. The trail sticks to the rugged bluff until you reach a right turn that takes you down to a broad bridge over the creek. This is your last chance to savor this beautiful waterway, so take a moment to sit and relax. The blue-blazed cross-trail comes in from the left just beyond the bridge, at 4.7 miles. The orange blazes swing to the right to lead you along Cypress Creek, with a veer to the left as the trail winds back through the forest. As you walk through a palm hammock, a flock of chimney swifts dart back and forth overhead.

At 5 miles, you return to the bluffs along the river, clambering up and down little slopes, skirting around more floodplain forest. The trail fills with nuts as pignut hickories begin to dominate the forest. After you cross two bridges in quick succession, the trail reaches a double blaze and turns left. Watch for an extremely gnarled old live oak with huge knobby protrusions, one of the oldest oaks along this walk. Just ahead, you'll pass a young loblolly bay on the right, covered in a variety of wild pine that looks just like hairy clusters of pine needles. A threatened species in Florida, this particular bromeliad shows off a spike of purple flowers when it blooms.

The river remains off to the right, beyond the forest, as the trail passes through a thicket of wild balsam apple. At 5.6 miles, you briefly emerge back onto the river bluff, hearing the distant sound of traffic from US 301. Leaving the river, the trail ducks into a scrub oak forest, then turns right to cross a bridge, returning to the hickory-dominated forest. After zigzagging along the soft sand bluffs, you cross a tall bridge over a deep side channel that weaves its way to the river. The trail swings to the left, where spiky saw palmettos lift their trunks 5 feet and more in the air. You've walked 6 miles. Don't stumble over the sole rock in the trail—a dark maroon-black slab of limestone, reminiscent of the rocks that create the rapids at Hillsborough River State Park.

The trail emerges out into the sunshine into a meadow broken up by smaller live oaks and slash pine. Growing in heaping mounds, smilax provides the ground cover. Your last glimpse of the river is off to the right. The wide mowed trail continues through the meadow, where raspberries and daisies fight for space. A zebra butterfly settles on the fluffy blooms of a Florida groundsel bush. After you cross the small bridge in the meadow, the trail heads toward a line of slash pines, then jogs right under the cool shade of a large live oak. Veering left, you walk down a tall corridor of slash pine into an oak hammock. Ferns and bay magnolia begin to appear on the right, signaling the end of the orange loop is near. Passing a fallen pine, notice how the vines from the tree to the ground are stretched taut like telephone wires. At 6.4 miles, you reach the end of the orange loop. Following the blue blazes in front of you, return through the tall ferns to the trailhead and parking lot.

DIRECTIONS

From Interstate 75 south of Tampa, take exit 240A, Sun City Center/Ruskin. Drive east on SR 674 through Sun City Center 3 miles to US 301. Head south on US 301 for 4.5 miles, crossing the Little Manatee River and turning on Lightfoot Road to the park's entrance. Before starting out on your hike, you must stop at the ranger station to pay admission, pick up a trail map, and get the combination to the gate for the hikers' parking area. Return to US 301 and drive 1.7 miles north, back across the Little Manatee River to the first turn (a dirt road) on the left.

CONTACT

Little Manatee River State Park
215 Lightfoot Road
Wimauma, FL 33598
813-671-5005
www.floridastateparks.org/littlemanateeriver

42

Alderman's Ford Preserve

Total distance (round-trip and circuit): 3.3 miles

Hiking time: 2 hours

Habitats: hardwood hammock, oak hammock, oxbow lake, prairie, river bluff forest

Trailhead coordinates (lat-lon): 27.879559, -82.170972

Maps: USGS 7½' Dover; Hillsborough County park map

Admission: Free

Hours: Sunrise–5 PM

As the Alafia River rises from marshlands south of Plant City, it descends through gently sloping hills toward Tampa Bay through a thick layer of limestone bedrock. Eroding a deep channel into this karst plain, the river tumbles over limestone boulders, forming noisy, churning stretches of hydraulics that are mesmerizing to hear and watch.

While the historic Alderman's Ford, a cattle-crossing point in the gentle shallows of the river, lies west of this particular preserve, Alderman's Ford Preserve is part of more than 10,000 acres of natural lands protecting the flow of this beautiful river. Many of Florida's rivers, including the Miami River, once sported stretches of whitewater, but early attempts at river commerce meant many of Florida's rivers lost their rapids to dynamite and dredging. As a result, this is probably the southernmost spot in Florida where you'll see Class II whitewater from a hiking trail.

Slip through the pass-thru from parking area to walk around to the kiosk to check out the trail route. The gate is closed and locked by a resident attendant, so be sure to time your hike to exit the trailhead before 5 PM. The trail system shown on the map isn't as extensive as what is currently actually in place, but this is a relatively new preserve managed by Southwest Florida Water Management District and Hillsborough County as a watershed for the Alafia River. It is open to hikers only, but you will see evidence of equestrian use. Much of the upper loop is in the open, so wear adequate sun protection. The lower

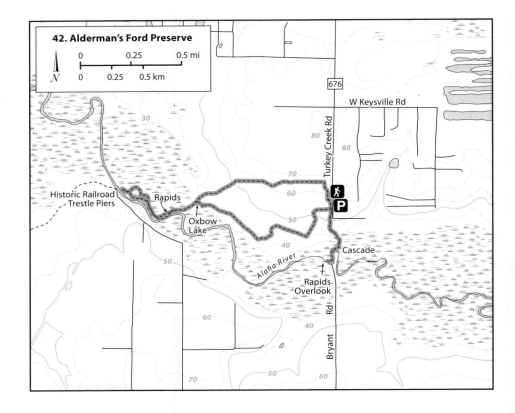

loop is in deep shade, so expect to encounter hordes of mosquitoes as well as poison ivy off-trail. Insect repellent is a must!

A large chunk of the landscape, including the part you're walking through to start, was formerly pastureland next to an orange grove. It has been replanted in places with longleaf pines that are just now tall enough to provide a small amount of shade. The trail is marked with diamond-shaped markers with a hiker in the middle. It turns right at the kiosk and parallels the tree line along Turkey Creek Road, which provides morning shade across an otherwise wide-open walk. Pass a trail intersection and continue on a gradual descent along the edge of the field. The trail turns to the left to slip into the deep shade of a hardwood

hammock. Braided alluvial streams course their way down through the lush forest as the trail heads downhill fast, through dense stands of cinnamon fern. Tree roots create a stair step effect as you descend quickly to a high bluff above the river, where a noisy cascade plunges down from a rocky embankment. A picnic table offers a spot to sit and take in your first glimpse of the Alafia River.

The trail shown heading west from this point on the official map does not yet exist. However, a well-beaten unmarked path atop the natural levee follows the river downstream. It's tricky footing in places, but worth the trek. You'll pass by a live oak of enormous girth that stretches out partway over the river like a living bridge. After a bit of a scramble

Rapids on the Alafia River

down to the river, the roar of rapids bounces off the bluffs as you climb back up and look down on a stretch of churning hydraulics, whitewater that a kayaker would salivate over. The trail peters out here after 0.4 mile, so turn around and make your way back to the picnic table and exit back up the steep hillside through the forest.

As you emerge from the shade, the cloud of mosquitoes lifts. Continue back along the fence line to the marked trail junction. Turn left. This is the lower portion of a loop trail that takes you along the rim of a former pasture. The trail keeps to the edge of the field, working its way around a drainage area dense with sweetgum and red maple trees and along the edge of an oak hammock. Colorful wildflowers appear in patches throughout the field, including stands of purple spiderwort. Take care not to step in the fire ant nests that dot the broad path through the grass. An oak

toad scrambles out of sight beneath a poison ivy leaf as a red-shouldered hawk cries out overhead.

A splash alerts you to the presence of an oxbow lake off to the left behind a screen of trees. It's a portion of the river left high and dry as it settled into its current deep channel, and is a gathering place for wading birds. After 1.5 miles, the trail comes to a prominent junction with a swale off to the right. Turn left to continue. Views of the oxbow lake are more open here, enabling you to watch for birds and be alert for alligators along its bank. Frogs are croaking amid the American lotus blooming on the surface. Underfoot, the trail becomes bright white sand as the habitat transitions into a patch of sand pine scrub. Take the left fork.

The sound of rapids travels well up the river valley and catches your attention about the same time you can see the Alafia River down the steep bluff to the left. Live oaks swaddled in resurrection fern arc well over the river. Here's another stretch of whitewater, a bit longer than the first and just as noisy. The trail widens into a forest road with glimpses of the river, pulling away into the sand pine scrub. At the next fork in the trail, keep left, passing a gopher tortoise burrow with prickly pear cactus growing at the mouth of it—a tasty treat for the tortoise. The forest crowds in as the trail continues downhill beneath large cedars and cabbage palms, reaching another prominent junction at 2 miles.

Continue forward past the junction just a little to emerge into an open area under a power line. Look to the left to see a pair of railroad trestle piers. Part of the original Plant System railway, these historic piers are built from brick and covered in Virginia creeper. This is the far western end of the trail system, so turn around and continue back to the trail junction. Turn left to explore the upper end of this loop. The trail is a bit squishy in places, with blue-eyed grass emerging from soggy spots. Spanish moss sways from massive live oaks, and a partridge dashes through the underbrush. The loop ends as the trail reaches the sandy forest road at 2.2 miles. Turn left.

Back along the straightaway, you have one last opportunity to check out the rapids on your way to the trailhead. Once again, you hear them well before you see them. From this perspective, peek through the trees, and you can see a place where you can clamber down to the edge of the rapids more safely than from the opposite direction. It's worth the short scramble to experience the splash of whitewater at the river's edge.

The trail continues along a palmetto-dotted open area. At the fork by the oxbow lake, keep left. You return to the intersection with the pasture loop at 2.5 miles. This time, continue straight to take in the north side of the loop. The trail drops through the swale and quickly rises up into the pastureland. Cows moo in the distance as you approach a fence line, with the lights of the Durant High School football field in the distance. The trail turns right to follow the fence line. Masses of wildflowers in bright pinks and purples lean out into the not-so-well-maintained trail. Dragonflies court overhead as the trail passes gigantic live oaks in this part of the pasture, some large enough to have started their own hammocks. Following a straightaway along the fence line, the trail ends up behind someone's backyard—the caretaker. Turn right and follow this fence line back to the parking corral, completing the 3.3-mile hike.

DIRECTIONS

From Interstate 75 exit 257, Brandon, follow SR 60 east for 2.7 miles. Turn right on Lithia-Pinecrest Road. Go 1.1 miles to the second traffic light and make a left on East Lumsden Road. Make an immediate right at the gas station to follow Durant Road, a heavily canopied road through residential areas, for 6.2 miles to the community of Durant. At the stop sign with Turkey Creek Road, turn right and drive 1.2 miles to the intersection with Keysville Road in front of Durant High School. Continue straight down Turkey Creek Road (signposted as a DEAD END) for another 0.4 mile to the well-hidden trailhead entrance on the right. Look for the NO PARKING signs along the road to find it.

CONTACT

Hillsborough County
Parks Recreation & Conservation
10119 Windhorst Road
Tampa, FL 33619
813-635-3500
www.hillsboroughcounty.org/parks

VI. Atlantic Coast

Crossing the Addison-Ellis Canal at Enchanted Forest Sanctuary

43

Ponce Preserve

Total distance (circuit and round-trip): 2.4 miles

Hiking time: 1 hour

Habitats: coastal scrub, coastal strand, dunes, mangrove marsh, maritime hammock, salt prairie, tidal marsh

Trailhead coordinates (lat-lon): 29.114660, -80.950067

Maps: USGS 7½' New Smyrna Beach; Trailhead kiosk map

Admission: Free

Hours: Dawn–dusk

One of the newest parks in the region, Ponce Preserve is a community park that protects a cross-section of barrier island habitats in a 40-acre ribbon between the Atlantic Ocean and the Halifax River south of Daytona Beach. Home of a significant archaeological site, it's also one of nature's last stands on the barrier island where auto racing was born.

Check the kiosk with the map before you start your hike. At the first trail junction, keep right to walk the loop counterclockwise. Marked with yellow blazes, the trail is a roller coaster over the midden and ancient dunes beneath a canopy of coastal scrub, with silvery-blue-tinged saw palmetto dominating the understory. Red bay trees and sand live oaks cast corridors of shade, but you do pop in and out of the sunlight while clambering up and down the steep slopes. Despite its short length, this is a rather rugged little trail.

The preserve bounds Atlantic Avenue (A1A), and while you can't see the cars, you can hear them rushing past. As the trail ascends through ancient dunes, the landscape opens to a broad view of substantial swales of silvery saw palmetto. To the right, you can hear the pounding of the Atlantic Ocean surf, and you might catch a glimpse depending on the height of the saw palmetto thicket. After a serious bit of scrambling you top out at a sun-drenched high point amid the saw palmetto, where sweet, light scents emanate from the forest below. Power lines to the right betray the presence of the nearby road. From this high point, the trail drops steeply down into a bowl with silk bay and red bay overhead, the corridor tightly defined by the saw

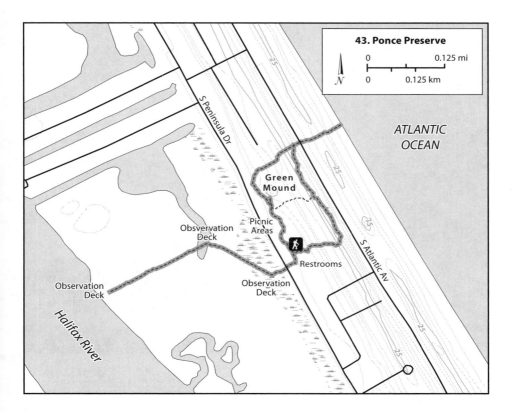

palmetto. It's still a major scramble, up and down, up and down, over sand ridges.

After a half mile, you reach a sign indicating a side trail down to right leads to the beach. There is a crossover on Atlantic Avenue leading to an access point to the ocean. To stay on the main trail, take the sharp left. The trail becomes more linear and flat, with softer sand underfoot. Prickly pear cactus sports big yellow blossoms. You enter a long corridor, shaded by the red bay. To the left is high ground, part of the midden hidden in the forest. This long tunnel of trail was the original access point for visitors to the Green Mound, prior to the preserve officially opening.

As you near the light at the end of the tunnel—Peninsula Drive—after 1.2 miles, a

sign directs you to turn left. Here, you encounter oyster shells underfoot. The trail snakes its way between the trees at the base of the Green Mound, the primary reason that Ponce Preserve exists. Once one of the largest middens on the Atlantic Coast, standing more than 50 feet high, the Green Mound is thought to have been originally built by late St. Johns Period cultures and was occupied between 500 B.C. and 1565 A.D. It was greatly disturbed prior to the 1940s—as many Florida middens were—by removal of materials for roadfill. These middens are ancient trash heaps, providing archaeologists clues as to the lives of the people who once lived along Florida's coast. Excavations in this midden have uncovered evidence of a village,

Atlantic Ocean view

including fire pits and postholes marking the corners of raised houses.

The mound contains layers of ash, sand, and clay, but what you'll see pouring out of the forest are spills of oyster shells from the edges of what remains of the mound. Living in such a bountiful landscape, the people of the Green Mound harvested oysters in the nearby estuary. The estuary breeds mosquitoes, so you'll encounter plenty of them here in this well-shaded portion of the preserve. The habitat transitions from the cedars and red bay of the maritime hammock to include more tropical vegetation, with wild coffee and acacia growing in the understory. The trail zigzags between the trees, crossing undulating terrain. Walking down a stately corridor of cabbage palms, you reach another sign. Turn left here to continue toward the parking area.

At the next sign, the Green Mound is off to your left, as is an ancient live oak, half-fallen and sprawling off the mound, limbs reaching out toward the Halifax River. There's a bench here for a place to sit and contemplate the ages. Just a little ways farther along the trail is a picnic spot under a canopy of tropical trees. Once off the mound, the trail winds through a dense forest of wild coffee and yaupon holly, past another bench and picnic table, and becomes a more substantial path, bolstered by crushed shells underfoot as you continue toward the parking area.

Passing several more picnic tables, the trail emerges at the parking area. Take advantage of the restrooms before you head out on the second part of the trek out to the Halifax River. The boardwalk is a delightful walk, especially to watch the birds flock in from afar as the sun sets over the river. Winding through a salt prairie, it passes many tidal inlets. When the tide is down, you'll see fiddler crabs scurrying about and oysters uncovered by the receding tide. As you walk the boardwalk, look down as well as ahead so you don't miss the teeming life in the marsh. Two observation platforms provide places for birders to keep watch from a shady spot and offer launch points for canoes and kayaks.

The farther you progress toward the river, the thicker the mangroves grow together until they create a dense forest along the river's shore. If you visit in July, you'll see the sweet-scented tiny white blossoms of the black mangroves. Looking down, you see their finger-like pneumatophores, breathing tubes rising from the tidal muck.

Arriving at the final observation deck along the Halifax River, you may spot an angler or two. This is a popular place to drop a line, the bounty of the estuary still in fashion after these many centuries. Local seafood plays a major role on menus of local restaurants throughout Ponce Inlet. Stand here long enough, and you'll see a dolphin chasing the wake of a powerboat, or a manatee poking its snout out of the water close to shore. One of America's most unique mammalian species, the manatee, or sea cow, often weighs more than a ton. These grayish giants float close to the surface of both saltwater and freshwater waterways, nibbling on water hyacinths, water lettuce, and seagrass. Normally a solitary creature—except during the chilly winter months and during the mating season—they range all along the Florida coastline and its rivers.

Decision point

DIRECTIONS

From Interstate 95, take exit 256 for Port Orange/Daytona Beach Shores. Drive east on SR 421 (Taylor Avenue), crossing the Intracoastal Waterway onto the barrier island. When you reach A1A (Atlantic Avenue), turn right. Continue 2.5 miles to Wilbur-by-the-Sea. Turn right at Old Carriage Road and drive down to Peninsula Drive, which parallels the Intracoastal Waterway. Turn left. Continue 0.4 mile to the preserve entrance on the left.

LAND MANAGER

Town of Ponce Inlet
4300 South Atlantic Avenue
Ponce Inlet, FL 32127
386-236-2150
www.ponce-inlet.org

44

Lyonia Preserve

Total distance (circuit): 2.1 miles

Hiking time: 2 hours

Habitats: oak scrub, rosemary scrub, sand pine scrub

Trailhead coordinates (lat-lon): 28.930217, -81.225438

Maps: USGS 7½' Lake Helen; Preserve map

Admission: Trails are free. Lyonia Environmental Center, $5 for adults, $4 for seniors, $2 for children 3–12, and free for children under 3.

Hours: Sunrise–sunset

Hidden away in the suburban neighborhoods of Deltona, Lyonia Preserve is a Volusia County park that's an unexpected delight. Covering 400 acres of relict sand dunes, the preserve hosts one of Florida's least common birds, the Florida scrub-jay. Set aside to protect critical scrub-jay scrub habitat in the center of Deltona, Lyonia Preserve is actively managed to encourage the growth of its avian population. Florida scrub-jays are only found in Florida, where we have a total population under 10,000. Of that population, more than 100 live here on Lyonia Preserve. Walk softly, and keep watching the oak trees as you hike to learn more about this unique bird. Start your hike in the early morning hours, before 8 AM, and you're guaranteed to see not just one or two of these colorful blue and white birds, but dozens of them, flitting through the oak scrub in search of breakfast.

The entrance and parking for the preserve is shared with the Deltona Public Library as well as an amphitheater for outdoor events and the new Lyonia Environmental Center. With all of these new buildings, the trailhead has been moved to the far eastern side of the parking lot. Make a right as you pull in, and you'll see the prominent sign in the corner. The nature center is worth visiting before your hike, if possible, to ground you in understanding the habitats along the trail system, the scrub-jays, and the unique karst aquifer beneath all this white sand. Pets are not permitted, so as to protect the scrub-jays.

The new trailhead is well marked, with an entrance fence and kiosk, and scrub plants

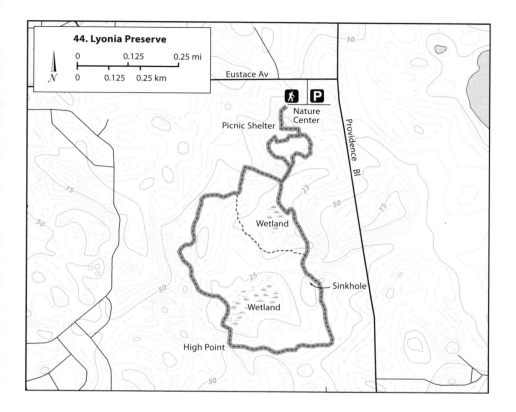

44. Lyonia Preserve

are identified beside the short walk along the fence line to a covered picnic shelter. When you reach the picnic shelter, turn left and follow the broad firebreak behind the nature center and amphitheater to the original entrance to the loop trail system. Turn right to start the Rusty Lyonia Trail, blazed orange. Although many unmarked trails still crisscross the stacked trail system of three loops, care has been taken to mark the main loops and intersections well. Take an immediate left at the T intersection. The trail rises through a young scrub forest dense with myrtle oak, Chapman oak, and rusty lyonia, the perfect height for scrub-jays to forage for acorns in the low brush. You hear the calls of many birds. If you see a flash of brown and black,

it's likely a rufous-sided towhee, which also prefers this high, dry habitat.

After 0.2 mile, you reach the upper end of the Rusty Lyonia loop. Continue straight ahead. You'll continue down the scrub-flanked corridor to the intersection with the Red Root Trail, which you now join. Continue straight to keep on the perimeter loop. After you cross a couple of old forest trails, used for access to maintain the preserve, you reach a lovely wetland cradled in the scrub and mostly hidden behind a screen of tall bluestem grass, its orange stalks waving in the wind. The trail jogs left around the wetland and heads up a noticeable rise.

This part of the preserve has been carefully stripped of its dense understory, and it looks a bit rough in places—the better to encourage young trees to sprout and provide the type of cover that the scrub-jays crave most. You may see this sort of ravaging of the forest in different places throughout the preserve at different times. It's intentional, and good for the scrub-jays. Until the original scrub restoration project restored the scrub-jays' natural habitat of low oak scrub, these hills were covered with tall sand pines like you see in yards the in the surrounding neighborhood. Florida's scrub ecosystem relies on frequent fires to regenerate the landscape you see here today. Because of the large suburban community of Deltona, fire has been suppressed, allowing sand pines here to grow to enormous heights. Manual restoration efforts at Lyonia Preserve ensure that there will always be patches of young oak scrub, a forest in miniature that the scrub-jays need for survival.

As the trail climbs a tall rise, young rosemary shrubs grow along both sides of the path in the bright white sand. Dark-leaved silk bay begins to appear along the trail. The leaves are a dark shiny green on top, with silky-haired red undersides. If you crush one, it emits the aromatic smell of bay leaves used in Italian cooking. This tree is a close relative, but is endemic to Florida. At the next trail junction, 0.5 miles into the hike, continue straight to walk the perimeter of the Blueberry Trail. Here, the elevation becomes especially pronounced, and with the cleared understory, you can see quite a distance. Keep alert for the shrill *shreep* of the scrub-jays. Watch for the slight depression on the right—a sinkhole, sometimes water-filled—as the trail levels out. Notice the scattered scrub palmetto, a relative of the saw palmetto. They differ in that the scrub palmetto leaf stem is smooth and continues into the leaf, ending in a point. Scrub palmettos also have fine tan fibers growing off their leaves,

which the Florida scrub-jay will pull and use to build its nest.

After a mile of hiking, you climb up a rise of 50 feet to the trail's high point to a bench, looking down on a grassy wetland below. Standing ankle-deep in water, two distant sandhill cranes consult each other, their haunting cries carrying across the scrub. Within moments, they take flight. As they glide overhead, notice the wingspan—7 feet across. It's a steep downhill to the marsh, where a handful of tall slash pines grow. As you round the bend, scrub-jays appear, close and curious. The Florida scrub-jay is a friendly bird, and when feeling no threat, almost tame. Within a few moments, the whole family appears, seven scrub-jays regarding you curiously from their eye-level perches in small sand pines and oaks. Each pair mates for life, raising its family with the aid of helpers, children of the pair with no mating attachment, who delay their own breeding to help raise a family. Families travel together across a territorial spread of 25 acres. The scrub-jays are

Florida scrub-jay

unexpectedly large, 8 inches tall, and so bright and colorful it's like having a flock of parrots surrounding you. Boldly, they hop to the ground, poke around at sticks, and whir past in a blur, landing on your head! But when the family's sentinel—on the lookout for danger—gives a sharp *shreep,* the birds melt back into the scrub, shuffling across the forest floor in search of acorns, insects, and lizards. During the acorn season, each family will gather a cache of acorns, as squirrels do, to feed themselves during the leaner times.

Crossing several more unmarked cross-trails, the trail rises up out of dense sand pines into taller oaks, with an understory of blueberries and deer moss. More frequent rosemary scrubs occur, creating small openings between the oaks. An aromatic plant, Florida's rosemary is *not* related to the culinary herb used in Italian cooking. Heading downhill through a corridor of young sand pines, the trail intersects with the Red Root Trail at 1.6 miles. Scrub-jay sightings are especially common along this stretch of the Red Root Trail, since it's presently still an ideal height for the scrub-jays to browse. Weaving a nest of scrub palmetto fibers and oak twigs, each family raises one or two groups of three or four hatchlings each year. Starting out with brownish-white coloration, the young birds stay with the family for at least a year. The availability of the perfect habitat limits the total population of Florida scrub-jays, as each family is extremely territorial, uninterested in migrating.

Head steeply downhill to reach a trail junction at a T intersection after 1.8 miles. Turn left. You're now back on the entrance trail into the loop system, the Rusty Lyonia Trail. Make a left at the next trail junction to walk the last perimeter trail, the other half of the Rusty Lyonia Trail. It scrambles uphill through a thick scrub of myrtle oak, rusty lyonia, and wax myrtle with scattered blueberries.

As the trail swings around to complete the loop, it passes through a thicker stand of oaks before reaching the end of the loop at 2 miles. Turn left, facing the back of the nature center, and walk down to the fence line. Turn left and follow your footprints in the soft, beach-like sand back to the picnic pavilion, and through a tiny stretch of scrub to exit at the trailhead. Don't be surprised, like we were, if some scrub-jays greet you at the trailhead, too! Where they show up is unpredictable, but you will see them. If you haven't checked out the Lyonia Environmental Center yet, do it now—it has fun interactive exhibits for the kids as well as an art gallery, café, gift shop, and restrooms. There is a small admission fee to the nature exhibits except on Sundays.

DIRECTIONS

From I-4 exit 114, Orange City, go south on SR 472 (Howland Boulevard) for 2.5 miles. Turn right on Providence Boulevard, turning right after 0.7 mile onto Eustace Avenue. The preserve entrance is immediately on the left.

CONTACT

Lyonia Preserve
2150 Eustace Avenue
Deltona, FL 32765
386-740-5261
www.lyoniapreserve.com

45

Smyrna Dunes Park

Total distance (circuit): 2 miles

Hiking time: 1 hour

Habitats: maritime forest, coastal dunes, mangrove swamp

Trailhead coordinates (lat-lon): 29.065864, -80.914742

Maps: USGS 7½' New Smyrna Beach; Park map

Admission: $5 per vehicle

Hours: Sunrise–sunset

Hidden in plain sight at the northern tip of New Smyrna Beach, the 250-acre preserve of Smyrna Dunes Park protects several fragile coastal environments from the ongoing encroachment of development that has marred most of Central Florida's beaches. No signs lead you to this park, and the parking area holds fewer than 50 cars, but Smyrna Dunes provides several significant facets of recreation—hiking, fishing, and the enjoyment of an unspoiled beach.

A 1.4-mile interpretive boardwalk circles Smyrna Dunes, lifting visitors well above the fragile dune terrain. An additional mile of boardwalk provides connections to the beach and a walk through a mangrove swamp. The entire loop is wheelchair accessible, although the side trails to the beach are not—they involve scrambles along sand paths, or staircases up and over the dunes. Adjoining the parking area, a pavilion provides a shaded picnic area with barbecue grills, open-air showers for bathers, and restrooms. Two kiosks show maps of the hike, along with interpretive information about the park.

One of Florida's original colonies, New Smyrna dates back to 1768, when Scottish physician Andrew Turnbull imported 1,200 indentured servants to tame the land—men and women from Minorca (a part of Asia Minor), Italy, and Greece. After a brief stop in St. Augustine, the fleet sailed down the Florida coast to Mosquito Inlet, which laps at the northern fringe of the park. They constructed canals and planted rice and indigo, but the harshness of the coast, along with mosquito-borne illnesses, killed off most of the settlers.

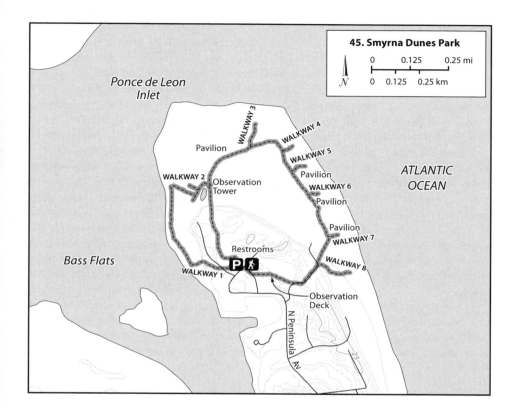

The colony was abandoned after 10 years.

To hike from high ground to low, follow the trail back toward the park entrance, where it soon climbs into the maritime forest. Don't be surprised to see stalks and stumps in places—the missing trees are a testament to Volusia County's continuing fight against invasive species. Although beautiful when it blooms, Brazilian pepper quickly chokes out Florida's more sensitive native species, like the Hercules' club. Several examples of this relative of the lime tree thrive in the maritime forest, easy to identify by its thorny trunk and compound, fern-like leaves. In spring, it attracts bumblebees with tiny clusters of greenish-white flowers. Red bay, very oak-like with a reddish tinge to its tight-grained bark, forms a spreading canopy overhead. Watch for small clumps of cinnamon fern and royal fern under the trees. A brown anole skitters across a fallen log, pausing for a moment to flutter its bright red throat fan to attract admirers.

Rising out of the maritime forest, the trail climbs the dunes, which are up to 20 feet high. Tangles of saw palmetto and catbrier hold these sand mounds in place. Watch for the first of many gopher tortoise holes. At home in this arid habitat, the gopher tortoise digs a burrow right into the side of a dune. In the heat of the afternoon, you'll see tortoises standing guard at the entrances of their homes; they browse the thickets in the cooler morning and evening, nibbling on prickly pear cactus, munching on sumac berries, and crunching down on ribbons of catbrier.

At Walkway #8, turn right and follow the boardwalk up and over the deep bowls between the dunes. Sea oats line the crests closest to the ocean; lone cabbage palms break up the landscape. Look closely at the sprawling prickly pear cacti–some have needles up to 3 inches long! On the climb over the last dune, notice how the sand catches and gathers around bitter panicum, the rough foredune grass holding the dunes against the wind. These white dunes look like mountains in miniature, with virtual glacial blocks of wind-hardened sand cracking away from the hillside, poised to break free. Sand cascades across the boardwalk, attempting to reclaim its territory.

This is the populated side of the peninsula. With beach driving permitted, cars crowd as close to Ponce Inlet as the landscape allows. Thankfully, a breakwater keeps them contained so although most of the Atlantic beaches have vehicles roaming along them, the beaches on the inlet side do not. Looking south, you catch the high-rise seaside sprawl of New Smyrna Beach; to the north, the skyscrapers of Ponce Inlet and Daytona Shores glisten. Smyrna Dunes provides a glimpse into what those places looked like just a few decades ago.

Save the beach walking for the protected shore–follow Walkway #8 back to the main trail. The boardwalk rises high over a deep basin between the dunes, where you catch a glimpse of a white geodesic dome off to the left–the NASA tracking station, used to monitor launches as they pass over this portion of the Space Coast. Scan the skies, and you might see an osprey plummet to grab a fish, or an American kestrel swooping down to the dunes to grab a mouse. Ring-billed gulls wheel past, screeching. Off in the distance, sails slip behind the dunes, a constant pa-

Gopher tortoise in the dunes

The oceanfront boardwalk goes on and on

rade of maritime traffic. Across the inlet, the tall brick form of the Ponce Inlet lighthouse towers over the landscape. Built in 1883, this lighthouse remained in service until the 1970s; it is now a museum and the tallest lighthouse in Florida.

Formerly known as Mosquito Inlet, these narrows provide access to the northern Indian River, a saltwater channel feeding Mosquito Lagoon. During the Civil War, the Union Blockading Squadron guarded this entrance, as it was a major target for blockade runners—profiteers who risked their lives to bring desperately needed goods (sugar and guns) along with luxury items (coffee, silks, and cigars) into Confederate waters. Sailing from Nassau, 191 miles away, blockade runners would sneak into the inlet under dead of night, slipping over the sandbar and out of the reach of the larger, less agile Union gunboats. In February 1862, the nearest militia, the St. Augustine Blues, marched south

to New Smyrna to protect a bounty of munitions that beat the blockade—abandoning their own city, which immediately fell into Union hands. The guns and gunpowder hidden here provided Florida's Confederate forces with a fighting chance of defending the state.

As you continue along the trail, it drops down into a low, barren, desert-like area. One row of dunes guards these lowlands from the ocean. Flocks of savannah sparrows cower close to the ground, blending into the dried grass as they chase insects across the sand. You'll pass more walkways to the beach, and pavilions outfitted with covered picnic tables and charcoal grills. Notice the tortoise tracks across the flat sands. It's easy to spot their homes from afar, as bursts of bright white from excavated seashells carpet the ground around each burrow.

As the trail turns south following the inlet, watch for the observation tower after 1.2

Smyrna Dunes Park

miles. A climb up this three-story tower gives you a sweeping view of the entire park and Ponce Inlet, including a cluster of tall sand dunes inland, across the river, broken only by the spikes of Washingtonia palms. The dead fronds of these tall palms fall downward but stay attached to the tree, forming a mound of material that looks like a hut around the trunk. Look toward NASA's geodesic dome—one lone specimen of Washingtonia rises from a dune within this park.

Take Walkway #2 to the right. It crosses an old road edged with very out-of-place granite boulders, perhaps a long-ago attempt at a jetty, and scrambles onto another boardwalk out into the mangrove swamp. Mangroves cluster around what looks like an old man-made canal. This is the northern extent of the red mangrove. Note the bean-pod-like "roots" at its base—miniature mangroves spawning, fully formed plants waiting to float off with the next high tide. Red mangroves often have a coating of salt on their leaves, as they naturally extract salt from seawater. Intermingled in this swamp, black mangroves (ranging north to St. Augustine) have shiny leaves and dark round seed cases. Both have suffered from abnormal deep freezes that affected the coast, so many mangroves look dead or dying.

Where Walkway #2 reaches the beach, you can turn right and follow the inlet around to the edge of the park—a beach walk of nearly 2 miles—back to Walkway #8, or head 0.3 mile south along the river to Walkway #1. Erosion of the dunes along the inlet exposes the bright pink roots of sea purslane, a succulent with a high salt content in its thick leaves. Its tiny flowers bloom all summer. Also known as sea pickle, the leaves of sea purslane have been used to treat scurvy and kidney disorders.

The canal feeding the mangrove swamp barely touches the upper edge of the beach, so the sea only nourishes the swamp at high tide. Oysters cling to the mangroves' exposed roots. This is the dog beach, so expect to see residents walking their dogs along the lapping waves. At the fishing pier, climb up the stairs to follow Walkway #1 back to the main loop, a 0.1-mile walk. On the main loop, turn right to return to the parking lot.

DIRECTIONS

From Interstate 95, take exit 249, New Smyrna Beach. Follow SR 44 east over the causeway into New Smyrna Beach, turning left on Peninsula Boulevard after 5.4 miles. Follow this road north for 2.7 miles through residential areas until it ends at the Coast Guard Station. Turn right to enter the park.

CONTACT

Smyrna Dunes Park
2995 N. Peninsula Ave
New Smyrna Beach, FL 32168
386-424-2935
www.volusia.org/parks

46

Merritt Island
National Wildlife Refuge

Total distance (five circuits): 8.9 miles

Hiking time: 5 hours

Habitats: tidal marsh, mangrove swamp, hydric hammock, palm hammock, oak hammock, scrub, pond, freshwater marsh

Trailhead coordinates (lat-lon)
Visitor Center Boardwalk:
28.641506, -80.735693
Hammock Trails:
28.644107, -80.716586
Scrub Ridge Trail:
28.694983, -80.715883
Cruickshank Trail:
28.678159, -80.771798

Maps: USGS 7½' Mims, Merritt Island NWR map

Admission: Free

Hours: Sunrise–sunset; closures possible during space launches

Adjoining Kennedy Space Center along the Indian River Lagoon, the Merritt Island National Wildlife Refuge offers some of the best bird-watching opportunities in Florida. Renowned for its diversity of species, the park offers several hiking trails on which you'll want to bring your binoculars and camera for an opportunity to see some of the 310 different types of birds, including Florida scrub-jays, bald eagles, black-necked stilts, and roseate spoonbills.

The trailheads are located off the three roads that create a loop through the south end of the refuge. After entering the refuge on CR 406, turn right to follow CR 402. From the entrance, it's 2.8 miles to the Merritt Island National Wildlife Refuge Visitor Center, 3.3 miles to the Hammock Trails, and 3.8 miles to the Scrub Ridge Trail, which is along CR 3 just north of CR 406. Head back from the Scrub Ridge Trail via CR 406 to access Black Point Wildlife Drive for the Cruickshank Trail.

VISITOR CENTER BOARDWALK

If you're new to the refuge or traveling with small children, a stop at the Merritt Island National Wildlife Refuge Visitor Center is a must to orient yourself to this marshy expanse along the Space Coast. The Visitor Center is open Mon-Fri 8–4:30, Sat: 9–5, and on Sundays Nov-Mar from 9–5. Birding is the top activity here on Merritt Island, especially during the winter months when the migratory birds settle in. For more than a decade, the Space Coast Wildlife and Birding Festival (www.nbbd.com/fly) has showcased the

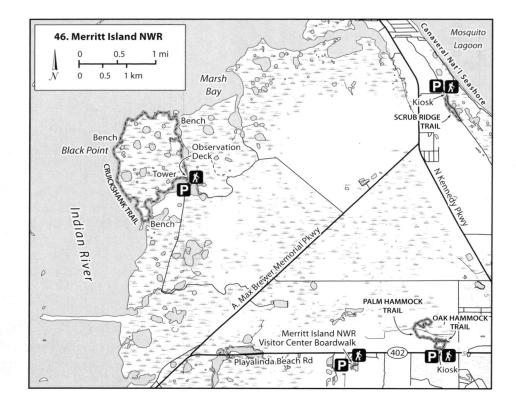

region's avian bounty along its trails and waterways, with Merritt Island swarmed with birders from around the globe every January. It's here you'll fill out that life list. At the Visitor Center, pick up guidebooks, checklists, and identification information to help you spot species. When the visitor center is open, a boardwalk trail gives you your first taste of Space Coast birding along a marshy pond out back. Look for purple gallinules hiding in the reeds and Louisiana herons stalking the shallows. The quarter-mile boardwalk ventures from pond to marsh to make a 0.4-mile loop through a shady oak hammock, providing access to a covered observation deck over a pond, perfect for picture-taking when the birds are within range.

OAK AND PALM HAMMOCK TRAILS

Continue another half mile down CR 402 to the Hammock Trails trailhead on the left.

Two trails lead away from the Hammock Trails kiosk—the Oak Hammock Trail (0.7 mile) and the Palm Hammock Trail (2 miles). Both are loop trails that return you to the parking lot. Start with the Oak Hammock Trail, a family-friendly interpretive trail to the right. Beneath the tall oaks, sword ferns crowd densely along the trail. Citrus trees grow wild here, a remnant of a homestead from the 1940s. Captain Douglas Dummitt established the very first citrus grove along the Indian River Lagoon near here in 1807, when he built a homestead along the eastern shore of the lagoon.

After crossing a bridge over a marshy ditch, you cross the NASA railroad line, followed by another bridge and a jeep trail. Continue on to the shade of a giant old water oak, where the trail splits in two directions. Follow the left fork through tall saw palmettos and up to a boardwalk. Turn left at the first intersection for a walk through a laurel oak forest. You'll start to see some unusual trees—their trunks are bare and smooth, with an orange hue. These nakedwood trees, also known as Simpson's stopper, grow profusely along all of the trails in the hammock. A dead-end side trail leads through a small grove of them. The "stopper" part of the name comes from the use of their bark to treat diarrhea.

The Oak Hammock Trail continues on a boardwalk through a hydric hammock. Beware of touching the trees that cozy up to the trail—many of them sport poison ivy! Islands of ferns break up the dark tannic swamp. At 0.5 mile, you meet the inner boardwalk—turn left, passing a short dead-end trail. The boardwalk ends, and the trail continues on a base of ground-up seashells. Wild coffee grows along both sides of the trail; some of the plants are more than 4 feet tall! Watch for its glossy leaves and distinctive reddish-brown coffee beans. A short boardwalk to the left leads to a swamp overlook with wild persimmon trees. The trail veers to the right, continuing back to the junction under the old water oak. Turn left to return to the parking lot, for a total 0.7-mile walk.

Leaving the kiosk to the left, the Palm Hammock Trail is for the more adventuresome hiker. Expect short stretches of muddy and wet hiking, including some stream crossings. Starting out under an oak canopy, the trail quickly crosses a small bridge over a ditch into a low area edged by a red maple swamp. It rises briefly through an oak hammock. Like the Oak Hammock Trail, it crosses a bridge, the railroad tracks, another bridge, and the

KEVIN MIMS

Along the Palm Hammock Trail

jeep trail as it heads out deeper into the forest. At 0.1 mile, the trail veers left into a dense hammock, where spreading laurel oaks shade an understory of tall saw palmettos. It's a damp area, with rich dark soil and roots underfoot. The trail rises and opens up overhead as it enters a corridor edged by saw palmettos, wax myrtle, gallberry, and young sand live oaks—another potential scrub-jay site—then drops back down into another palm hammock. A boardwalk begins at 0.6 mile, with a bench to the left. The boardwalk carries the trail through a swamp forest mostly dominated by red maple and Virginia willow, ending at another palm hammock. Where the trail becomes indistinct due to palm fronds on the ground, veer right, following fiberglass markers with brown directional arrows. When you are confronted with so many cabbage palms at once, the distinct knobby patterns on their trunks stand out in sharp relief.

The trail turns right into a maze of tall palms, where you weave your way through to another boardwalk over a mixed oak and maple swamp forest. Twisting and turning sharply, the boardwalk continues for more than 900 feet and ends in another palm hammock. A crashing in the underbrush announces the scurrying of wild hogs, leaving their deep furrows in the trail while digging for grubs. Follow the green bands through the forest. The trail sticks to the edge of the hammock, along a line of young magnolia trees and Simpson's stopper. At 1.2 miles, cross a boardwalk that accesses NASA instrumentation for space shuttle landings—this trail is directly in line with a landing strip. Passing through another palm hammock, the trail rounds a bend and crosses over some large limestone rocks.

At 1.4 miles, you'll see the first directional sign for the trailhead. Turn right, walking up a causeway edged by swamp on both sides, the trail crowded by tall asters. The profusion of wildflowers attracts many zebra longwing butterflies. Turn right at the TRAILHEAD PARKING ½ MILE sign, crossing a short bridge and fording a narrow swampy stream under a canopy of oaks and maples. At 1.8 miles, a bridge crosses a swampy ditch, where tall stems support clusters of the orchid-like blossoms of duck potatoes. Cross the railroad tracks. If debris blocks the line of sight to the trail, walk around it and look for the bridge. The final section of trail continues through an oak hammock ornamented with exotic plantings. After 2 miles, the trail ends at the parking lot.

SCRUB RIDGE TRAIL

Continue along CR 402 to where it meets CR 3. Turn left and drive past CR 406. The trailhead entrance road is on the right. Drive 0.4 mile down this road to the trailhead. Just a mile long, the Scrub Ridge Trail offers expansive views across lagoons between the ridge and the beach, as well as the opportunity to see Florida scrub-jays living near the sea.

From the parking area, follow the broad path into the open coastal scrub. There is little shade, since there are few tall pines to provide any. The trail is headed straight for a distant line of tall slash pines, and there is a sameness to the landscape that you just can't deny. The understory is dense with saw palmetto. Curving to the left, it comes to a T intersection with an unmarked trail. Turn left to return along the loop. A Florida scrub-jay lands in a sand live oak, boldly curious at your approach. Merritt Island National Wildlife Refuge and the adjoining Canaveral National Seashore host the state's largest population of this endemic bird, whose numbers continue to diminish as population squeezes out their requisite habitat, this not-so-pretty but pretty important open scrub.

As you walk north along the trail, a wall of vegetation screens your view of the marsh. The road broadens after 0.7 mile as you return to the trailhead, completing the 1-mile hike.

CRUICKSHANK TRAIL

If you've ever wondered what it would be like to drive on water, Black Point Wildlife Drive comes close. It's a one-way hard-packed limestone road edged on both sides with water—tidal marsh, mangrove swamp, and open lagoon—and few pullovers. An interpretive brochure explains different points along the route. The trailhead is 3.4 miles down the road; watch for the PARKING sign at marker 8. A composting toilet is provided at the trailhead.

Palm-lined marshes along the Scrub Ridge Trail

Start your hike on the Allan Cruickshank Memorial Trail with a stop at the interpretive kiosk. It's tempting to run over to the observation deck, but save it for the end of the 4.8-mile hike, after you've savored a walk along the Indian River Lagoon and its tidal marshes. The trail follows a levee around several impoundment areas and is the on-foot equivalent of Wildlife Drive—narrow, surrounded by water, a perfect place for quiet bird-watching. Wear sunscreen and a hat, as there is little shade on the trail. Brisk salt breezes make up for the open environment; you'll have few problems with mosquitoes.

Listen for the sounds around you. An alligator splashes into the water from its lazy spot beneath a mangrove, causing peeps and squawks in the bushes. A mullet propels its entire body into the air, landing back into the water with a great plop. A cabbage palm rustles in the wind. An osprey calls out with its distinctive cry.

Small rattlebox, with its bright yellow pea-shaped flowers, clings to the sides of the levee, soaking up water and sunshine. Bracken ferns grow in the shade of wax myr-

tles. A roseate spoonbill glides overhead, delicate pink. An immature bald eagle hovers, curious about the hikers below. Louisiana herons, with their distinctive white bellies and deep blue plumage, wade through the shallows in search of small fry, poking through islands of perennial glasswort swathed in autumn colors—browns, reds, yellows, and greens.

At 0.8 mile, it's your first chance to sit and relax on a shaded bench. There are several along the trail. Once you pass the instrumentation station, the trail grows rough. No longer a jeep track, it becomes uneven and hummocky, although the park staff keeps the grass trimmed. Expect to walk more slowly for the next 4 miles. The thick succulent leaves of saltwort peek out of a sea of red-tipped glasswort. Used as a medicinal herb and as a tea, saltwort is thought to relieve asthma, constipation, and gout.

White mangroves edge the trail on the right, providing a windbreak against the open waters of the lagoon. Sea rocket shows off its tiny purple blooms. The mangroves part briefly at 1.4 miles for a sweeping view of the lagoon. Tall clumps of big cordgrass grow along the levee's edge. When the wind picks up, the waters of the impoundment area whip to waves. On the right, a long, narrow mangrove island creates a canal between the levee and the lagoon. Swamp hibiscus towers up to 10 feet tall, waving its massive pink flowers in the breeze.

When you reach marker 3, you've walked slightly more than 2 miles. Almost 3 more to go! A wood stork swoops down, its large frame with black-and-white plumage distinctive against the blue sky. It frightens a flock of purple gallinules off a small island. After the trail curves around a small lagoon, another covered bench appears at 2.2 miles. On the right, an opening in the mangroves provides a sweeping view of the north end of Titusville. On the left, NASA's Vehicle Assembly Building comes into view in the distance. One of the world's largest buildings—covering 8 acres and enclosing 129 million cubic feet of space—the Vehicle Assembly Building is where NASA builds, repairs, and outfits rockets and space shuttles for travel.

A belted kingfisher skims the mangrove-edged canal. In the impoundment, grassy islands give way to more substantial islands anchored by mangroves. Passing marker 2, expect less than 2 more miles of hiking. The levee veers in an arc toward Wildlife Drive. Take a moment to look into the water as you veer left around the far corner, where tiny fish and seashells are visible against the white sand bottom. The lagoon itself is dark, stained with tannic acid. Don't stare into it too long—the undulating blue-black surface of the impoundment can become hypnotic!

Just before the next covered bench at 3.6 miles, a juniper grows along the water's edge, bright with waxy blue berries. The levee zigzags for the next quarter mile as it returns to the beginning of the arc; across the water, you can clearly see where you've been. An osprey flies over, mullet grasped firmly in its talons. As the levee veers right, the marsh on the left resembles an open prairie, with tall cordgrass swaying on each island. Young mangroves struggle to take root. Pass marker 1, and you soon see the observation platform far to the left. On the right, a telephone pole provides a preferred perch for cormorants drying their wings.

Heading up to the observation deck, the last stretch of the levee has open water on both sides. Watch the grasses carefully, as this area easily camouflages the wintering whimbrel, distinctive with dark stripes on its narrow head and its curved bill. At 4.6 miles, you reach the broad, tall observation deck. Climb up and survey the marsh. You've skirted the impoundment area, and the natural salt marsh lies off to the east, beyond the levee.

Return to the kiosk. A long black racer appears from the underbrush, chasing a marsh rat out into the open as it stalks its meal. Turn right to the parking lot, ending your walk at 4.8 miles.

DIRECTIONS
From Interstate 95 exit 220, Titusville, follow SR 406 east for 8 miles over the causeway to Merritt Island. Pass the entrance gate to the refuge. Because of heightened security around Kennedy Space Center, you may be asked for identification or may be subject to a vehicle search. After 3 miles on CR 402, you'll reach the turnoff for CR 406—your decision point for whether you're headed to Black Point Wildlife Drive or the Visitor Center hiking areas.

CONTACT
Merritt Island National Wildlife Refuge
P.O. Box 2683
Titusville, FL 32781
321-861-0668
www.fws.gov/merrittisland

47

Enchanted Forest Sanctuary

Total distance (circuit): 2.5 miles

Hiking time: 1.5 hours

Habitats: floodplain forest, freshwater marsh, hardwood hammock, hydric hammock, oak scrub, pine flatwoods, wet prairie

Trailhead coordinates (lat-lon): 28.533350, -80.802283

Maps: USGS 7½' Titusville; Park map

Admission: Free

Hours: 9 AM–5 PM Tues. through Sun.

A wonderland of big trees, geologic oddities, and historic sites awaits just outside Kennedy Space Center at the Enchanted Forest Sanctuary, the flagship conservation land that kicked off Brevard County's Environmentally Endangered Lands program more than a decade ago. This is a magical place for children and adults, scarcely a mile west of the Indian River Lagoon to the south of Titusville, protecting 470 acres of diverse habitats along its well-marked trail system, with the spine of the Atlantic Coastal Ridge a prominent landform down the middle.

The entry road is part of the Hernandez-Capron Trail, an old military trail laid out by General Joseph Hernandez and built by his men in 1837, during the Second Seminole War, to link the fortresses at St. Augustine and Fort Pierce. Built atop the elevated prehistoric sand dunes known as the Atlantic Coastal Ridge, the road persisted as an immigrant trail to South Florida through the late 1800s.

Head toward the Education Center to start your hike. You can tell right away this is a hiker-focused preserve—there's a Hike Desk for you to sign in and grab a map. Pets are not permitted on the trails here. The Education Center is particularly busy on weekdays with school groups, but provides an excellent overview for all ages of the habitats, flora, and fauna of the preserve, including such rarities as the Florida scrub lizard and the eastern indigo snake. The center is also where you'll find restrooms, classrooms, and a gift shop run by the Friends of the Enchanted Forest.

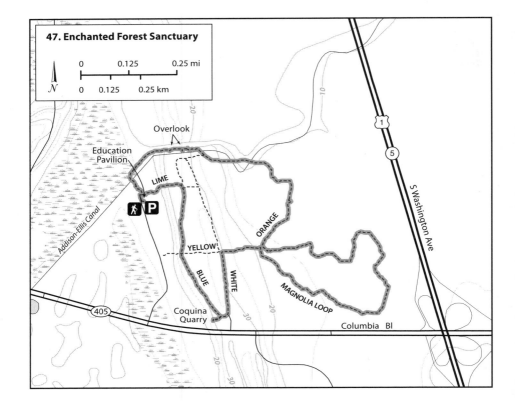

47. Enchanted Forest Sanctuary

Since the first edition of this guidebook, the trail system has expanded a little and has been re-blazed and renamed. Each trail carries a name that echoes the surrounding habitat and its inhabitants. The trail system now starts behind the Education Center. Leaving the center, turn right and walk toward the native land garden; turn right again to walk behind the building. Follow the trail into an oak hammock along the Biodiversity Loop, which is the first of several trails you'll be stitching together to keep to the perimeter of the trail system. At the junction with Enchanted Crossing, continue straight ahead along the Biodiversity Loop. The trail immediately reaches a T intersection. To the right is a gate leading out to the parking lot. Turn left. You're walking along the edge of a scrub forest on a well-groomed footpath, with aromatic silk bay providing some shade. The oak canopy is much thinner than it was before the hurricanes of 2004–2005, but it's still a good representative upland forest with a lot of young shrubs in the understory. A splash of bright red among the dusty green draws your eyes to a coral bean's blooms. Watch carefully as a small lizard vanishes under a colorful lupine. A relative of the fence lizard, the threatened Florida scrub lizard, *Sceloporus woodi,* lives only in Florida, and only in upland scrub habitats, dry sandy hilltops like this ridge. Growing up to 6 inches long, the grayish-brown lizard has dark brown stripes down its sides.

As the trail continues up a gentle slope,

you come to a junction with a bench atop the Atlantic Coastal Ridge. Turn right. The Ridge Trail works its way along the ecotone between the high open ridge and the upland forest. You pass a bench, and there's a tall magnolia tree up ahead. Dropping downhill, you come to the Tortoise Trail at 0.3 miles. It crosses over the Ridge Trail, leading downhill to the parking area, and was the original access trail when the preserve opened a decade ago (then called the Lime Trail). Cross it and keep to the Ridge Trail.

When you reach the Coquina Quarry Trail at 0.5 mile, you're within sight of a busy local airport, which accounts for the frequent buzzing overhead, especially on weekends. Follow this spur trail down into an old coquina quarry, shot through with solution holes, formed by the slow drip of water through weak spots in the limestone. This outcropping of rock is part of the Anastasia formation, a long shelf of limestone stretching along Florida's Atlantic coast from south of Jacksonville to north of Palm Beach. Like sliced butter, the quarry walls show the precision scooping of machines that once cut the rock for building stone.

After you retrace your steps up the spur trail, turn right to continue along the Ridge Trail as it loops back north around the ridge. Watch for a flowering paw-paw on the right, a relative of the soursop, a fruit often seen on Caribbean menus. At the next junction with the Tortoise Trail, there are a couple of benches. Turn right to head downhill into the shade. The Tortoise Trail makes a quick descent from the scrub into a forest dense with magnolias, oaks, cabbage palms, and saw palmetto. Cabbage palms tower overhead as you reach the junction with the Mesic Trail. Continue straight. The trail ascends up a slight rise and a reaches a multitrail junction with a kiosk and a gathering of benches.

Turn right to start walking counterclockwise along the Magnolia Loop. This is one of the highlights of the preserve, so don't miss it! Lushly canopied, it starts off by passing a large live oak with an unusual curl to its trunk. Wild coffee fills the understory, and cabbage palms rise high overhead. As the trail descends, it winds under southern magnolias more than 100 feet tall and massive live oaks. A floodplain forest hides off to the right behind a screen of trees; in winter, the red seedpods of red maple betray its presence. Wild citrus, including oranges and grapefruit, grow in this part of the forest. The trail comes up to a magnificent oak, an oak that would take quite a few people holding hands to encircle it, with a cabbage palm growing straight up the middle. The sharp smell of fungi is in the air as you walk past many fallen logs. Sword ferns, marsh ferns, and royal ferns carpet the deep, rich soil; the trail is mushy in places. A thousand shades of green delight the eye.

The trail enters an unusual "forest within a forest" at 1.1 miles, a dense stand of yaupon holly. This holly is notable for its tiny leaves and for the use of its berries to create cassina, the highly caffeinated "black drink" of the Seminoles and other more ancient Floridians. Keep to the right at the fork in the trail. Emerging into a paradise of palms, oaks, and ferns, the trail leads you down a corridor of tall cabbage palms. There's dark earth underfoot, an area that may get damp after heavy rains, with more massive oaks spreading their thickly knotted root systems across the trail. The swamp in the forest, downhill and to the right, becomes more obvious around 1.4 miles, with bubbles rising to its surface from gases emitted by rotting leaves beneath the water. The trail continues to rise away from it. After you pass a bench, you're back at the clearing where the Magnolia Loop began, after 1.7 miles.

Turn right to follow the Tomoka Trail to stay on the outer loop of the trail system. The trail

Atop the Atlantic Coastal Ridge

immediately drops down through a tunnel of vines, with cabbage palms providing the canopy. There is a bench at the beginning of a zigzagging boardwalk that works its way through the floodplain forest. Strap ferns sprout from fallen logs like bright green feathers. Open pools of clear tannic water are edged by ferns. Reaching the Biodiversity Loop junction, turn right to stay on the outer loop. It immediately becomes a boardwalk through more floodplain forest. An interpretive sign provides information about the Addison-Ellis Canal, which affects the hydrology of this landscape.

Just beyond the junction with the Mesic Trail, the Coquina Trail veers to the right. Turn and follow it downhill. It has a nice narrow descent and a wooden bridge over the canal. The water is tannic but clear, with oranges floating in the mild flow. Benches on the far side of the canal provide a scenic view. As the trail turns left, it parallels the canal, and it's a very steep drop—an actual cliff—down to the bottom of the canal. Several cleared spots in the cabbage palms provide an excellent view of the canal. Started in 1912, the Addison-Ellis Canal was probably meant to drain the extensive wetlands between the St. Johns River and the Indian River Lagoon for development. Remains of the canal stretch from the Canaveral Marshes along SR 50 under I-95 to the Enchanted Forest, where construction abruptly ended when the diggers hit the impenetrable Atlantic Coastal Ridge, ruined their equipment, and went bankrupt.

Here's where you need to keep an eye on the kids. Steep cliffs and poison ivy provide hazards off to your left. After 2.1 miles, the landscape opens up in front of you—you're back on the top of the Atlantic Coastal Ridge, with scrub a sharp contrast to the leafy glade of cabbage palms along the canal. A shaded bench sits off to the right, and unmarked trails vanish into the distance. Ignore them and continue paralleling the canal, and you'll be rewarded with some excellent views of the geologic formations where the ridge was deeply cut. Strap fern clings to boulders on the far rock face. As the trail drops down off the ridge, it is soft sand underfoot, much like climbing down through dunes. A large gopher tortoise burrow is off to the right.

As the trail narrows, curves, and drops down lower, it is lined with young cabbage palms. You emerge within sight of the Education Center and a historic marker for the canal. Slices of coquina, shot through with solution holes, are centerpieces in a garden of native plants. The odd look of these rocks evokes moonscapes, appropriate given you're just a mile or two from Kennedy Space Center. Work your way through the garden and back past the nature center. Be sure to sign out at the Hike Desk on your way out!

DIRECTIONS

From I-95 exit 215, Titusville, drive east on SR 50 to the first traffic light. Turn right onto SR 405. Follow it for 4.4 miles to the park entrance on the left. If you reach the US 1 overpass, you've gone too far.

CONTACT

Enchanted Forest Sanctuary
Management & Education Center
444 Columbia Boulevard
Titusville, FL 32780
321-264-5185
efs.eelbrevard.com

48

Maritime Hammock Sanctuary

Total distance (circuit): 2.8 miles

Hiking time: 2 hours

Habitats: coastal strand, hydric hammock, mangrove forest, maritime hammock

Trailhead coordinates (lat-lon): 28.011213, -80.530452

Maps: USGS 7½' Melbourne East; Park map at kiosk

Admission: Free

Hours: 7 AM–6 PM Oct. through Apr., 7 AM–8 PM May through Sept.

Bordering and managed by the Archie Carr National Wildlife Refuge—the first wildlife refuge in America established to protect sea turtles—Maritime Hammock Sanctuary showcases maritime, or coastal hammock, marshlands, and mangroves along the Indian River Lagoon. It's 150 acres preserved from the residential development that has otherwise spread up and down A1A along this barrier island, and shows signs in places of having once been a former nursery. Eradication of nonnative species continues. According to one interpretive marker, "This is the place where the North meets the South" . . . biologically speaking. You'll find that out along this hiking-only trail as you discover species that are comfortable in Naples or Key West while following a twisting, winding, sometimes narrow and soggy, and mostly a most excellent adventure.

Start your hike at the North Trailhead, where there are several grassy parking spaces on the slope above the bike path. Stop at the kiosk to pick up a map. The preserve is shaped like a bridge, with an incursion of subdivision in the middle section, although the houses are well hidden from view. The trail starts by skirting a sinkhole or pit that was part of a nursery that once occupied this spot. You'll see some escaped nursery residents like snake plant and Norfolk Island pine growing in the hammocks, but most of the invasive species have been rounded up.

Snaking around and down, the trail enters a lush hammock. Look up into the high canopy for orchids, primarily butterfly and

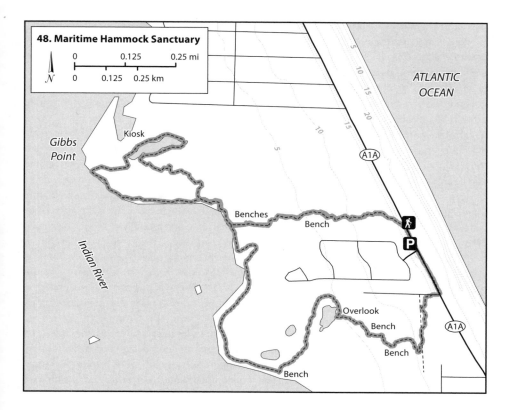

greenfly orchids, which bloom in the summer months. Even off-season, their leaves are rather showy. As the corridor narrows, you're surrounded by more tropical trees and shrubs in the understory. A natural archway rises over the trail; you may need to duck under it. The trail twists and winds through the dense forest beneath tree limbs outstretched in graceful windswept arcs like ballet dancers. Becoming mushy underfoot, the footpath crosses a series of bog bridges surrounded by pennyroyal and giant leather ferns. After a sharp right turn at a fence line, a short spur trail provides a shaded bench from which to look out and savor a view of a creek hidden under a tunnel of tropical vegetation.

At the trail junction, the "You are Here"

marker provides a map to show where the trail system goes. Turn right to head up along the stacked loops on the north end of the sanctuary. The trail is right behind the mangrove roots along the Indian River Lagoon, and can get wet at times. A half mile in, you encounter your first gumbo-limbo tree. The gumbo-limbo is also jokingly called the "Tourist Tree" due to its distinctive red, peeling bark. This is the northernmost preserve in which I've encountered this tropical tree.

Keep right at the next trail junction, where there is another map. Sprays of shoelace fern and goldfoot fern emerge from the tall cabbage palms. You emerge from the hammock into a beauty spot. at the next trail junction, a panoramic view of open marshes framed by cabbage palms and giant sprays of sand cordgrass in the foreground. Turn right to circle the marsh. Mounds of coreopsis and aster are in bloom throughout the open areas. This is an excellent spot for birding. A little blue heron squawks and flies away at your approach. Cormorants crowd the branches of mangroves on a small island in the middle of the marsh. Easily confused with the anhinga, the cormorant is a more social bird. You'll see them hanging out in groups. The anhinga prefers solitude, and has a longer, leaner frame. Its neck looks enough like a snake that "snakebird" is a colloquial name for the anhinga. Both birds dive underwater for prey and then retreat to a perch to stretch their wings to dry, since they do not have oil glands to waterproof their feathers.

The breeze off the lagoon across the marsh makes this part of the hike naturally air-conditioned. Pass the side trail to a residential neighborhood and loop around the marsh, crossing it on boards atop a concrete weir. Turn right. After a mile, the trail turns left and you're along the lapping shoreline of the Indian River Lagoon. Here, the mangroves grow substantially taller. A boardwalk leads through a wet area. Sea wrack and oyster

Indian River Lagoon

shells are spread across open spots between the mangroves, and some of the sea wrack is in Technicolor—beyond the normal "dead grass gray" to shades of orange and purple. Bog bridges carry you across damp spots. Complete the double upper loop, returning to a junction with a map. Continue forward across the bridge to reach the initial junction at 1.4 miles.

The next part of the trail isn't as interesting as what you've hiked so far. It's a necessary connector between the two preserved hammocks within this sanctuary, skirting the residential area, and as such, is a long walk along a tall levee next to the mangroves that line the Indian River Lagoon. You may spot ibises in the mangrove limbs, and a massive alligator lives at the base of one sharply banked turn in the levee, so don't hike this piece on autopilot, as you may be tempted to do. A long straightaway leads down to this left turn. Reaching an interpretive sign about the impoundments, which were created for mosquito control many decades ago, watch for a bridge on the left that finally gets you off the long dike at 2 miles and back into the tropical hammock again.

You encounter benches more frequently as the trail passes through a forest of young gumbo-limbo. Passing an interpretive sign about the tropical plants, the trail is infused with a damp, skunky aroma. The young tropical trees are skinny, smooth-barked, and packed densely through this part of the forest, reminding me of the tropical hammocks of Key Largo. Branches curl into bizarre inchworm shapes overhead as the high canopy fills in with red bay and live oak again. A spur trail leads off to the right at 2.3 miles to an observation deck that opens up onto a lagoon. If you can tolerate the mosquitoes—which are more intense here than along the rest of the loop—take the time to look for wading birds roosting in the mangroves.

A northerly tropical hammock

tinue walking through the shade of the hammock, past another bench. At 2.5 miles, the trail makes a sharp left and goes down a corridor with a scrubby feel. Still twisting and winding, the trail passes beneath oaks arching from left to right, undulating fingerlings of branches spreading to provide deep shade and shelter for more bromeliads and orchids. The footpath gets hilly, as if you're climbing up and over middens. Passing another old baffle in a fence, the trail pops out under a power line. A marker ushers you to the right, where you emerge out on the paved bicycle trail at the South Trailhead.

Turn left and walk up the paved trail past the inholding—Mark's Landing—as traffic zips past at high speed along A1A. Reaching the North Trailhead, you complete a 2.8-mile loop.

DIRECTIONS

From Interstate 95, take exit 180 for Melbourne. Follow US 192 east 8 miles through downtown and continue over the causeway to Indialantic. When the highway ends at the beach, turn right and follow A1A for 10.3 miles, passing a variety of public beaches en route to the community of Melbourne Shores. Park at the north trailhead (you'll have to pull across the bicycle path to do so, so watch for pedestrians and bicycles) and start your hike there.

CONTACT

Maritime Hammock Sanctuary
6200 South Highway A1A
Melbourne Beach, FL
321-723-3556
www.eelbrevard.com

Through the next stretch of maritime hammock, the canopy isn't looking especially healthy. Florida's red bay trees, the primary hardwood found in the maritime hammock, are under attack by the redbay ambrosia beetle. Introduced into the Southeastern United States in the past decade through foreign trade of lumber and wooden packing materials, *Xyleborus glabratus* first made its appearance through a path of destruction in the maritime hammock of Jacksonville's Timucuan Preserve in 2005. It's since spread to other sites around the state. Introducing a vascular fungus into trees in the *Lauraceae* family, which also includes silk bay, it kills off the host tree within a few weeks. It's an ecological disaster poised to decimate our coastal hammocks.

More shells crunch underfoot as you con-

49

Turkey Creek Sanctuary

Total distance (circuit): 1.6 miles

Hiking time: 1.5 hours

Habitats: sand pine scrub, hardwood hammock, oak hammock, floodplain forest

Trailhead coordinates (lat-lon):
28.016912, -80.604775

Maps: USGS 7½' Melbourne East; Park map

Admission: Free

Hours: 7 AM–sunset daily. Margaret Hames Nature Center open 9–4 daily.

Surrounded by suburbia in Palm Bay, Turkey Creek Sanctuary is a precious preserve of 117 acres, protecting the gentle bends of Turkey Creek as it carves a deep path through sandy banks on its winding course to the Indian River Lagoon. Manatees graze in the clear tannic waters of the creek in spring and summer, delighting visitors as they swim in search of eelgrass and water lettuce.

Your hike starts at the front entrance with its small butterfly garden. Look for Gulf fritillary butterflies with wide orange wings with white spots below and zebra longwing butterflies with wide black and yellow wings. Sand pines tower overhead; myrtle oaks and saw palmettos crowd the understory. You quickly reach a kiosk with a map of the sanctuary, off to the right. On the left is the Margaret Hames Nature Center, with interpretive displays, research materials, and restrooms. Stop in the center to pick up a trail map and a copy of the interpretive guide.

Continuing along the trail, you reach a gated entrance into the sanctuary. Turkey Creek Sanctuary is open seven days a week 7 AM–sunset; the exact hour the gate is locked is posted next to the gate. Follow the bark-chip footpath as it winds behind the public library into the dense sand pine forest, passing a side trail to a picnic pavilion. When you come to the intersection with the jogging trail, make a left, then a right to start the boardwalk. Stop and sign the trail register.

The boardwalk at this preserve is somewhat unique in that it isn't there to keep your feet dry—it keeps the footpath off the habitat, allowing wheelchair access to most of

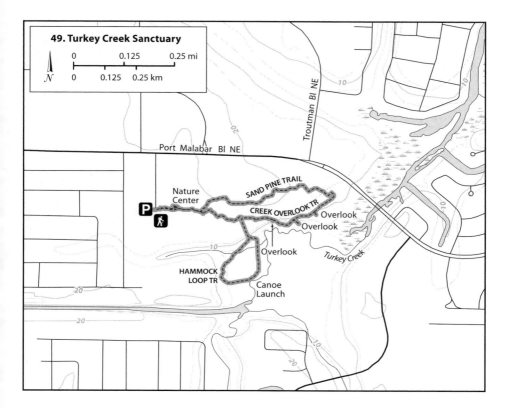

49. Turkey Creek Sanctuary

| 0 | 0.125 | 0.25 mi |
| 0 | 0.125 | 0.25 km |

Troutman Bl NE

Port Malabar Bl NE

Nature Center

SAND PINE TRAIL

CREEK OVERLOOK TR

Overlook

Overlook

Overlook

Turkey Creek

HAMMOCK LOOP TR

Canoe Launch

the park. It also memorializes residents and visitors who've helped with the construction effort, their names or messages permanently carved in the boards, a humorous distraction as you walk. There is plenty to read along the trail besides the boards themselves, as this is an interpretive trail, with numbers to match the guide and tags on many of the trees, shrubs, and plants. The boardwalk zigzags through the sand pine scrub; overhead, the tall sand pines are thick with ball moss. Greenbrier snakes across open patches of bright white sand. Turkey oaks add a splash of fall color in the lower canopy.

Frequent benches make this an easy walk for hikers of any age. After you pass the first bench, the boardwalk swings to the left and comes up to a gazebo. Just beyond, the boardwalk forks; keep to the right to follow the Hammock Loop Trail. At the next fork, turn left. The boardwalk drops down, and you catch your first glimpse of water—Turkey Creek, bordered on the far shore by steep sand bluffs, the remnants of ancient sand dunes. As the boardwalk turns a bend, you enter the hardwood hammock, dominated by live oaks, cabbage palms, red maple, and elms. Bromeliads and fungus decorate the tree limbs. The boardwalk begins to parallel the water, affording you two viewing platforms from which to watch for manatees. Saw palmettos dip their fronds in the dark water; turtles cluster together on a fallen log, drying their shells in the sun. You pass under a grapefruit tree that drops its heavy yellow

Boardwalk above Turkey Creek

fruits across the trail. Although this tree grows wild, its original stock came from Spanish homesteaders in the 1500s, who were ordered to bring citrus trees to Florida when claiming their land grants. Native Americans soon discovered the flavor of citrus and scattered seeds throughout the wild. Like most wild stock, these grapefruit are sour, appreciated only by the raccoons and insects along the creek.

As the boardwalk curves along an elbow of the creek, it comes up to a canoe landing at 0.5 mile. Visitors are welcome to enter the park by canoe or kayak, paddling up from the Indian River Lagoon or from a launch point in Palm Bay, the city boat ramp at Bianca Drive. Pignut hickory trees pepper their nuts across the boards. The canoe landing straddles a side channel of the creek, a floodplain channel hosting wild coffee plants rising up to 7 feet tall. Passing under a power line, you reach the other end of the jogging trail, with

a HACKBERRY TRAIL sign. Stay on the boardwalk as it winds around a sugarberry tree, wandering deeper into the hardwood hammock, a dense canopy of red maples, sugarberry, laurel oak, and black tupelo. Rounding a bend, the boardwalk spans over a marshy area. Marsh ferns, pokeberry, and Spanish needles dominate the forest floor. Two leaning red maples create an arch over a curve in the boardwalk. Watch for tall American beautyberry bushes and dogwoods that bloom in early spring. As the boardwalk rises back into the sand pine scrub, it reaches the beginning of the loop at 0.7 mile. Continue straight. When you return to the junction in front of the gazebo in the sand pine forest, turn right.

This portion of the boardwalk parallels Turkey Creek downstream, providing numerous overlooks from which you can watch for manatees. Take the time to stop and savor the views. Above you, sand pines rise to the sky. Deer moss grows in scattered clumps across the pine needles on the forest floor. Two different types of rosemary favor this scrub environment—the Florida rosemary and the large flowering rosemary. While the Florida rosemary has thick, dark green bottlebrush-like branches, the flowering rosemary is a more delicate plant, with light green foliage. Unless you see its delicate purple blossoms, you might mistake it for a variety of St. John's Wort.

Each overlook gives you a unique view of the creek. From the first overlook, you can look back down along the creek's route you traced along the beginning of the Hammock Loop Trail. Set on a high sand bluff, the second overlook provides a sweeping vista of a lazy bend in Turkey Creek. Looking straight down, you can see that although the water is laced with tannins from oak leaves, the tea color doesn't spoil its clarity. The boardwalk descends down the sand bluff, so the third overlook sits close to creek level, along a sharp bend. At 0.9 mile, a short side trail leads to a platform under a spreading live oak tree. Look up. Butterfly orchids decorate the tree, showing off in springtime with their tall yellow-green flowers, each with a purple-striped white lip.

Returning to the main trail, turn right. This section of boardwalk is wider, continuing along the boundary between the sand pine scrub and the hardwood hammock nourished by Turkey Creek. An overlook provides a vista on a floodplain channel of the creek, a oxbow lake nourished whenever Turkey Creek overflows its banks. Up in the surrounding trees, cardinal wild pine shows off its light green needle-like foliage in preparation for spring flowers.

After 1 mile, the boardwalk ends, but the trail continues. A sign warns that this part of the trail is not wheelchair-accessible—it's a natural footpath defined by logs on the edges. It winds through an oak hammock, drawing close to Port Malabar Boulevard. You can see cars rushing by before the trail swings back on itself to parallel the boardwalk through the sand pine forest. Sand live oaks arch over scattered wiregrass and rosemary. Silkgrass grows in a clearing between bluejack oaks; wasps swarm around an opening in a snag. Watch for the footprints of raccoons in the white sand. Emerging on an old jeep trail, the trail continues on a straight course for a short distance, making a sharp left to complete the loop at 1.5 miles. Turn left at the T intersection to retrace your steps back past the jogging path, the picnic pavilion, and through the gate. If seeing hundreds of names underfoot has you wanting to be immortalized on the boardwalk, stop by the Margaret Hames Nature Center and make a contribution to the cause. When you return to your car, you've completed a 1.6-mile walk.

DIRECTIONS

From Interstate 95 south of Melbourne, take exit 176 and turn left onto CR 516 (Palm Bay Road). Follow it 2.3 miles to Babcock Street (CR 507). Turn right, driving 1 mile to Port Malabar Boulevard. Turn left. From I-95 northbound from Vero Beach, take exit 173. Turn right on Malabar Road (CR 514). Make a left onto Babcock Street. Follow it 1.4 miles to Port Malabar Boulevard. Turn right. Drive 1.1 miles down Port Malabar Boulevard to Santiago Drive, just before the park sign. Make a right. Parking is on the right, across from the park entrance and just before the library entrance.

CONTACT

Turkey Creek Sanctuary
1518 Port Malabar Boulevard Northeast
Palm Bay, FL 32905
321-676-6690
www.palmbayflorida.org/parks

50

Oslo Riverfront Conservation Area

Total distance (circuit): 3 miles

Hiking time: 1.5 hours

Habitats: coastal hammock, palm hammock, pine flatwoods, mangrove swamp

Trailhead coordinates (lat-lon): 27.587051, -80.375452

Maps: USGS 7½' Indiro; St. Johns River Water Management District Recreation Guide to District Lands

Admission: Free

Hours: Sunrise–sunset

Coffee-lovers, rejoice! On this hike, you'll see more coffee that you ever have in your life, a dense jungle of wild coffee plants packing the understory of a tropical hammock. Florida is home to several varieties of wild coffee, including *Psychotria nervosa*, with glossy green leaves, and the less-common *Psychotria sulzneri*, with silvery blue-green leaves. You'll see both varieties along the preserve's trails. In the summer, clusters of white blooms attract butterflies and bees to pollinate the plants. By October, the glossy coffee beans appear, ranging from dark crimson to a chestnut brown.

As you start the Herb Kale Nature Trail, stop at the kiosk to pick up a map and sign the trail register. Throughout most of the hike, the trail is well marked with multicolored signs; interpretive signs explain the plant and animal communities within the preserve. As you walk on the dark earthen path into the hardwood hammock, spreading live oaks form a dense canopy overhead. The trail crosses a boardwalk over a marshy area crowded with ferns, reaching a fork. Turn left, crossing a small bridge. The trail jogs left at another sign, continuing through tall ferns and wild coffee to a sharp right turn. Colorful wildflowers edge the trail—tall white aster, tropical sage with blooms waving like red flags, and the multicolored blossoms of lantana.

Watch where you put your feet! Less than a half inch high, delicate white magnolia-cone mushrooms burst out of the footpath. Known for its diversity of unusual plant species, Oslo Riverfront Conservation Area

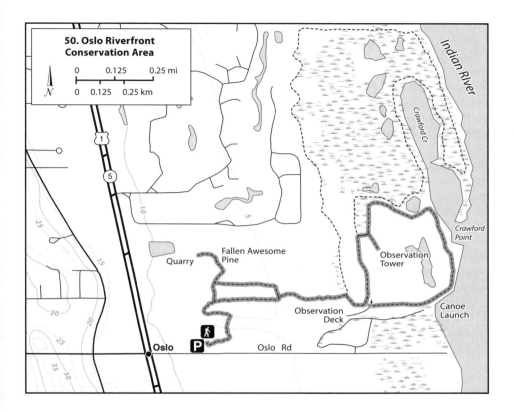

has at least 20 rare species identified, including Simpson's stopper, coral-root orchid, and whisk fern.

The next trail junction is at 0.3 mile. Continue straight, heading toward the coastal wetlands and flatwoods. After you pass through a stand of silvery-green saw palmetto, the trail gains a little elevation and emerges into the white sand of the pine flatwoods. Old multibranched slash pines tower overhead. This is the land of epiphytes, where colorful air plants and orchids cloak the spreading live oaks, and bromeliads dangle like chandeliers from hanging vines. Most bromeliads grow only on trees, with the pineapple a notable exception. Bromeliads of this girth have a natural cup in the center,

called the tank, where the plant collects water. As insects and leafy matter fall into the tank, the plant nourishes itself. It does not tap nutrients from the tree, but uses it only for support. Florida has nearly 20 species of native bromeliads, falling primarily into the *Tillandsia* and *Catopsis* families. Difficult to distinguish from the ground, these include such varieties as the fuzzywuzzy air plant, the cardinal air plant, and the giant air plant, seen here. Unfortunately, importation of tropical plants from Central America led to the introduction of *Metamasius callizona,* a bromeliad-eating weevil, along Florida's east coast during the late 1980s. Its ravenous eating habitats have put most of Florida's once-common native bromeliads, including the giant air plant, on the endangered species list.

When you pass the side trail of bog bridges that leads to the Pine Flatwoods, head straight. You'll come back to this point to explore later in the hike. As you cross the bridge, notice the giant leather ferns choking up the swampy channel. The trail enters a palm hammock with dark, mushy earth underfoot. The tall corridor of cabbage palms rustles in the wind. Shoelace ferns dangle like long ribbons from the palm's smooth trunks. You catch a whiff of salt air; the lagoon is not far away. Cross a bridge into the mangrove swamp and turn right. Swing past the interpretive kiosk to the trail junction, and turn left, following the sign to the observation tower. Make the first right to walk over to the observation tower. It's not your typical tower—it's a ramp reaching for the sky, providing a perch from which you can watch ibises in the trees, anhinga stabbing at fish, and roseate spoonbills winging their way overhead.

At the bottom of the ramp, immediately turn right on the causeway between the mangroves, a slip of land surrounded by swamp. As the causeway veers to the right, you catch a glimpse of the Indian River lagoon through the dense thicket of mangrove on the left. Rising slightly, the footpath becomes grassy. The roar of falling water comes from a culvert draining one impoundment into the next. Created for coastal mosquito control, these mangrove-lined impoundments now serve as an outdoor laboratory for the University of Florida Medical Entomology Laboratory, which adjoins the preserve. Students study mosquito life cycles and the transmission of disease. Always wear a strong insect repellent when hiking through coastal impoundments.

The trail swings right again, coming up to the canoe dock on the left, with its sliver of an entrance to the Indian River lagoon. Sea purslane and saltwort grow along the edges of the footpath as it changes back to sticky

Observation deck over the mangrove swamp

marl, full of holes made by sand fiddler crabs. Watch as the crabs scuttle under the mangroves. At 1.7 miles, turn right onto the observation platform, a surface deck on the open waters of the impoundments. You can see the observation tower off in the distance.

Back on the trail, turn right, quickly completing the coastal wetlands loop. Keep following the trail straight ahead of you, turning right past the interpretive kiosk. Make a left onto the bridge to retrace your steps back through the palm hammock. After you cross the second bridge, watch for the PINE FLATWOODS sign. Turn right and walk along the narrow boards laid across the flat saw palmetto trunks, climbing up into the oak and palm hammock. After the end of the boardwalk, look up to see another wonderland of bromeliads high overhead in the cabbage palms. As the canopy closes in on the trail, an incredible variety of small epiphytes and orchids grow on the scrub live oaks and wax myrtle, and massive ferns rise over your head. The trail becomes sandy underfoot, rising into an area with larger slash pines. Spreading live oaks play host to myriads of ferns and bromeliads. Wild coffee rises tall on both sides of the trail as you reach the intersection with the PINE FLATWOODS sign at 2.2 miles. Turn right, following the trail up to the remains of the Awesome Pine. Felled by one of the hurricanes that hit in 2004, this former National Champion slash pine was more than 11 feet around its base. Even fallen, it makes a pretty impressive log.

Turn left to follow a short and rugged spur trail to an old water-filled quarry pit where workers dug out coquina, a conglomerate of compressed seashells making up the underlying Anastasia limestone along this part of the Atlantic Coast. The rock became the base for the original US 1 through Vero Beach. Turn around and return to the AWESOME PINE

sign. Turn right, retracing your steps back past the PINE FLATWOODS sign. Notice the goldfoot ferns sprouting out of a fallen cabbage palm. These ferns grow out of the soft material from which the palm fronds sprout, and you'll often see them mimicking palm fronds on dying palm trees. At 2.6 miles, you return to the main trail. Turn right, following the familiar trail back to its junction with the Hammock Loop. Take the left at the junction to enjoy a shady wonderland of tall ferns and the ubiquitous wild coffee plants. The dark crimson and bright red of the coffee beans stand out against the deep green foliage, as do the deep purple American beautyberry and white blooms of marlberry. With so many berries to choose from, rufous-sided towhees and ruby-crowned kinglets flit through the forest, feasting. The trail ends at the parking lot, completing your 3-mile hike.

DIRECTIONS

From Interstate 95 exit 147, Vero Beach, head east on SR 60. At the intersection of US 1 and SR 60 in downtown Vero Beach, head south 3.8 miles. Oslo Road (CR 606) is at the traffic light in front of the South Vero Beach Square Shopping Center. Turn left at the light, and left into the trailhead after two openings on the left—one for the shopping center, the other the exit from the trailhead. The small parking area easily fills up with visitors' cars, so use the shopping center parking as an alternative.

CONTACT

St. Johns Water Management District
Palm Bay Service Center
525 Community College Parkway, Southeast
Palm Bay, FL 32909
321-984-4940
www.ourorca.org

Recommended Reading

Alden, Peter, Rich Cech, and Gil Nelson. *National Audubon Society Field Guide to Florida.* New York: Alfred A. Knopf, 1998.

Bartram, William; Francis Harper, ed. *The Travels of William Bartram.* Athens: University of Georgia Press, 1998.

Bell, C. Richie, and Bryan J. Taylor. *Florida Wild Flowers and Roadside Plants.* Chapel Hill, NC: Laurel Hill Press, 1982.

Belleville, Bill. *River of Lakes: A Journey on Florida's St Johns River.a* Athens: University of Georgia Press, 2000.

Brotemarkle, Benjamin. *Beyond the Theme Parks: Exploring Central Florida.* Gainesville: University Press of Florida, 1999.

Comfort, Iris Tracy. *Florida's Geological Treasures.* Baldwin Park, CA: Gem Guides Book Co., 1998.

Dietz, Tim. *Call of the Siren: Manatees and Dugongs.* Golden, CO: Fulcrum Publishing, 1992.

Derr, Mark. *Some Kind of Paradise: A Chronicle of Man and the Land in Florida.* Gainesville: University Press of Florida, 1998.

Fergus, Charles. *Swamp Screamer: At Large with the Florida Panther.* Gainesville: University Press of Florida, 1998.

Friend, Sandra. *Sinkholes.* Sarasota, FL: Pineapple Press, 2002.

Green, Deborah. *Watching Wildlife in the Wekiva River Basin.* Longwood, FL: Sabal Press, 1999.

Nelson, Gil. *The Ferns of Florida.* Sarasota, FL: Pineapple Press, 2000.

Nelson, Gil. *The Shrubs and Woody Vines of Florida.* Sarasota, FL: Pineapple Press, 1996.

Nelson, Gil. *The Trees of Florida.* Sarasota, FL: Pineapple Press, 1994.

Ripple, Jeff, and Susan Cerulean, eds. *The Wild Heart of Florida: Florida Writers on Florida's Wildlands.* Gainesville: University Press of Florida, 1999.

Rawlings, Marjorie Kinnan. *Cross Creek.* Atlanta, GA: Mockingbird Books, 1969.

Rawlings, Marjorie Kinnan. *South Moon Under.* Atlanta, GA: Mockingbird Books, 1977.

Sanger, Marjory Bartlett. *Forest in the Sand.* New York: Atheneum, 1983.

Stamm, Doug. *The Springs of Florida.* Sarasota, FL: Pineapple Press, 1994.

Taylor, Walter Kingsley. *Florida Wildflowers in their Natural Communities.* Gainesville: University Press of Florida, 1998.

Tekiela, Stan. *Birds of Florida Field Guide.* Cambridge, MN: Adventure Publications, Inc., 2001.

Tinsley, Jim Bob. *The Life & Times of Bone Mizell: Florida Cow Hunter.* Orlando, FL: University of Central Florida Press, 1990.